Great Deals online

We are Unbeatable.co.uk. You may not have heard of us yet but we have over 95,000 customers already and the vast majority were recommended by a friend or their family. We shop around for deals so that you don't have to.

We've been supplying great deals on branded consumer electronics and home entertainment products for over 26 years now ! With more than 7000 lines from over 200 of the best Brand suppliers, we offer an alternative to the High Street for real value, from Aiwa to Zanussi, via Philips , Sony and lots more

Unbeatable.co.uk prices

Without the costs of Town Centre sites, we offer typical savings of up to 60% off High Street prices. We're confident that we offer the best prices and value anywhere.

Unbeatable.co.uk stock

We carry over £5M worth of stock to ensure that the majority of our orders are shipped within 3 days.

Unbeatable.co.uk service

We are a founder member of the Which? Web Trader scheme launched in 1999 to promote easy and secure online shopping, and remember we have 26 years experience of building our business on satisfied customers' recommendations.

Unbeatable.co.uk satisfaction guaranteed

We're proud to offer a simple no-quibble 14-day money back guarantee, meaning you can return your purchase if you change your mind. All we ask is that the product remains unused.

Unbeatable.co.uk staff

We're only as good as our staff, so should you need to talk to us we ensure each member is trained to the highest standards so we can offer you the very best assistance.

Unbeatable.co.uk customers

Over 95,000 registered customers regularly shop with us and recommend us to their family and friends.

Unbeatable.co.uk customer service pledge

Our aim is complete customer satisfaction and if your shopping experience with us is anything other than enjoyable, we'd like to know.

Please take a look at our website to see our full range of products –
www.unbeatable.co.uk

You can contact our customer service team by
email – abc@unbeatable.co.uk or phone 01293 543555.

We look forward to adding you to the growing list of people who save time and money by becoming an unbeatable.co.uk customer.

Also, don't forget to take a look at our online auction site
www.unrepeatable.co.uk where you can scoop a 'bargain priced' clearance line by bidding in one of our online auctions. Bids start from just £1.

the complete guide to
letting
property

2ND EDITION

liz hodgkinson

KOGAN PAGE

Author's note

For simplicity and clarity, I have throughout referred to landlords as 'he' and tenants as 'she'. Although obviously landlords can be either male or female, all laws on the subject relate to 'landlord and tenant' and not 'landlady and tenant'. Also, the term 'landlady' has other connotations. Use of the female pronoun to distinguish 'tenant' is simply to avoid using 'he/she' or any other such clumsy nomenclature in the main text, where I have referred to tenant in the singular. No sexism is intended in either case.

First published 2000
Second edition 2002
Reprinted 2002

Kogan Page
120 Pentonville Road
London N1 9JN

British Library Cataloguing in Publication Data

A CIP record for this book is available from the British Library.

ISBN 0 7494 3674 3

Typeset by Saxon Graphics Ltd, Derby
Printed and bound in Great Britain by Thanet Press Ltd, Margate

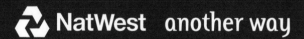
Advertisement feature

NATWEST MORTGAGE SERVICES

Buy-to-let packages are enjoying huge popularity at the moment because of a happy combination of three positive factors.

Firstly, low interest rates have cut the cost of finance. Secondly, lenders have produced a series of innovative, flexible, buy-to-let packages.

But it is perhaps the third factor, the potential both for regular income and capital gains, which is driving the market forward. In many cases the mortgage costs can be met by rental and, if property prices continue to climb as rapidly in the future as they have in the past, there is the prospect of substantial capital gains.

If, like many others, you are thinking about a buy-to-let proposition, here are some of the points you should consider.

Choosing a property
Leave all your personal prejudices about the sort of home you like to live in at your garden gate as you set out on your search. You might enjoy gardening, for example, but for many tenants, gardening is seen as a bind. To broaden your property's appeal to a wider range of tenants, keep garden maintenance to a minimum. A paved area, for instance, is easier to look after than a lawn.

Just as high maintenance gardens are to be avoided, so are high maintenance homes. Period properties can be charming to live in but, for landlords, they can be an expensive drain on their income stream.

Location is important too. Tenants don't look for the most prestigious address in town but they do want convenient transport links, easy access to local shops and schools and a neighbourhood which has a comfortable feel to it. (It's a misconception, incidentally, that students want to live in rough areas. Like everyone else, they don't).

If a convenient location is essential, so is a convenient lay-out. Bungalows are often highly sought after in the rental market because their convenience appeals to both young families and older people. Plenty of storage space is also always welcome, especially to those renting in between homes.

Presenting the property
Once you've found the right property, you need to present it properly. Clearly, any repairs and maintenance jobs will be carried out first and then you can start on decorations, floor coverings and curtains. Even 'unfurnished' properties usually have carpets, curtains, a fridge and a washing machine.

For walls, painting in a neutral colour to complement the carpet is usually better than wallpaper. Choose plain rather than patterned carpets that clean easily and preferably good quality man-made ones (which are usually no more expensive than cheap wool carpets) or ring the change in some rooms with stripped and varnished floors if you hope to attract younger tenants.

In bathrooms, kitchens and halls, tiles or lino are best. They are easy to keep clean and minimise carpet damage. Ready-made curtains in plain colours are good because they are easy to replace.

Avoid reconditioned or second-hand electrical goods. If you don't buy new, you must have them checked by an electrician to ensure they are safe.

Furnished or unfurnished ?

There's often very little difference in the rental you can expect from a furnished as opposed to an unfurnished property. Yet, to equip a three-bedroomed house fully furnished could easily cost up to £8,000.

If you do choose the fully furnished route, beware of cluttering it up with your cast-offs which may make it appear dowdy and unattractive. Choose solid, functional furniture and use loose covers to protect sofas and chairs.

Kitchen equipment should be well made but basic and easy to replace. Plain, stainless steel cutlery, white crockery that won't chip easily and sturdy pots and pans are best.

Legal points

It's useful to take advice on the type of tenancy agreement you should have. Single Assured Shorthold Tenancy Agreements, set for a fixed term, are very popular. Ask your solicitor or, if you intend to use one, a letting agent, for advice. Both you and your tenants need to know your rights and responsibilities and these are best set out in writing in your agreement.

The agreement should cover your rights of access as landlord. In addition to access for repairs, you may well need access for inspection, to carry out works to services, which are common to your property and others, to conduct inventories or, towards the end of the letting, to display re-letting boards or to show the premises to prospective tenants. In the interests of courtesy and legal correctness, the agreement should say that, as landlord, you will give 24 hours' notice before entering, except in emergencies.

Regular visits, every three months or so, are a good idea to check for any faults that have developed, particularly if you don't employ a letting agent. Tenants will not always tell you when something is wrong and it can be much more expensive to repair something at the end of the tenancy than to fix it three months earlier.

In conclusion choose, decorate and furnish your property with the needs of your tenants in mind. Concentrate on the business aspects of your investment and you will be poised to maximise your potential.

ROOM TO LET

SELF STORAGE GIVES YOU MORE S P A C E

access
storage solutions

If you've got a storage problem, we've got the space. With rooms from as little as £5 per week, access offers an affordable and secure environment to store your valued possessions. Over 13,500 customers already entrust their belongings into our care, you can too. Call us for a free quotation.

access *phone* 0800 122 522 www.**access** *storage*.com

The Letting Game

Self-storage is a necessity of 21st century living. We live in a transient society where moving is the norm. No longer do we live in one house for the majority of our lives; have a job for life; live in the city where we were born; or stay with one partner. We are constantly on the move.

We have more belongings than ever before and finding space to store all these belongings can be a problem. Access Storage Solutions has the solution to this problem – space. And that's why self-storage is becoming the latest 'must have' accessory.

The self-storage business is one of the fastest growing markets in Europe and Access is market leader in the UK, and Europe. In America, self-storage has taken off but in the UK we are just realising its potential.

Access has 45 stores in Great Britain stretching across a network that reaches London, the Southeast and the Midlands. Thirty-one of the stores are in London alone. For all that this industry is relatively new in the UK, Access has a staggering 13,500 customers occupying over 1 million square feet of storage space in the UK alone. In mainland Europe, it currently has 23 centres spread across France and Germany – 14 of which are in Paris.

People that use self-storage are those that need more space, temporarily or permanently and there are plenty of reasons why:–

People letting their homes furnished and want to store precious items.

People letting their homes unfurnished and need to store their furniture.

People who move into rented accommodation as an interim measure when moving house.

Young families with growing children who need somewhere to store toys and nursery equipment that isn't needed at the moment.

Middle-aged householders who are storing their grown-up children's belongings.

People who are de-cluttering, either to help sell their house or because they are relocating.

Young flat dwellers that only have a limited amount of space.

People who have inherited furniture from relatives and don't want to sell it.

Students who need to store their belongings during the holidays.

Homeowners who are renovating their homes and need space to store furniture during the building work.

People working from home who need more space.

People who have active hobbies and need space to store their equipment – bikes, windsurfs, skis and snowboards.

People who want to store seasonal items, such as garden furniture.

Self-storage is the easy option – it's not about putting things in the attic or garage to gather dust – it's about placing your belongings in a room where they will be safe, secure, clean and dry. It's about giving you peace of mind.

With Access, you can rent as much or as little space as you need; from a locker measuring a few square feet, to a warehouse-sized room as big as a football pitch. The service is so flexible that you can use it for a matter of days, months or years, from as little as £5 per week.

It's called self-storage because essentially, you 'do it yourself', but there is help available if you need it and moving equipment is available free of charge. If you require help moving your belongings, Access will help you direct or find a recommended removal company.

You're the only key holder so you can access your room whenever you want. Each store offers extended opening hours and certain stores offer 24-7 access. There is 24-hour security, plus CCTV monitoring and security gates. All staff are fully trained storage professionals, who can provide you with answers to all your storage problems and other useful services, such as, comprehensive insurance at competitive rates and a wide range of useful packing supplies.

Not only does Access provide all that as the norm, there is another service you can take advantage of.

Pack 'n' Go is a quick and simple way to store things that take up too much space at home. Access will deliver a specially designed trailer to your home for you to pack. When you're ready, they'll come and pick it up and drive it to your nearest Access store, where you will be able to store it safely and securely. When you need it back, it can be delivered back to your home or you can collect it yourself. No need to hire a van – simple!

Most people would like to make more room at home and self-storage is the sensible solution. So next time you're about to put more clutter away, think of Access Storage Solutions, because garages are for cars, attics for insulation and bedrooms for beds!

Buy-to-let mortgages

for properties in need of renovation prior to letting

Ecology Building Society

provides specialist mortgage finance across the UK for properties and projects that generate an environmental payback, whether in town, city or countryside.

We want to see run-down, derelict properties brought back into use and many of our mortgages are to finance renovations or conversions, for owner occupation or buy-to-let.

If you are a private individual and need a renovation mortgage, talk to us, even if your property has been turned down by other lenders. Call our helpful mortgage team on

0845 674 5566 *or see*
www.ecology.co.uk

Ecology Building Society
FREEPOST
18 Station Road
Cross Hills
Keighley BD20 5BR

THE WORLD HEALTH SERVICE

trust

There are times in our lives when we depend on other people - utterly, completely and without compromise. For one million people in 190 countries around the world, BUPA International provides the same assurance. Wherever you are, whatever you do, you can rely on us to look after your health needs. BUPA International - trust us to care.

www.bupa-intl.com
+44 (0) 1273 208181

BUPA International

GLJ1/11

Contents

Becoming A Landlord
Hamptons International Top Tips

Property has become a mainstream form of investment. In the past 10 years returns on property have out-performed most other forms of investment. The key to choosing any investment is ensuring that it matches the requirements of the investor. This is very much the case when approaching property investment. Listed below are some of the key issues Hamptons International has identified from our experience with our portfolio of property investors:

How much time and effort are you prepared to allow for the property? If this is limited then it would make sense to choose a new property in top condition or consider buying a property that has an existing tenant in place. Alternatively you could appoint an agent to manage redecoration and furnishing. A professional lettings and management agent (ARLA member) can deal with most of the routine work.

Budget carefully at the outset to ensure you can cover possible repair costs, or the mortgage should the property be vacant for any period. Ensure you include details of all costs including service charges and ground rents. Rental properties require redecoration on a more frequent basis than your own home.

Owning a successful rental property starts with choosing the right property and area:

- Buy the right property for the market. Get to know what sort of tenants are common to the area and what level of rent is paid. Would you consider a property for Short Lets?

- Once you have chosen your target tenant group, choose properties that will appeal to them. You might prefer a quirky old cottage, but corporate tenants generally prefer new apartments with good transport connections. On the other hand a family will not be interested in a third floor walk-up.

- The choice to provide the property furnished or unfurnished should also be governed by the requirements of the target tenant group.

- The choice of area will largely depend on budget. Our experience would indicate that for the same budget, a small but prime property in a good location can provide better financial returns than a large secondary property in a less desirable location. It also follows that a smaller property will costs less to maintain.

- Once you have chosen a property, review the rent levels being achieved for similar properties by asking for details from a mix of lettings agents in the area.

- Personal taste in decorating has no place in property investment. Follow the advice of the experts. Neutral really does work.

John Rockel
Director – Lettings & Management

Hamptons International wishes you the best of luck with your property investing. If we can assist with any of the following services please do contact us:

PROPERTY TO LET?

Save legal fees! Law Pack Publishing, the country's leading self-help legal publisher, can provide you with a range of solicitor-approved do-it-yourself tenancy publications.

Legal Form Packs*: (£4.49 inc VAT) ready-made legal forms for:

- Assured shorthold tenancies
- House/flat share agreements
- Notices to terminate
- Household inventory
- Holiday letting agreements

Legal Form Packs also contain guidance notes with completed example.

'Residential Lettings' software (£9.99 inc VAT): provides essential background information and advice for landlords, with ready-to-complete agreements, notices, etc.

Rent Book (£1.59 inc VAT): legally required if rent is paid on a weekly basis.

Publications are available at WH Smith, Ryman and other leading high street stationers.
Or buy online at: **www.lawpack.co.uk**

Publications valid in England and Wales
*Scottish versions available

Law Pack Publishing Limited
76-89 Alscot Road London SE1 3AW
Telephone 020 7940 7000 Fax 020 7940 7001

The National Approved Letting Scheme

Thinking of letting your property? If so, for peace of mind, use an agent who is a member of The National Approved Letting Scheme.

The National Approved Letting Scheme (NALS) is a voluntary accreditation scheme for letting and management agents. It was established in 1999 with the objective of giving owners the confidence to let their property by appointing qualified agents who, in joining the Scheme, have agreed to abide by a set of minimum service standards for letting and management.

The NALS scheme was set up to provide much-needed benchmark service standards that would enable landlords and tenants to avoid the pitfalls of dealing with rogue letting agents.

Three of the industry's leading professional bodies support the scheme – the Association of Residential Letting Agents (ARLA), the National Association of Estate Agents (NAEA) and the Royal Institution of Chartered Surveyors (RICS). The scheme is also endorsed by the DTLR (Department of Transport, Local Government and the Regions), the Housing Corporation and the British Property Federation.

In summer 2001, NALS was awarded substantial government funding to support its nationwide growth. Whilst it is part-funded by government, the scheme remains independent.

Hugh Dunsmore-Hardy, Chairman of NALS, explains the significance of the Government funding to all sectors of the private rented property market. "NALS' service standards are the consumer's benchmark against which to judge the performance of letting and management agents operating in the private rented sector," he says.

"The financial support being made through the DTLR underlines the Government's commitment to raising consumer confidence within the private rented sector, and thereby increase the supply of rented accommodation as an alternative to home ownership."

Requirements of membership

Membership of NALS is open to letting and management agents that have a director, principal or partner who is a member of one of the three professional bodies – ARLA, NAEA or RICS – or are registered social landlords or a housing association. In future, it is intended to see the scheme widened to include any agent who meets the NALS criteria for accreditation.

It is a prerequisite of membership that organisations should have in place a customer complaints procedure underpinned by an arbitration scheme, Professional Indemnity Insurance and Client Money Protection cover. Currently, around £1 billion of UK tenants' deposits remains unprotected.

All members undertake to offer residential letting and management services on written terms which, at the least, meet the service standards prescribed by NALS and provide their clients with a written statement setting out the services to be provided and their charges.

For further information on NALS and to obtain details of an agent in your area please contact:
The National Approved Letting Scheme
Warwick Corner
42 Warwick Road
Kenilworth CV8 1HE
Tel: 01926 866633
Fax: 01926 866644
Email: info@nalscheme.co.uk
Web: www.nalscheme.co.uk

BUPA International
– peace of mind wherever you are

No-one likes to dwell on the prospect of ill-health. But if you're thinking of moving abroad or managing and letting property overseas, then health insurance should definitely feature on your 'to do' list.

Making decisions is difficult when there are so many alternative ways to go about it. Some people choose local health insurers and others rely on UK health agreements to see them through. However, it is important to bear in mind that health care systems differ greatly from country to country and even region to region. It is easy to find yourself facing waiting lists, excessive medical charges and standards of care that may be inferior to what you're used to at home.

More and more people are turning to large international health care providers like BUPA International, the UK's leading health care organisation. With over four million members of 115 nationalities in over 190 countries worldwide, BUPA International provides comprehensive and flexible schemes that you and your family can rely on.

Depending on your requirements, there are a wide range of flexible high quality global health insurance options designed for people living and, working abroad for six months of the year or more. The schemes can be tailored to meet your needs, offering primary care, maternity cover, home nursing, routine and emergency dentistry, as well as hospital treatment and accommodation, emergency road ambulance and cover for sports injuries.

There are three levels of cover to choose from with BUPA International's Lifeline Scheme, each one appropriate for different circumstances. Whichever level you choose, you can be sure that BUPA International will be there when you need them. Bill Ward, Managing Director at BUPA International explains why:

"Moving abroad can be stressful enough without having to worry about how to access quality healthcare for yourself or your family. With BUPA International, our members are only a single phone call away from expert help and guidance, 24 hours a day, 365 days a year. Should they need our help they know that they will get quality care comparable to that which they are used to in the UK, and can choose to be treated in the UK if they specify that option. We also have a network of over 4,000 hospitals and medical centres worldwide with whom we have direct payment arrangements - so our members don't have to worry about settling bills and can concentrate on getting well instead".

BUPA International staff have experience and knowledge of local facilities all around the globe and are aware of any potential problems. Having invested £15 million in customer service technology, they can be contacted by phone, e-mail or by using our call-back service from our website.

The 'Membersworld' website is a fully secure site designed exclusively for BUPA International members, enabling them to check their claims status online. Other handy features include online claim forms, full access to membership details and instant quotes. There is a wealth of useful information for people travelling round the world, with country profiles, details on local embassies, hospital networks and even general health care tips. Members can also look at case studies, link to the BBC World Service Radio, look at up-to-date international weather forecasts, and check out the latest world news. Visit the site for a preview on www.bupa-intl.com.

For further details on all of BUPA International's products and services both for individuals and companies, please visit: www.bupa-intl.com or contact: +44 (0) 1273 208 181.

Why choose BUPA International?

- Experience and reputation – the world's largest expatriate health insurer
- Quality of service delivery
- Financial security . Network of overseas service/contact centres and medical providers with whom direct settlement arrangements have beenorganised
- Price/value for money
- Scope of coverage offered by the schemes. . Flexibility in terms of collection of premiums (method of collection and currency), product design, and service
- Transportability
- 24-hour multi-lingual helpline, 365 days a year
- Quick turnaround of claims - settled within five working days .
- Internet services, providing easy access to information and support wherever you are

Emergency Assistance Around the Globe

What happens if you are living abroad and require urgent medical attention, far from adequate medical facilities?

BUPA International members with assistance cover have the reassurance that wherever they are in the world and whatever happens, they can be evacuated to the nearest centre of medical excellence, should their condition require it.

For example, when Mr Jaysingh suffered a serious heart attack while working in Russia, BUPA International evacuated him to a hospital in Finland, where he received the expert attention and recovery care he needed. Mr Jaysingh said later, "the treatment I received was highly professional and BUPA International handled the complex medical and travel arrangements with ease".

Buying to Let – *Good judgement and good advise*

The last twelve to twenty four months has shown an explosion of interest in the buying to let market. Increasingly investors have been disappointed on the returns provided by their banks or by the yield of investments on the stock market and have turned increasingly to the property market in order to achieve what would appear to be the most dependable blend of the decent return on a month to month basis in terms of yield and steady capital growth which can basically be assured. The result of this interest has been an explosion in house prices in many parts of the country with the net effect that the traditional first time buyers have been priced out of the housing market in many neighbourhoods.

Is buying to let all that it is cracked up to be? It can be in spite of the increasing number of landlords and properties available for rent. However one must proceed with caution because it is not as simple as buying a house with or without specially tailored mortgage then letting it out.

First there is tax advise. A property which you don't live in will be subject to capital gains tax when it is sold assuming a profit has been achieved. Proper accounts needs to be kept of the rental income together with details of expenditures incurred as a result of owning the property so that income tax can be properly assessed. You must make contact with the revenue at the appropriate time and provide them with the necessary information and all this may require the services of an accountant. There are questions such as whether the property should be in the sole name of a wife perhaps because she is not liable to income tax or at least income tax at 40% Should you set up a private limited company? Are there tax advantages involved in doing that?

It is of course very important to choice the right property. Only a small percentage of properties available for sale are appropriate for buy to let in terms of their potential yield. A yield of between 5%-10% per annum makes sense but anything less than that does not. You have to build in for those months in the year when there may not be a tenant. On average regardless of the length of the term of an assured short hold tenancy a property can expect to have seven tenancies in ten years. There is therefore quite a turnover and every time one tenant leaves and another one comes in expense will be incurred and rent will be lost.

It is important to have the correct short hold tenancy agreement. You can obtain copies from law stationers but equally you may want to take the advise of a solicitor on a appropriately tailor made document. It is crucial to make sure that any covenants and restrictions that you wish to be imposed are evidenced in that tenancy agreement. The tenancy forms the totality of the contract between landlord and tenant. You need rights if the tenant fails to pay his rent properly or if he outstays his welcome beyond the end of the term.

There is a vast number of mortgage products now available on the market for people who are buying to let. You must disclose to the mortgage lender that you are buying to let. The products available are not necessarily more expensive than those for owner occupiers but advice from a financial advisor maybe prudent in order to get the right product for you. Again assuming you need a mortgage and you are not a cash buyer you must be careful as to structure the package in appropriate financial terms in order to secure the appropriate financial rewards.

Finally there are the questions as to whether you employ a managing agent. Again this is expensive but managing agents can be useful particularly if the property you buy to let is in a different town or city or if you are busily engaged with full time employment and want someone to assist with the day to day problems of a tenancy such as getting in building contractors, plumbers, electricians etc when things go wrong. The managing agents can be expected to charge something in the region of 10% of the rent for the provision of an ongoing service.

Many people are asking themselves whether buying to let is a good pension option in view of the poor performance of pensions funds the lacklustre returns of annuity investments. It has to be said that history has shown that if there is a down turn in the economy the property market is normally the first to feel it. Those who remember the recession of 1989/1990 will recall the horrendous problems of negative equity and those unable to pay their mortgage instalments when interests rates were peaking at 15%. That risk can never be avoided and a view has to be take on the current state of our economy. However for those who need to raise a mortgage there needs to be a sufficient margin of comfort in order to continue to make financial sense should interest rates rise and should property prices flatten out. Generally speaking you would not be able to raise anymore that 85% of the purchase price by way of mortgage and generally the length would have to be 130% of the mortgage instalment in order to give sufficient margins.

In all we would say that buy to let has got a lot more steam in it yet and can provide a first class investment.

About this book

At some time in their lives, just about everybody will come into contact with the private rented sector, whether as a tenant, a landlord, or both. Most people rent property at some stage in their lives, and very many wonder from time to time whether they could successfully let property for profit.

This book demystifies the lettings game and tells you all you need to know to become a successful landlord. It is for anybody who might be considering, however vaguely, buying a property to let, for those who have already done so, and those who may wish to expand their investment portfolio.

Although detailed financial and legal information is included, this book also gives many insights into what it *feels like* to be a landlord, from the perspective of those who have already taken the plunge. The many anecdotes and case histories contained in the book, all true stories, make amusing, inspiring, and sometimes painful reading.

As an investment landlord myself (admittedly on a very small scale) I have experienced all the emotions connected with being a landlord, from wild excitement to lurching fear, anticipation and anxiety. Being a landlord in the modern world is much like sailing round the world: you get moments of intense activity and stress, and then long periods of great peace and calm. The job definitely has its ups and downs.

Speaking purely personally, I find that being a landlord adds an exciting dimension to life because at the same time as — with any luck — making useful extra money, you are also providing that most necessary of all services: a roof over somebody's head.

Introduction

A short history of rented property

From medieval times to Rachman

From medieval times until the end of the First World War, around 90 per cent of property in the UK was rented. Renting was quite simply, for the majority of people, a way of life, and although an Englishman's home has long been said to be his castle, most of these 'castles' were owned by people other than those living in them. Even noble and titled people very often lived in rented accommodation.

The situation was similar in most of Europe. In fact, for most of history, very few of those who lived in societies where homes were relatively permanent, immovable structures, have owned the land on which their dwellings stood.

In the days when the majority of homes were rented from private landlords, many people lived in daily terror of being turned out in the streets for some real or imagined misdemeanour, as there was little security of tenure and most tenants had very few rights indeed. For hundreds of years the landlord was king, mightily feared by his tenants. He owned the property and held most of the rights in the land. In the case of farmers, landed gentry and mill-owners, for instance, the landlord was very often the employer as well, an all-powerful personage who could hire and fire at will, and there was little redress available. Until recent times, many hundreds of thousands of British families lived in 'tied' cottages or houses, where the home went with the job. If you lost your job, that meant you automatically lost your home as well.

Because of their almighty power over the lives and fates of others, landlords were popularly seen as wicked, and much classic fiction contains heartrending stories of poverty-stricken families being turned out into the streets with their pathetic bundles of goods, having fallen foul of a heartless, grasping landlord. Dickens, Thomas Hardy and Mrs Gaskell all made much of the plight of the poverty-stricken jobless tenant being driven out by a landlord with a heart of stone. In present-day popular historical fiction, such as that of Catherine Cookson for instance, the all-powerful landlord continues to be a recognizable villain.

But however terrifying fictional landlords appear, few could compare with the real-life Peter Rachman. No novelist could have dreamt up such an ogre. During the 1950s, Rachman, an expatriate Pole, bought up hundreds of slum properties in the now-fashionable West London areas of Notting Hill and Bayswater, and let them out mainly to newly arrived Jamaican immigrants who found it difficult in those days to get accommodation of any kind, because they were black. Rachman overcrowded and overcharged his many tenants, and then enforced his rule by means of hired thugs. His tenants had no recourse to the law and were in any case grateful for having a roof over their heads, even such a roof as Rachman provided. Rachman, who began life as a landlord by finding rooms for prostitutes, became a multi-millionaire by this means.

He was also a bit-player in the Profumo Affair, the biggest British political scandal of the early 1960s, and the teenage Mandy Rice-Davies was his mistress for nearly two years. In fact, his name only came to public light because of his involvement with the 16-year-old Miss Rice-Davies, a protégée along with Christine Keeler of osteopath Stephen Ward, whose 'night job' was that of procuring young attractive girls for men in high places. Paradoxically, Rachman's name has become a household word when those of Ward, Profumo, Lord Astor and others involved in the scandal are all but forgotten.

In the late 1950s, Rachman's income from slum rentals amounted to nearly £80,000 a year – not a bad return nowadays, but an unimaginable sum in those times. However, the life he led – continuously threatening and harassing tenants, salting money away in offshore funds, seeking out teenage lovers – was stressful in the extreme, and Rachman died, unmourned and unmissed, of a massive heart attack at the early age of 42. He has been immortalized, however, by an entry in the *Oxford English Dictionary,* where 'Rachmanism' is defined as 'exploitation of slum tenants by unscrupulous landlords'.

To this day, anybody who buys up a property to let, thus becoming a landlord, risks being called a 'Rachman', even by people who no longer have any clear idea who the real Rachman was. The name 'Rachman' with its word-association of rack rents, sounds evil in any case to our ears, and the term has vilified landlords for ever as being greedy, exploitative and amoral. Even the nicest landlords can hear themselves being called 'Rachman' at parties and other gatherings, by would-be wits.

From Rachman to Rent Acts

However, around the same time that Peter Rachman was making his millions by such dubious means, things in the housing world were starting to change for ever, with ordinary people being able to buy their own homes, and tenants gradually accruing ever more rights. In fact, the seeds of change had begun many years earlier when the private rented sector began to give way to social housing during the 1920s and 1930s. The number of private landlords gradually began to diminish as local councils built subsidized housing for those who did not have enough money to buy their homes. Most of these new homes were provided with modern conveniences such as bathrooms, running water and electricity – none of which was routinely provided by the private landlord at this time.

When the landlord was the local council rather than an awesome, powerful individual, it was far less easy for tenants to be evicted, if only because the council would then have to find them other accommodation. For a number of very sound reasons, chief of which were cheaper rents and better-quality housing, most people who had to rent their homes now preferred to be a council tenant, rather than getting into the clutches of a private landlord. Council housing was, in the main, well constructed, well looked after and offered a 'proper' modern home, with a front and back garden, three bedrooms and a separate living and dining room. Council flats, which came later, were also extremely serviceable dwellings and were certainly a dramatic housing advance on the grim tenement blocks that preceded them. Although rarely of architectural merit, council properties were warm, clean and spacious, at least when newly built.

Not all social housing was erected by local councils, however. At around the same time as councils were embarking on ambitious housing programmes, a number of rich philanthropists also started to provide better-quality housing for the working classes. These were often models for their time. The Guinness and Peabody Trust buildings are famous, of course, but there were also lesser-known developments such as The Grampians, a large block of flats in Shepherd's Bush, London, which was built in the early 1930s by Sir Thomas Grampian to provide working-class people with decent, albeit modest, homes.

The growing provision of philanthropic and social housing, which gave some security of tenure, as well as warm, comfortable, well-appointed homes, had the effect of turning the attention of the government of the day to the private rented sector. At the time, socialist ideas such as the notion that 'property is theft' were in the air, and it seemed about time, to 1950s governments at least, that those paying rent should have some rights and security of their own. The result was a series of Rent Acts, whereby power began to be wrested from the landlord and pass into the hands of tenants.

From 1957, when the first Rent Act came into force, tenants could no longer be turned out on a whim, but were protected by law. If they felt they were paying too high a rent, or that their landlord was not keeping the place in good repair, tenants could apply to a Rent Tribunal for a 'fair rent' which, in effect, almost always meant a vastly decreased rent. The 'fair rent' decided on by the tribunal was usually considerably less than the market rent for that particular property. Landlords could also be ordered by the Tribunal to carry out repairs.

At this time, many tenants became regulated, or controlled tenants, which meant they could neither be turned out nor have their rents increased. As late as the 1980s, there were still significant numbers of people in rented accommodation all over the country who were paying less than £10 a week rent, having won their right to remain in the property forever by the provisions of various Rent Acts, the last of which came into force in 1977.

Although Rent Acts may have been good news for the tenant, they shifted the balance of power so much in the tenant's favour that before long nobody wanted to be a private landlord. By the 1960s, most small-scale landlords were desperate to sell their properties for anything they could get. The days when a Peter Rachman could institute a reign of terror were over. But because rents became so low, and tenants might remain in the property for ever, landlords could not afford to repair or maintain the property in good order. By the 1980s what remained of the private rented sector was, in the main, the utmost in undesirability. Properties available for rent were usually dilapidated, dingy, often with outside toilets and no running water. Most remaining private landlords were very small-scale property owners indeed, with a portfolio of perhaps two or three houses.

As late as the 1960s, my grandparents were living in a rented terraced house without a bathroom, electricity or hot water. The landlord, a local builder, who owned a small row of houses originally costing a few hundred pounds the row, could not make enough from rents to carry out any refurbishment. Although the property was in many ways unsatisfactory, as it had severe damp in addition to all its other problems, on the plus side the rent had not increased for many years. Such a property would be considered unfit for human habitation today, although both my grandparents lived until well into their 90s in the place. Now, of course, it is an expensive and highly desirable tarted-up bijou property.

So by the 1970s, more or less the only long-term tenants in privately rented property were protected tenants paying a tiny, never-increased rent. These people, who could not be evicted by any means, became known as 'sitting tenants'. In those days, such tenants often went with the property, so that purchasers had to take on the unmoveable tenant as well as the other burdens of home ownership. As recently as the 1980s, a friend of mine owned a large Victorian house containing a sitting tenant in the basement paying £6 a week rent. He had been there since the Second World War.

It was by now almost impossible to get anywhere smart to rent, as everybody was terrified of becoming a landlord, fearing they would never be able to get bad tenants out, or command a market rent. The term 'low rent' came to describe anything or anybody of inferior quality. At the same time, it had become extremely easy to get a mortgage and, with tax relief available on mortgages, the majority of people now preferred to own their own houses. The effect was that the private rental sector shrank almost into non-existence. By 1989, just 7 per cent of housing in Britain was in the private rented sector.

Because it had become impossible either to evict tenants or raise rents, such private landlords as remained now tended to let their properties as 'holiday lets', whereby they were let out for short periods only. Although such lets were theoretically available only for a month to the same person, landlords and tenants would often tacitly agree with each other to keep renewing the agreement with the same tenant. These 'holiday' tenants were not protected by any laws; the term was often used so that landlords could evict tenants at will, and the tenant was not necessarily occupying the premises for purposes of a holiday. This was, strictly speaking, against the law, but everybody turned a blind eye, such was the shortage of properties to rent. The whole system was a complete mess.

Otherwise, almost the only other type of private landlord at the time was the so-called 'reluctant landlord', a business executive for instance who would let his house for a year or two when being relocated abroad by his company. This type of property was usually well-appointed, and was almost always let to incoming temporary relocaters. It was, therefore, an upmarket concern, and rents here were high, as they were usually paid by the executive's company. In the early 1980s business in this area was brisk enough to result in a proliferation of letting agencies, a phenomenon which culminated in the formation of the Association of Residential Letting Agencies (ARLA) in 1981.

The other main type of landlord at this time, also 'reluctant', was the homeowner who wanted, or had to move to another location, but was unable to sell his or her own property because of the 1988–89 house price recession. During this time, many house prices fell so steeply that thousands of homeowners were in negative equity. Letting the temporarily unsaleable house was a way out of the problem, and it also provided lucrative business for many newly established letting agencies. Again, the property in negative equity was often furnished to a high standard, desirable, and let for a high rental.

The 1988 Housing Act

Everything in the private rental sector changed yet again when the 1988 Housing Act became law on 15 January 1989. This Act introduced dramatic changes intended to make the rented sector fairer for both landlords and tenants, and bring more rental properties onto the market. The Act still tended to favour the tenant over the landlord; for instance, the landlord had to give two months' notice to the tenant, while the tenant only had to give one month's notice to the landlord. However, it gave potential landlords the confidence to start letting again by introducing the concept of the Assured Shorthold Tenancy, a legally binding agreement whereby properties were let out for six months at a time.

All Assured Shorthold Tenancies of the future had to be of six months' duration, capable of termination by either party at this time so long as due notice each way had been given and accepted. Rents, according to this Act, could only be increased on a yearly basis. Although shorthold tenants could, and often did, renew their tenancies and stay in the same property for several years, the legally binding time of the contract was never to be more than six months. At the end of each six months, a 'break' occurred, whereby the agreement could be renewed or terminated, provided the proper notice was given by each side in writing.

The concept of the Assured Shorthold Tenancy, which was an imaginative leap and a dramatic departure from previous landlord and tenant regulations, has stood the test of time and become standard for most people operating in the private rented sector. In the main, it works extremely well and is one of those rare successful pieces of legislation that pleases everybody, as, theoretically at least, everybody wins.

Once landlords realized they could now legally evict tenants after six months at the very most, and also set market rents which could not easily be challenged by Rent Tribunals, the rented sector began to improve vastly in both quality and quantity. Those who had become tenants before 1989, the pre-Housing Act tenants, still held on to their protected status, if applicable, but this did not apply to tenancies starting after this date.

The 1988 Housing Act distinguished between furnished and unfurnished lettings, and also brought in legislation concerning the flammability of furniture and fittings. As sofas, chairs and so on now had to conform to regulations, this had the effect of introducing better-quality goods into furnished accommodation. Gas and fire safety regulations were also introduced. Reputable letting agencies will not take on properties where furniture and fittings do not conform to current regulations, and as ever more private landlords are now letting through agencies, rental properties are becoming very smart and attractive indeed.

At first, there was slightly more security of tenure attached to unfurnished than furnished properties, so most landlords preferred to furnish their places so that they could evict unsuitable tenants. This anomaly was swept away by the 1996 Housing Act and nowadays there is little to choose between furnished or unfurnished properties in terms of rents or in security of tenure.

Recent developments

Because of the ever-changing demands of the market, another category has recently entered the lettings business, that of the 'sparsely furnished' or 'part furnished' property. This is fast becoming the most popular category of all, as it provides the absolute basics for living such as kitchen appliances, beds, tables and chairs, yet gives tenants the scope to make a home of the place.

The other factor that has revolutionized rental properties in the UK has been the introduction of the Buy-to-Let scheme in 1996. Before this date it was not possible to rent out mortgaged property, at least not without the express permission of the mortgage lender. You were not supposed to buy property on a mortgage with the intention of renting it out, and high-interest bank loans were the only means of raising revenue for investment properties. But through an ARLA initiative, it has become possible to obtain a mortgage especially devised for the investment landlord, and related only to property not intended as a home for yourself. In fact, you are not allowed to live in a Buy-to-Let property yourself. This scheme, which has proved extremely successful, has brought a new type of landlord into being: the middle-class small investor who is neither grasping nor greedy, but who wants to do something more interesting and tangible with some spare money than putting it into pension schemes, stocks and shares, or savings accounts at the bank. The intense media attention focused on the scheme at its outset also had the effect of encouraging many people with legacies or redundancy money sitting in the bank to take the plunge and become first-time landlords.

Although there may still be some mini-Rachmans in existence (no amount of legislation can thwart the really determined fraudster) today's typical landlords are most likely to have perhaps one or two rental properties, to furnish and appoint the investment property with as much care and taste as their own home, and who are looking to make not a killing, but a safe, steady extra income. Present-day landlords most often view their rental properties as a sideline and while being landlords continue the day job.

At the same time as a new type of landlord is emerging, the housing market is changing yet again. During the 1960s and 70s, an enormous stigma was attached to renting, and it was very much seen as the poor person's choice of living option. Anybody who was anybody bought as soon as possible and with 100 per cent mortgages available on some properties, what was the advantage in renting? Mortgage repayments were very often cheaper than paying out rent, and during the 1980s, the Thatcher government encouraged house purchases still further by introducing the Right-to-Buy scheme whereby council tenants could purchase their homes at very low prices. Now, however, there is an increase in the number of people wanting to rent property.

The new renters are, in the main, not people who cannot afford to buy their own properties, as was usually the case in the past. By contrast, they are people who have decided, for one reason or another, that they prefer the flexibility of renting. The pattern nowadays, at least for a growing number of young professional people, is a preference for renting properties to which they have little or no commitment and which they can quit in a month or two. Whereas up to the late 1980s most people in their early 20s wanted to buy, the average age for purchasing property is now around 30.

There are also more professional people, particularly those in the IT industries, being relocated to other areas or other countries for perhaps a year or two, and these people do not want to buy, either. These days, companies tend to relocate single people rather than whole families (it's much cheaper, for a start) and such employees are often looking for a rented pied-à-terre, a hotel room plus, while their families remain in the family home. This is again a new type of client for the private rental sector, and an area in which there has been rapid growth.

There are high-powered workers in modern industries coming to the UK from countries where it is still the preferred pattern to rent. (On the continent, over 40 per cent of people still rent their homes. In the UK, just 11 per cent of housing is in the private rented sector.) These professionals are mainly young, single, highly paid and working long hours, and they want to rent something smart, well-appointed, clean and efficient. Most of them do not see themselves as permanent fixtures in the host country, which is another reason not to buy.

The increasing number of divorces and relationship break-ups also means that there are now more people than ever before living on their own. Often, these newly single people do not want to buy either, at least while they are not in a long-term relationship. Many cannot afford to buy another property while the former spouse remains in the marital home, especially if maintenance and mortgage payments still have to be met.

Many of these 'new renters' are looking for a temporary home, and the Assured Shorthold Tenancy suits them perfectly. But because they are very often high-earning professionals, or at least used to a good lifestyle, the new renters are extremely fussy, and the demand now is for high-quality rental properties, not dismal, damp, dilapidated places with stained carpets, miserable wallpaper and junk furniture. As one estate agent put it, 'The flat has to look like the interior designer moved out last week.'

During the 1980s, when there was very little decent property available for private renting, there were always at least 10 tenants chasing every available property. When rented properties were in very short supply, there was little incentive to make them attractive to tenants. The rents could also be sky high, as properties tended to go almost before they were advertised. But now that very many thousands of people have bought up properties especially for the purposes of renting, the tenant once again has choice, and landlords have to offer something extremely desirable to attract a high-quality tenant.

By mid-1999, lettings agencies were reporting that, for the first time ever, they had an excess of quality properties over tenants, and there were no longer five or six potential tenants chasing every property. Another factor at this time was that money had become extremely cheap to borrow, interest rates were low, and so there was increased interest in buying at the lower end of the market, where most investment purchases are made.

The combination of the Buy-to-Let scheme, the popularity of owning investment properties, and low interest rates has meant that for the landlord, the rental market has become highly competitive. Tenants now want chic, smart, well-located homes, and to borrow from a well-known advertising slogan, today's landlord must never forget that the tenant has a choice.

But, then, so does the landlord. As a potential or actual landlord, you can choose to buy a studio flat, a one- or two-bedroom flat, a family house or a whole block of bedsits, for instance. You can take tenants on an Assured Shorthold Tenancy, on a short let or a holiday let. You can be an absentee landlord, or let a flat within your own home. You can take in paying guests, lodgers, or buy a holiday cottage to let out in the season. You can let a caravan, a mobile home or take in overnight guests. You can specialize in letting to students, or to those on Housing Benefit.

There are very many ways of being a landlord today and each one has its own set of rules and regulations, its pros and cons. And if the service of providing others with rented accommodation is no longer an automatic licence to print money, those who are successful at the lettings game can do very nicely indeed out of renting their property to others.

There always has been, and there always will be, a rental market. Providing people with a roof over their heads in exchange for money has been a fact of life from ancient times. From Biblical times, when Mary and Joseph were temporarily lodged in a stable, to today's sophisticated and critical tenants looking for somewhere to park their laptop and PowerBook, the need for people willing to rent out their property for others to inhabit, remains.

Renting, unlike buying, is a fixed cost that can be budgeted for over a finite term. This, according to the Association of Residential Letting Agents, makes it a very flexible housing option for those who do not want, or who are not in a position to commit themselves for 25 years or so of a mortgage.

It can be exciting and challenging to be a landlord in today's dynamic, ever-changing rented market. But – is it for you?

1

Is letting for you?

As we have seen in the Introduction, the era of the private, small-time landlord is with us once again and we are back to the days when it is possible to make a useful income from renting out properties to tenants.

Some heavily advertised Buy-to-Let schemes have made the whole thing sound extremely seductive. According to much current hype, all you do is buy up a property at the lower end of the market, do it up, then let it out at a huge rent. You then sit back and watch the money roll endlessly in, at a vastly higher rate than you could possibly achieve from any other type of investment. You just can't lose.

But is letting property really as simple and foolproof as it is often made out to be? In one sense of the word, yes. Anybody at all, provided they have the money or are able to borrow it, can buy an investment property and then rent it out, or attempt to. You do not need any particular training or qualifications and, these days, not even the ready money. So long as you have enough for the deposit and can satisfy the income requirements of lenders, you can now get a specialized mortgage for the purpose of buying an investment property.

So far, so good. But precisely because so many small investors are now entering the private rented sector, the market is becoming ever more competitive, streamlined and professional. Tenants can now pick and choose, and in the lettings game, as with any other type of commercial enterprise, the bungling amateur risks making a loss rather than a profit.

Where property is concerned, you are talking about very large sums of money indeed. Even the most modest investment property will cost at least £30,000. If you are considering signing up for a Buy-to-Let scheme, you can put another £25,000 on top of that for the interest repayments on your loan.

By contrast, you can buy a car or a computer for £1,000 or less and still pick up a saleable artwork for a few hundred pounds. If you make a loss on these, it is hardly a major financial setback. But if you buy the wrong property at the wrong price at the wrong time and in the wrong place, you can end up with very considerable losses indeed.

Jason Cliffe, marketing and sales manager of the Leaders group of letting agencies, which operate mainly in the South-East, said: 'We are always prepared to give advice to potential landlords but very often, they don't listen to a word we say. Then they wonder why they can't let the property they may have bought and refurbished at enormous expense.

'There's some folklore,' he added, 'which says that any old property can be rented out to somebody. If that was ever true, it's certainly not the case now. Not only do you have to buy the right property, but you have to be the right kind of person to be a landlord. As we have learned from our own experience as letting agents, not everybody has, or can acquire, the qualities needed.'

What it takes to be a landlord

So what are these qualities? Over a number of years of being a landlord myself, talking to other landlords, and spending many hours gleaning wisdom from letting agents, I would say that in order to be successful at the lettings game, you need to possess the following attributes:

- First and foremost, you must absolutely love and be passionate about property.
- You must be businesslike and efficient.
- You should possess people and management skills.
- You should have a problem-solving turn of mind.
- It helps to have an extrovert, rather than introvert, type of personality.

We'll take each of these points in turn and explain why each is essential for success in the modern, highly professional and competitive lettings market.

You must love and be passionate about property

One of the first rules of financial success is: when thinking of something that might make you money, choose something in which you already have a natural interest. Why? Because if you are already interested you will, almost without realizing it, have developed and built up a considerable level of expertise. If not, you will constantly be at the mercy of those who have, and they will be able to run rings round you.

To take a personal example, it would never do for me to invest in the computer world, simply because computers bore me to death. Although I know there are vast fortunes to be made, as people like Bill Gates and Clive Sinclair have conclusively proved, I cannot readily understand these machines. I have to use computers, but for me they are a necessary evil. I would never willingly attend a computer exhibition, and shudder each time I pass a computer shop. Therefore, for me to invest in computers would be like swimming in shark-infested seas. I would not even begin to know the difference between a bargain and overpriced rubbish.

Similarly, I am not remotely interested in cars. Again, I have to use them, but in the four years that I have owned my present vehicle, I have never once opened either the bonnet or the instruction manual. It has simply never occurred to me to do either. Yet a car-mad friend actually drools over car engines, and slavers over car magazines, hardly able to wait until the new ones come out. Not surprisingly, this friend has been successfully dealing in cars as a sideline for many years, and always drives something a little bit special, a little bit different. This same friend, though, has always made disastrous deals on property.

I'm not interested in antiques either, another area where it is possible for the canny to make a killing. I hate antiques fairs and am never tempted to browse in antique shops. Again, a friend who finds antique and junk shops irresistible has made some very useful sums from buying and selling junk-shop finds.

Because of my total lack of interest in these three commodities, it would be financial suicide for me to invest money in any of them with a view to increasing my capital. Stocks and shares are another area in which I have no natural interest, so I leave those well alone as well.

When it comes to property, this is a different matter altogether. Ever since I was a small child, I have been fascinated by houses and homes. I used to love my doll's house and was always rearranging furniture and fittings in it. (If you think about it, buying investment properties is only an adult extension of organizing your doll's house.) I also used to love designing and decorating my bedroom and my student bedsit, seeing how nice I could make them on nil resources.

As an adult, I welcome the challenge of turning a horrible tip into a wonderful living space, and wherever I go I embarrass my companions by peering into people's windows to glimpse their choice of interior design and to get ideas from them. Also, whenever I pass an estate agent's window, wherever I happen to be, I automatically glance at the prices and properties on offer, much as my antique-loving friend cannot see an antique shop anywhere in the world without going inside. An exciting weekend for me would be one spent viewing potential properties, always asking the important questions: could I live in this myself? If not, why not?

I am also a sucker for property and interiors magazines and always have a huge stack of them in my home. I find those endless, widely derided house make-over shows on television compulsive viewing as well.

I have also been quite successful at buying and selling my own homes. All have sold at a considerable profit, and most were in terrible condition when purchased. But because I could see their potential, I was willing to take the plunge. It's a mistake to imagine that because house prices generally rise, that you can never make a loss. My former in-laws have managed to make a loss on every single house they have ever bought because, in the main, they bought houses which suited them, rather than having an eye to resale value at the same time.

Not everybody can spot a good location, or assess a good price. So if, on looking back at your personal property purchases, you have tended to make a loss, then maybe investing in rental flats is not for you.

Although big-time investment landlords are extremely hard-headed financiers who, very often, do not ever see the rental properties they purchase, most people are simply not like that, and any investment has a degree of emotion tied up in it. In order to become a successful landlord on a small scale – and the vast majority of private landlords own four or less properties – it helps if you have already had extensive, and successful, experience of buying, selling and refurbishing homes. If, by contrast, you have lived in the same house for several decades and have hardly touched it in all that time, becoming an investment landlord may not be the best choice for you. In my own case, when I had a little bit of spare money to invest, putting it into property seemed a sensible choice.

A love of homes and interiors is an essential consideration as, these days at least, the market is constantly changing and has to be carefully watched all the time. If you have already got your hand in, then you will be in a better position to make the fast decisions that may be needed in a constantly fluctuating market.

For example, a particular property may let extremely well for a year or two, then you cannot seem to find tenants for love nor money. Why? It may be that a large organization, employing many hundreds of people looking for temporary accommodation, has just closed down. It may be that more people in the area are now buying rather than renting. It could be that just too many rental properties have come on the market for the number of tenants available. When something like this happens, it may be wise to sell your property and use the money to buy another one in a better area for renting. In one sense, investment property has to be considered almost as a share certificate, rather than a once in a lifetime, permanent purchase.

Looking good

It will be difficult to keep your eye on a changing market unless you have a natural interest in the matter. If you have good taste and enjoy harmonious surroundings, you also put yourself ahead in today's market. Present-day tenants tend to be extremely fussy and turn their noses up at rental properties that are decorated in the wrong colours and have the wrong curtains or carpets for their particular taste. All lettings agencies report that, even nowadays, when so much advice is readily on offer, the number of properties which gladden the heart are pitifully few and far between.

'So many landlords simply have no idea,' said Catherine Cockroft, Lettings Director at the upmarket London agency, Aylesford. 'I often view properties which landlords tell me have only just been refurbished, and my heart sinks when I discover that there is a different carpet in every room, gaudy colours on the walls and unmatching sofas and chairs. I know that my tenants simply won't take such a place, however new the furnishings and however expensive the refurbishment programme.'

A vitally important question to ask when considering embarking on investment properties is: am I reasonably competent at DIY? Although you do not have to be a professional-standard painter and decorator yourself, it certainly helps if you have some knowledge of building and decorating. Again, if you have refurbished many of your own homes in the past, you will have already built up valuable expertise. Unless you are aware of short-cuts and cheap but effective ways around property problems, you risk spending a fortune on refurbishment, money that you cannot hope to recoup in rents for many years.

One investment property I bought had a bathroom which, although new and smart, screamed bad taste. It had shiny black and gold tiles, a black vinyl floor and cheap orange pine bath panel, cupboards and units. The whole thing was a mess and I knew that the chic, smart type of tenant I was interested in attracting would not go for it. What to do? It would have cost well into four figures to retile the walls and replace the flooring, so instead I put up a pair of exotically printed black, orange and red curtains, painted all the nasty cheap pine eggshell black, and put in black towels and a black bathmat. The result was that my hideous bathroom looked like a designer statement, as if it was all intended, and I ended up spending around £100 instead of over £1,000. My tenants, I'm glad to say, love it!

Another flat I bought had a hideous bathroom suite which, as well as being old and stained, was a livid pink. The bathroom also had pink tiles, a sticky pink nylon carpet, and pink walls. A pink rose-patterned blind was at the window. With such a bathroom, the flat was quite unlettable, but again, installing a new one would cost thousands. In this case, I cleaned the stained bath by filling it with bleach and leaving it overnight, and painted the walls aqua. The skirting board was painted a navy blue that exactly matched the cheap cord navy carpet I put down, and a smart navy-blue Roman blind with rope-effect edging went at the window. I put in dark blue and pink towels, and painted the cupboards navy and white. The finished bathroom had a 1930s ocean liner effect (a few large posters of liners also went up) and looked smart and clean. This refurbishment cost less than £300.

In another property, however, there was simply no way of rescuing the tired avocado bathroom. Everything had to come out, and be replaced by a new white suite, new tiles, a new power shower and new vinyl on the floor. Sometimes you can tart up, sometimes you can't – and the trick lies in knowing which.

In the cases where the refurbishment cost a matter of a few hundred, I did it myself, but when I had to replace an entire bathroom, I used professionals. Clearly, the more you can do yourself, the quicker your property will come into profit, but at the same time the place should not look botched and amateurish, and I would not advise messing around with plumbing and electrical items yourself. These highly skilled and potentially dangerous jobs always need experts.

Today's discerning tenants appreciate clean, trendy, designer furniture and to get this look, it will save you a lot of money if you can face going to Ikea, or similar furniture warehouses, and assemble flatpack furniture yourself. When equipping an investment property, you have to know by some kind of sixth sense where you have to spend and where you can safely economize. I know that a cheap Ikea coffee table, costing perhaps £50, does the job just as well as an expensive antique or hardwood one. But I also know, or at least have learnt, that you simply cannot get away with providing tenants with an exhausted, clapped-out sofa. Although sofas and chairs do not have to be top of the range, they do have to look new and be comfortable.

Tables, kitchen chairs – in fact anything that can be painted or covered – can be cheap and cheerful, but the bed, if one is provided, should be smart and newly bought, not salvaged from a junk shop or car boot sale.

When embarking on investment properties you have to know by instinct whether a bleak-looking flat can become a dream home by the simple addition of a large green plant in the corner, or by rearrangement of the furniture. Arnaud Cheung, a Director of Foxtons Estate Agents, said: 'In one flat we viewed, the place looked totally different with some magazines on the coffee table and a big vase of fresh flowers at the window. These little touches can make all the difference between a property being instantly lettable and hanging around on our books for months. Even something apparently very tiny, such as the landlord providing a Tenant's File, containing instructions, guarantees, useful phone numbers, local restaurants and so on, can ensure that a property is instantly let, as it shows that the landlord cares, and is not just money-grubbing.

'But so many landlords,' he added, 'just never think of things like that. You can't just be after the money, but have to give that little bit over and above the basic minimum to be successful.'

You must be businesslike and efficient

In the lettings business, it is essential to be able to move quickly, and to be able to have all the important paperwork readily to hand. (And don't be under any false impression: landlord and tenant transactions generate far more paperwork than you would have ever thought possible.) As a landlord, you will be responsible for preparing the inventory, for checking the tenancy agreement or contract, for repairs, and for informing the utilities companies of incoming and outgoing tenants. If you have a leasehold flat, you may also have to deal with managing agents, Residents' Associations, freeholders, service charges and levies. There will, in addition, be tax and accountancy matters to deal with, solicitors, local boroughs, and possibly County Courts if things go wrong. And each one produces its own mountain of paperwork.

So, if you feel you have the property interest and expertise to become a successful landlord, you now also need to know whether you are efficient and organized enough. Answer the following questions to discover your efficiency rating:

1. When receiving potentially stressful or tedious mail, such as bank and credit card statements, tax returns and so on, do you open and deal with them at once, or put them unopened in a drawer where they risk being forgotten?
2. Do you have an efficient filing system for your domestic bills and important documents, so that you can instantly retrieve them?
3. When there are boring jobs around the house that need attention, such as a leaking tap, a patch of damp or faulty wiring, can you shut your mind to it, or do you deal with the problem at once?
4. Do you follow up telephone calls, enquiries and so on right away or leave them for days on end?
5. Do you keep your accounts tidily and efficiently, or are they always in a terrible mess?
6. Do you find that domestic administration, such as paying gas, electricity and telephone bills, comes easily to you or gets on top of you? As a landlord, this kind of stuff will multiply a millionfold, and the more properties you have, the more you will have to handle this kind of detail.
7. Are you always losing things like keys and important telephone numbers, or are they always to hand?

If you can answer a confident 'yes' to all of these questions, then you are halfway towards being a successful landlord. In my own case, such efficiency did not come easily or naturally, but I soon learnt the hard way and now have separate, easily-accessible colour-coded files for each of my properties and spare sets of keys where I can find them when needed. You would not believe the number of times that tenants lose their keys and can't get into their property. Often the lettings agency does not keep a spare set and even when it does, tenants tend to lock themselves out at midnight or 3 in the morning, rather than when agencies might be open.

Apart from making life easier, efficiency and a good business sense will recommend you to lettings agencies. All have their 'white' and 'black' lists, and if you are blacklisted, you may discover they are unwilling to deal with you. Also, those people who are known to be good landlords tend to attract better, higher-paying tenants.

Do you possess people and management skills?

If you are, or ever have been, on the receiving end of glossy brochures from lettings agencies, you will notice that they all stress one thing above all else, and that is that 'we are in the business of people, rather than property'.

Because as a landlord you are involved in providing that most essential service of all – a roof over somebody's head – you cannot leave out the personal element. If you are a pleasant person to deal with, if you have an instinctive understanding of what a tenant might need, and possess enough empathy to put yourself in the position of a tenant, then you will race ahead in this business.

People working as estate agents and lettings agents learn to be pleasant, however they might be feeling, and they are also, in the main, in professions where a smart appearance is still considered essential. A tenant who is about to hand over an extremely large sum of money to a landlord (and to a tenant, all sums paid in rent are enormous) will be happier when dealing with a sociable, easy kind of personality than somebody who is difficult, defensive or bullying. The landlord–tenant relationship has always been a particularly difficult one to handle, which is why there are so many laws and Acts of Parliament on the matter. Landlords have a reputation for always complaining about their tenants, and tenants have an equal reputation for complaining about their landlords. In fact, it is almost a *sine qua non* of being a tenant that you complain endlessly about the landlord. Where money changes hands on such a personal matter as a home, there is always plenty of scope for misunderstanding, arguments and threatening behaviour.

All professional agencies know that the relationship between tenant and landlord is a tricky one to get absolutely right, and their business is to put some crucial distance between the two. But however great the distance, there is always a possibility that you will have direct contact with your tenant.

The skill lies in being neither too friendly nor too cold. All lettings agencies are adamant that the great majority of problems arise when the landlord and tenant become too friendly. 'The friendlier at the start, the more acrimonious at the finish,' pointed out Jennifer Reigate, a professional inventory clerk. 'My heart always sinks when I hear either a landlord or a tenant say they get on famously with each other, as I know that is going to create problems later.'

Letting property is both intensely personal and a business run for profit. The secret is to be pleasant but not over-friendly, and to have as little to do with the tenant as possible once the formalities have been completed. It is not a good idea to appear ruthless, in the mistaken impression that you are being professional, and it is certainly a grave mistake to treat the tenant as a close personal friend.

The best way to look at the relationship is that of slight professional acquaintances, or as neighbours. There is nothing wrong with exchanging a few friendly words with your tenant if you happen to pass her in the street, but it is not a good idea to invite her in to dinner. There should not be any scope for either side to take advantage.

How do you know whether you have the requisite people skills? If you are in a management position at work, where you have to handle many disparate individuals, or if you have kept many friends over a long period of time, then you most probably do possess people skills, although you may not be aware of it. It is an advantage to be of an equable, optimistic turn of mind, as there are many ups and downs in this game.

Relationships established in this business can become very close for a short time, and in this they can be compared to relationships with people you meet on holiday, where you can be extremely friendly, even intimate, for a week or two, and then they walk out of your lives forever.

Arnaud Cheung of Foxtons took a physics degree at London University and originally had no intention of becoming an estate agent. But now he says: 'After graduating, I realized I was not a natural physicist, and much preferred dealing with people.' His instinct was correct, as three years after joining his agency, he became a director.

As an absentee landlord, you will, with any luck, not have to have all that much to do with your tenant. But you will still have to deal with agencies, officials, inventory clerks and so on – and in a business where there is so much margin for error, so much to go wrong, those possessing people skills will find the whole thing so much less daunting.

If you are considering letting rooms in your own home, or renting out a flat or bedsit in your house, then you will inevitably have much more contact with your tenants. Not all of these may be people you would naturally choose as friends, and the more you can remain pleasant but detached, like the best hotel managers, the better for everybody concerned.

It is essential to have a fairly tolerant turn of mind, to be even-tempered and have an ability to remain calm. Those forever on a 'short fuse' may like to consider some other way of making money.

You should have a problem-solving turn of mind

Again, you will probably already know from previous experience whether this is among your attributes. If, when a problem arises – on any matter at all – your mind immediately turns to possible solutions rather than getting into an automatic panic, then you will already possess this skill.

Problems are endemic to the lettings business, and unforeseen circumstances may arise all the time. The lettings agency may go out of business, your tenant may refuse to pay rent or sublet to somebody else. You may find that your immaculate investment flat is overrun with cats and dogs when you specifically stated 'No pets'. The shower may flood the downstairs flat, and you find yourself being sued for the damage. You may have void periods when you cannot let the place. The washing machine may flood the flat. Neighbours downstairs may complain about noisy parties held by your tenants. If you have a leasehold flat, the freeholder may change and you could find yourself with a massive bill for your share of painting the outside.

All the things that can happen in your own property can happen with an investment property. These are equally subject to all the ills that bricks and mortar are heir too – and then some, because with investment property, you always have to look at the difficulty from another person's point of view as well as your own.

However skilful lettings and managing agencies may be, at the end of the day the property remains yours and you have ultimate responsibility for it. It's your investment, not theirs, and it's up to you to look after it. Others, such as tenants, agents and the like, can just walk away from it if they want to. You can't; at least not until you sell it and move on.

There are many complicated landlord and tenant laws, and you may be unsure of your rights when a dispute crops up. Would you know how to solve these or other problems instantly, or how to get accurate help or advice?

As a landlord, you must be efficient in finding a way round all the problems that are likely to arise. It must be said, though, that practice makes perfect and although the rookie landlord may initially panic when nasty problems develop, you soon gain expertise in dealing with them.

It helps to have an extrovert type of personality

As a landlord, you will be dealing with a large number of different types of people with whom you must develop an instant relationship. You will often find yourself ringing up and contacting complete strangers.

You may have to cope with pushy lettings agencies, wayward tenants, brusque managing agents. The more sociable and outgoing you are, and the pleasanter you can remain, the easier you will find these transactions.

Again, when assessing your own suitability as a landlord, look back to your own life and experience. Do you prefer, like an Anita Brookner hero or heroine, to live on your own in a hermetically sealed flat, rarely admitting visitors? Or are you always giving parties, putting people up overnight, ringing up friends and chatting to strangers?

The chattier and more sociable you are by nature, the easier you will find it to be a landlord, as most of the people you are dealing with will be, and will remain, comparative strangers. You may become extremely friendly with a particular letting agent, for instance, and establish a very good relationship, only to find that the next time you need to find a tenant, that person has moved on and a stranger is at the desk. The lettings world is ephemeral, fast-changing and nothing stays the same for very long, including personnel. You will constantly find yourself dealing with a new set of people. Even if you are lucky enough to have a wonderful tenant who stays three years, eventually she will move on and a stranger will take her place.

Nowadays, very long-term tenants are usually only found in the public sector. The trend in the private sector is towards ever shorter rentals, with some lasting only a few weeks. In some ways, the introduction of the Assured Shorthold Tenancy has encouraged this, but also we are following the United States, where people tend to rent an apartment for an extremely short time.

So don't expect any kind of permanency. On the whole, the shyer and more introverted people are, the more they prefer things to be as permanent as possible. As a landlord, you will be buying into an extremely dynamic, very people-oriented business rather than something slow and steady.

At the same time, patience is a virtue as property investment is seen as medium to long term, rather than something where there are instant enormous returns.

It must be said that by no means all landlords have the wonderful qualities outlined in this chapter – which may be why there is so much strife between landlords and tenants generally. But unless you possess most of the attributes outlined, you are likely to find investing in rental properties a hugely stressful business. It's not an automatic way to riches, and emphatically not a licence to print money.

As one former landlord told me: 'I had an investment flat for a time, but found it just too much hassle; keeping inventories, interviewing tenants, making tax returns, trying not to have void periods.' This person sold his investment flat and was relieved to go back to having a savings account at his bank. The returns are far lower, but he reckons, having tried the business of letting, that it's worth it not to have to deal with tenants and their problems.

If you are still keen, the next important question is: what kind of property should you buy?

In response to increased demand for American refrigeration appliances, Euro Marketing has widened the choice available to you by stocking the entire range from world's leading manufacturers of major home appliances: Whirlpool, Maytag, Admiral & General Electric.

The new range of American Fridge Freezers has been carefully designed to give maximum flexibility and accessibility while still offering the largest possible storage capacity. These fully vented, frost-free fridge freezers offer superb storage results, with temperature controlled drawers, and external humidity controls for the large crispers.

Unique new features, combined with quiet operation and easy-clean design, make the new generation of fridge freezers ideal for a large family.

Our refrigerators give you chance to revolutionise the way you decorate your kitchen. The range includes models in white and black and also offers three optional levels of stainless steel to match the latest exciting ideas for kitchen décor.

Choose stainless steel door panels or even fully clad stainless steel doors, both ideal for built in kitchens. For the ultimate in modern styling, a fully clad in stainless steel fridge freezer will look stunning as a freestanding appliance in a large kitchen.

You don't have to stick to the modern look of black or stainless steel. Some side by side models can be fitted with optional door trim kits to accept coloured panels to match your own décor. If you would like a blue fridge freezer in a blue kitchen, all you have to do is ask for door panels to match your kitchen. The door panels are easily attached to the fridge freezer and can be changed as often as you change your kitchen.

So you don't have to follow fashion, you can follow your own taste.

2

Finding the right property

Supposing you have decided that you want to buy an investment property, and before taking the plunge, you go into a nearby lettings agency for advice. This is a good idea anyway as agencies will be able to give you all kinds of useful preliminary information on the most popular streets, average rents and so on.

Every single agency will tell you exactly the same thing, which is that by far the easiest properties to let are studios and one-bedroom flats. The bigger and grander the flat or house, the more difficult it can be to let.

'We often get potential landlords coming into our offices, telling us they want to buy the biggest property they can, so as to get the highest rent,' said Arnaud Cheung of Foxtons. 'And our advice is always the same: instead of buying one big property, why not buy two or three small ones for the same amount? Around 60 per cent of requests in our lettings departments in every one of our branches are for studios or one-bed flats.'

The reason for this is that nowadays, the person most likely to want to rent rather than buy is a single professional person, usually between the ages of 25 and 35, who has a busy lifestyle and who does not, for the time being, want the hassle or permanency of buying. These are people who have outgrown student and shared accommodation, have usually repaid their student loan, and are looking for a place where they can be on their own.

These days, people paying premium rents prefer to live on their own rather than to share, if they can possibly afford it. Even those in relationships very often prefer to have their own pad – and demand for single-person apartments is increasing all the time. Conversely, demand for three-bed-plus flats and houses is diminishing. And the fewer tenants you have in the one apartment, the less risk there is of trouble and strife therein. The more tenants crowded into one space, the greater the potential for damage, unpaid rent and illegal subletting.

Apart from being easier to let, maintain and decorate and furnish, small flats usually give, pound for pound, a better return on the initial investment than, say, a five-bedroomed house with a massive garden. You may be lucky enough to land a fantastic long-staying tenant right away for your big house but you might also find yourself with lengthy void periods. In a well-chosen location however, a studio or one-bed is unlikely to remain empty for long. Even in a highly competitive market there is still, report agents, a serious shortage of this type of property, and still more tenants than suitable properties available.

The two main considerations to bear in mind when looking for a suitable investment property are:

1. Could I, at a pinch, live in it myself?
2. Location, location, location, or the three Ls.

Could I live in it myself?

The standard advice when buying property is to put location first, but my feeling is that with investment properties, the principal factors to be taken into account are different from those applying to your own home. And the gut reaction as to whether you could live in it yourself is actually more important, initially, than the location.

You might reasonably point out that since you are highly unlikely ever to live in the place yourself, why should you worry about whether you could bear to live in it? The answer to that is: if you couldn't live in it, why should you expect some-body else would want to? But more than that, if you are looking for something which you could inhabit yourself, you are much more likely to make a sensible buy and a sound investment. Although of course there is less emotion tied up in an investment property than in your own home, there is still some. Very few people are completely rational when making up their mind about properties – and potential tenants are the most irrational people of all.

The kind of thing that is likely to put you off will most prob-ably put a potential tenant off as well. I once viewed an ex-council flat that appeared to be a wonderful bargain and was in an ideal location for letting. But once I saw it, I knew I could never market it with any confidence, because it was completely clad, floor to ceiling, in wood. Even the agents selling the property referred to it as 'the sauna' and although they tried to persuade me that it would be 'fantastic for letting' I knew that it would be hard for me even to set foot inside the place, let alone rent it out. Whatever sort of tenant could I hope to attract when I hated the interior so much myself? Yet if you like the place, those being asked to pay rent will most probably like it as well.

Other personal aspects apply when I am looking for an investment property. For example, whenever I am viewing I would never, ever consider a studio flat that had a sofa bed or pull-down bed as the only sleeping arrangement. Because I know that I would hate to get a bed out, make it up and then put it back in the morning to provide living space, I would not ask anybody else to do so. I know that if I lived in such a studio, I would have the sofa bed out all the time, making the place look untidy and cluttered. A studio with a pull-down bed is a slightly better idea, but it would still never do for me because I would always have to make sure there was a 6½ foot empty space in front of the bed when I came to pull it down, and that might mean rearranging furniture all the time.

Nor would I go for a studio flat which only had room for a single bed. I would expect, however theoretically, that I might like somebody to share my bed, at least on occasion. Also, a studio with a double bed can at a pinch be let to a couple, whereas you are definitely restricted to one person if there is only a single bed. And as the biggest current tenant market is the single 20 and 30 somethings, they too are extremely likely to want a boyfriend or girlfriend to stay over sometimes.

Because of these considerations, I never consider square studios converted from a living room, but always look for oblong shapes where you can divide the space into sections for sleeping, living, dining, working – however small they may be. Somebody who has no objections to manoeuvring a sofa bed twice a day may not have the same objection as me. But I could not bring myself to part with upwards of £80,000 to buy a place I hated.

When looking for an investment one-bedroom flat, I always go for those with eat-in kitchens. Because I personally like eat-in kitchens and would never buy a property to live in where I had to cart my food to another room, I expect that any tenants would have the same turn of mind. They might not – but you've got to go on something, and I have found that personal preference works every time.

Assuming you have decided to go for a studio or one-bed flat, there are still very many decisions to be made, each with its own advantages or disadvantages. It makes sense to view a number of potential properties in your price range before you decide to take the plunge, and not to exclude any because of unfounded prejudices. Don't, for instance, automatically turn your nose up at the prospect of buying an ex-council flat as a rental investment. You may, as I do, generally prefer character properties to purpose-built and ex-council flats. They are more aesthetic, more upmarket and more appealing. For me, when I started considering becoming a landlord, my overwhelming preference for Victorian and Georgian properties was so ingrained that at first I refused to look at anything else. I have to have something beautiful, I told myself, even as an investment. Yet as I looked, I soon discovered that the best studios and one-beds were often to be found in 1930s, 50s or 60s blocks, where the studios were purposely designed, rather than being converted from small rooms in the attic or basement.

If you are thinking of buying an investment property in a large town or city – where the biggest rental markets are to be found – you will usually have a choice of:

- conversion;
- mansion block;
- purpose-built block; or
- ex-local authority block.

All of these will be leasehold properties. If looking for a studio or one-bed, you are unlikely to be able to purchase a freehold house, although one-bed starter homes do exist. Sometimes, though, the leases are 999 years, so in effect are little different from freeholds. Average leases will be 125 years.

Conversion

'Conversion' is the name given to properties where a previous single-occupancy house has been converted into flats. A conversion will most likely be a Victorian or Georgian terrace, but it may also be a 1930s or later property built as a house and later divided into flats.

The advantages of a conversion are that rooms are likely to be grand, or at least interesting, and may retain attractive period features such as large windows, ornate ceilings, working fireplaces and cornices. Service charges on conversions (which the landlord has to pay) are usually fairly low, as there is unlikely to be a lift or resident porter, both of which push up maintenance costs.

Disadvantages of conversions are that partition walls are often very thin and noise comes through from other flats. Kitchens and bathrooms are usually very tiny, and the common parts are often extremely dingy. These properties are also usually more expensive to buy than purpose-built blocks, as you pay a premium for the 'character' that you may not be able to realize in extra rent. Generally speaking, conversions do not fetch higher rents than more utilitarian properties. It's the *space*, not the wonderful fireplaces or high ceilings, that tenants are prepared to pay for.

Another disadvantage of conversions is that if the place is very old there may be damp penetration, flaking plasterwork and a battered front door. As all refurbishment to old buildings is expensive, they are often not carried out by the freeholder. In addition, if the building is listed, it can be difficult to get planning permission for improvements. Planning permission takes time, and if you undertake repairs without obtaining the requisite listed building permission, you risk having to undo all your good work.

Very many smaller conversions, such as those with three or four separate units, may be self-managed rather than employing professional managing agents, and as well as the leasehold, you may also be purchasing a share of the freehold. This has its pros and cons. Generally speaking, although not always, professionally managed blocks are better maintained than self-managed blocks. It is also common to get much bickering and rivalry where there is self-management and, as an absentee landlord, you may not be willing to play much part in management.

You should also bear in mind that very many conversions, particularly those carried out during the 1960s and 70s, when planning regulations were less strict, are very badly done indeed. So, if looking for a property in which to invest your money, don't set your heart on a conversion and believe that you must have a character property at all costs.

Mansion block

Mansion blocks are those imposing edifices, usually Edwardian, that are common in central London and other big cities.

The advantages of these, as with conversions, are that you get high ceilings, period features and, very often, well-proportioned rooms. As these apartments were purpose-built, you are unlikely to get thin partition walls, as may be the case with conversions. Flats in mansion blocks are usually expensive and as they are considered desirable residences, the blocks themselves are usually well maintained, with impressive common parts and, very often, a resident porter. There will almost always be a lift. The blocks are very secure and services such as rubbish collection and cleaning of common parts are standard. Very often, gardens and flowerbeds, if any, are meticulously looked after.

Mansion blocks were originally designed to be upmarket residences and as such, frequently have features that add to their luxurious feel, such as mirrors in the hall, deep-pile carpets and expensive thick wallpaper in the common parts. *You as a landlord will be paying for all these!* However, studios and one-beds in mansion blocks are usually cheaper than those in conversions, for one very good reason: the service and maintenance charges are often extremely high, and you may not be able to recoup this in extra rent. In many mansion blocks, heating and hot water are supplied via a central system and included in the service charge. You may not be able to pass the cost of these onto your tenant.

Also, as mansion blocks were built to be grand, small units such as studios and one-beds are often found in the worst positions, such as the lower ground floor where there is very little natural light, making them rather dark and gloomy. Kitchens may be poky and bathrooms old-fashioned. Also, as many mansion blocks are now getting old, renovation programmes, always added to your service charge, can run into several thousands extra. Again, you are unlikely to be able to recoup this on rent, although it must be said that mansion block flats usually resell at a profit.

Purpose-built block

The term 'purpose-built' usually refers to blocks constructed from the 1950s onwards, and these almost always have a square, utilitarian, immediate post-war look.

The advantages of buying into a purpose-built block (PB) are that all the flats inside are designed to be studios, one-beds or whatever, and are not cut-downs from larger spaces. Properties in these blocks tend to be cheaper than in mansion blocks, and service charges are correspondingly lower as well, as there is not the same standard to maintain.

In a block of any size there will almost always be a lift, and there may be a resident porter as well. As with mansion blocks,

PBs are almost always professionally managed, although in recent years there has been a tendency for the block to be managed by a voluntary Residents' Association formed of owners. In most cases, non-resident landlords are not allowed to become part of the management team, as the property is not their main home.

Flats in PBs are usually cheaper than in mansion blocks and, depending on the whim of the architect at the time, may or may not be well designed. Much 1950s and 60s domestic architecture has not stood the test of time, and many PBs suffer from internal problems not easily addressed, such as all the reinforced concrete central to the construction of the building going rusty.

Other disadvantages to PBs may be: flimsy walls, low ceilings and metal windows that have rusted up and refuse to open. These blocks are not as pretty as conversions, or as imposing as mansion blocks, but they do have a 'modern' look and the flats are usually smart, clean and easy to maintain. PBs are extremely popular with tenants, and flats in these buildings, provided the location is right, usually let extremely well.

Ex-local authority block

The final option is to go for a flat in an ex-local authority block. At the time of writing these are the cheapest of all, but they are rapidly catching up with PBs and mansion blocks in purchase price.

For a long time there was a serious stigma attached to local authority properties, especially as in a block of any size the majority of residents would be renting from the council. However, the Right-to-Buy scheme, introduced in the 1980s by Margaret Thatcher, has had the effect of making many former council properties almost as desirable as any other, as owners have often made considerable efforts to improve the appearance of the block, with window boxes, hanging baskets, well-kept gardens and clean communal areas.

The advantages of ex-local authority flats are these: they are around 10 per cent cheaper to buy than other investment properties, and as the freeholder is usually the local authority, service charges are often very low as well. As nobody is making a profit out of these blocks, you are unlikely suddenly to find yourself landed with a huge levy for outside painting, or mending the lift, for instance.

Ex-council flats are very often extremely well designed, with large kitchens, spacious living rooms, bedrooms and bathrooms. Many have small balconies, and some may have private gardens as well. They are often well equipped with built-in cupboards and wardrobes, and the block is often very secure, with magnetic keys issued only to owners and residents.

In a small block where every resident is an owner, as is increasingly the case, the common parts are usually clean and well maintained, although basic. You are unlikely to find carpets or expensive wallpaper there. Another advantage is that if you buy into a block consisting only of one-bed flats, there are unlikely to be hordes of children rushing around.

These blocks are also often in excellent locations. Penthouse flats in high-rise blocks (now becoming desirable again after being derided for years) often have fantastic views, and can represent a real bargain.

The disadvantage of ex-council flats is that from the outside they always look 'local authority' and are usually built to a very basic design indeed. They are emphatically not pretty, and have no frills or designer touches. Their appearance does not gladden the heart, and if you feel that under no circumstances could you ever bear to live in one yourself, you may be better off avoiding this option. But there are council blocks and council blocks. I could not bring myself to buy a property in a council block that looked forbidding and bleak, where there was graffiti scrawled on the walls and where I could hear children screaming. A small, low-rise block where everybody is an owner–occupier, though, may be a different matter.

When purchasing a leasehold property for the purposes of subletting, you must discover whether this is allowed in the lease. Some leases specify that tenants must stay for a minimum of one year; others discourage the idea completely.

Blocks of flats that have a preponderance of middle-class, middle-aged owner-occupiers may not look kindly on transient populations of people holding noisy parties, coming in at 3 in the morning and otherwise disrupting their peace and quiet. Although every owner in a block of flats has a duty not to cause a nuisance, if you are an absentee landlord, you may not be aware of the nuisance your tenants might be creating.

Other options

Another type of investment property is now becoming available, and this is the inner-city block converted from a former warehouse, bank, fire station or other commercial building. These properties often make very attractive living spaces and as they are central, tend to let extremely easily. In central areas of London, these blocks are often entirely bought by investment landlords who never even see the properties, but buy them long before completion. But as these landlords are usually big-time investors from Hong Kong, Singapore or similar, these properties may not be an ideal choice for the timid first-time investor.

The other problem with these properties is that as there may not be anything in the street to compare as to price, you may not know whether you are buying a bargain or not. I myself would not have the confidence to buy into one of these blocks, as I would feel too daunted by the big business and high finance going on all around me. But they may be worth looking into, if they are going up in an area you already know well.

These properties are trendy, 'cool', designed to a high standard, usually with wooden floors, stainless steel kitchens and stone-flagged bathrooms for instance, and they will attract high-powered tenants.

Buying a house for your student children

Nowadays, many parents may consider buying a house for their student children to live in during their university years. Income on the investment is generated by charging other students to live there, and when the university course is over the parents can decide either to sell the house, or keep it going as an investment property. For those with enough money to spare, this is worth considering, as it ensures that your student children have a decent roof over their heads, and the money the other student tenants pay gives a little extra income, as well as providing an interesting alternative to having money on deposit. In many parts of the country, especially where house prices are rising fast, this can be an excellent investment.

Buying a house for student children is often the first step on the way to becoming an investment landlord, and many middle-aged people who never previously saw themselves as landlords are now entering the market by this means.

Matthew Munro of Knight Frank said: 'If you buy a house for your student children, you know the offspring are safe and secure, they don't have to worry about a rogue landlord and they won't find themselves out in the street just before finals.

'Those who have chosen to educate their children privately and have spent a great deal of money doing so, can at least expect to break even.' According to Mr Munro, it makes 'frighteningly good sense'. Many parents with almost-adult children will have paid off their mortgages, but of course such a property would also be available on a Buy-to-Let scheme, in cases where the rents would more than cover the mortgage.

One major advantage of investing in this kind of property is that you know in advance who the tenants will be – your daughter or son, and their friends. If the flat or house belongs to Mummy or Daddy, there is also a greater incentive to look after it.

What is the best kind of property to look for here? Estate agents mainly recommend a classic three-bedroom terrace or semi, especially as the dining room in a three-bed terrace can be converted to a fourth bedroom. Of course returns on the investment depend on area and price paid for the property, but rents of around £1,500 a month all told (in 2001) are about average. New houses lend themselves particularly well to this purpose, so long as they are in the right location. New houses being built near stations, universities and colleges are worth considering if you have a student son or daughter.

In order to be popular as a student home, houses must be no more than a mile from the university. Anything further out is likely to prove difficult to fill up with students.

The choice is yours, and there is no overwhelming single advantage to any of these types of property. Super landlord Greg Shackleton, who owns more than 40 investment properties in Brighton, always goes for conversions in terrible condition, which he then renovates. His feeling is that conversions are more attractive to premium tenants than flats in PBs, and that the vastly lower service charge is a distinct advantage.

In London, one landlord I know buys up flats in terrible condition in ex-council blocks, then renovates them to a high, modern standard. Although the blocks he buys into are often disgusting in themselves, they are always in prime locations, which brings us onto the second important aspect of successful buying to let – location.

Location, location, location

If you are very new to buying investment properties, you may be unsure of the difference between a good location and a bad one. George Humphreys, of the rental investment department at Hamptons estate agents, said: 'Landlords always think they know what makes a good location, but in our experience few of them do.'

If you have always lived in a leafy middle-class suburb, in a large detached house with a double garage and a lawned garden front and rear, this to you may seem a good location: quiet, sedate, away from traffic and noise and near to good schools, churches and shops. But such a favoured spot may not be so good for transient tenants. On the whole, with very few exceptions, the kind of people looking for rented property want to be very near to public transport, no more than 5 minutes away from the station or underground, and within walking distance from shops. Most tenants do not have a car, and as they are single people living alone, will not be making an almighty weekly shop at an out-of-town supermarket. They are much more likely to want to pick up their dinner on the way home, or phone for a takeaway.

Most tenants are not interested in gardens or garages, and prize convenience above all. They are not looking for a lovely thatched cottage with roses round the door, but somewhere smart, chic, modern, easy. In some cases, they want to be no more than 5 minutes away from their place of work, especially if they are working long hours.

When looking for investment properties, it is essential to have potential tenants in mind, rather than just buying somewhere and then hoping that somehow a top-paying tenant will take it. When looking for properties in London, I always make sure that anything I buy is no more than 5 minutes walk away from a tube station, and is in Zone two, at most. Zone five? Forget it. By far the biggest group of London tenants are those working in the City or the West End, and they are looking for living accommodation in a location within easy reach of their work.

My most successful investment flats in central London have been those that are extremely near Central Line underground stations. I have found that high-earning, busy professional people do not object at all to ex-council flats. In fact, if they come from abroad they positively like them, as they remind them of home. The only conditions this type of tenant stipulates are that the flat itself should be spotlessly clean and with everything working as it should.

If buying an investment property outside London, the same considerations should apply: the flat should be very close to the shops and other amenities. Anything else is a plus, but properties with shops in easy walking distance will let far more quickly than those that are miles from any convenience of this type. A golden rule for location, wherever you are thinking of buying is: the property should be no more than 5 minutes away from main transport links. If it's a good quarter of an hour's walk to the nearest station or bus stop, forget it, as it won't be easy to let. Holiday cottages, of course, come into a completely different category, and we will be discussing these later.

In London's Richmond and Chiswick, too far out to tempt most City workers, there are good links both in and out of London, and the places are attractive in themselves. These areas also have the advantage of being very near Heathrow. Which brings us to another location point: properties that are very near major airports tend to let well, because airports employ many thousands of people, not all of whom want to make a long journey after work – especially if they are shift workers.

Those whose jobs involve frequent flying may also prefer to live near to an airport rather than in a quiet, difficult-to-reach village in the country. One landlord of my acquaintance owned some studio flats in a rather bleak 1960s block right near Heathrow. They were always let, because the airport was only minutes away, within walking distance.

A town that has many language schools will attract foreigners, many of whom will be rich young people prepared to pay premium rents. Very often, their rents are paid by Daddy, who wants to know that his son or daughter is temporarily housed somewhere nice, safe and convenient. I once let a flat to a Japanese student who, quite literally, had a suitcase full of money.

Go for what you know

A question new investors often ask is: should the investment property be very near to my own home? Well, there are considerable advantages to this. By far the greatest number of investment landlords start by buying property in an area they already know well. Big-time investors from the Far East are a different matter, as they frequently buy properties when they are no more than a hole in the ground. But for those of us not in this league, different considerations apply.

It makes sense to buy an investment just round the corner from where you live for a number of reasons. First, if you have lived in a particular area for a long time, you are likely to know the price structure of that location, and whether a particular property represents a bargain or not. I currently live in Hammersmith, West London, and my London investment properties have always been in this borough. I know the shops well, I know the transport links, I am aware of the advantages and disadvantages of living in the area, and I keep a keen eye on prices by obsessively looking in agents' windows. As I am on hand, it is also relatively easy for me to view and snap up a bargain should I come across one. I am not on hand to readily view properties in Shoreditch, for instance, and a property that seems a bargain in an unknown area of London may actually be in an area which has hidden horrors of which I know nothing.

A friend who lives in Putney, south-west London, always buys investment properties in Putney, for much the same reason. Although SW15 is not such an obviously good letting area as W14, he feels more confident buying into an area where he has lived for many years than, say, Hackney, which he does not know at all.

Most people working in the City or in central London would not want to rent a place as far out as Putney, but on the other hand, it is a busy place and there are many people working locally, in banks, schools and offices, who are looking to rent. Although Putney is only three miles away from Hammersmith, it represents a completely different kind of rental market. These are all factors that the novice investor should bear in mind when considering any specific purchase.

Greg Shackleton, the super-landlord who has over 40 investment properties, always buys in Brighton, where he lives. He is on hand to view and snap up bargains, he knows precisely whether a particular property is in a good location, and he can quickly call on local agents, builders, handymen and so on.

If you do not know an area at all, it is best to leave it alone, at least until you are in a position to do some research and assess the pros and cons of the place. Very many people who enthusiastically bought investment properties in the Docklands area of London thinking they couldn't lose subsequently found them hard to let. Although they were in one sense central, there were very few facilities, very few good shops and, after work, no 'life' in the area at all. Tenants felt marooned there, and almost as if they were in prison. Most tenants coming to a new area will want to sample at least some of the local life on offer.

Don't forget that the majority of incoming tenants will be strangers to the area and, being mainly young, they like to live in a place where they have access to pubs, cinemas, night life, clubs, theatres and other entertainment. They do not, generally speaking, want to be in a sterile ghetto with security gates and nothing but other new developments as far as the eye can see.

I bought a holiday home on the South coast and, once I got to know the area, I also bought an investment property. Before buying, though, I enquired at a number of letting agents as to the extent of the rental market. I learnt that a couple of multinationals had recently opened up premises nearby and were employing hundreds of IT and computer workers. Most of these were recent graduates, new to the area, and would be looking for smart, easy to maintain rental homes. That decided me. Although rentals were far lower than in London, property prices were correspondingly lower, and so the gross yield was about the same, maybe slightly higher.

The investment property, a small but perfectly formed studio, was soon let to a young man, a recent PhD who had been headhunted at university by an IT firm. He was brand new to the town but as the flat was central, in a pretty seafront location, on major bus routes and near to all the town's amenities, he soon made friends and established a busy social life.

Locations that may not lend themselves to an idyllic family life can work extremely well as a letting proposition. For instance, it is very well worth looking at properties over shops. For most of the time that your tenant is in residence, the shop will be closed, and in the evenings and on Sundays, when they are mainly at home, there will be peace and quiet. Also, shops are usually situated in shopping areas.

A friend bought a rental property in a 1970s block where trains ran very close by. Although this might not be desirable for an old person confined to the home, it was perfect for a tenant who was out all day. The other big plus of this property was that it was right near the station – only 2 or 3 minutes away. For tenants who took the place, the proximity of the station more than made up for the noise of the trains.

Keep your eye on the market

Although successful rental properties must be very near to stations and shops, this does not mean to say that every property in such a location will let easily. Before buying, it is essential to establish whether there is a serious rental market in this particular area, and how big this market might be. In some suburban areas, full of young marrieds with families who prefer to buy rather than rent, there may not be much of a market at all. Also, markets may change dramatically. Near where I live in London, two huge premises, each employing literally thousands of young workers, suddenly closed down and established themselves elsewhere. This meant that a vast potential rental market had suddenly vanished.

These are all things which, in the lettings game, have to be watched carefully. Few things stay the same forever and the essence of success in the investment property market is a willingness to buy and sell as markets change and develop.

Most estate agents maintain that the rental market and the sales market are rarely both good at the same time. If sales are good, rentals are down and if rentals are good, this means that sales are down, usually because of increased interest rates. But if you have a smart, clean property in a location where many people are always looking to rent, then the risk is that much less. And remember, whatever the gloom and doom there *always have been* and there *always will be* people looking for homes to rent.

One important tip: when considering buying investment property, always avoid properties described by estate agents as 'a good rental investment'. Barry Manners, a director of Chard Letting Agents, advises:

> Estate agents always describe properties as good investments when they can't find anything nice to say about them. Steer well clear of any property being marketed as an investment buy.
>
> Also, never go for advice on rental investments to estate agents, who are only interested in selling you something and taking their commission. Instead, ask dedicated letting agents for their views on a particular property or location.

I once narrowly avoided this mistake myself. A very cheap, very well-located property that looked a real bargain was advertised in an estate agent's window as 'a good rental investment'. Just what I'm looking for, I thought, but before arranging to view I had the good sense – as it turned out – to contact a letting agent in the area. She was very clear: 'Never ever buy a property in that block', she shuddered. 'It's terrible. We can't let anything in that building.'

Whether temporarily good or bad, the rental sector will never entirely disappear, and in a sought-after area there are always more tenants than properties. If you are very, very new to the lettings game it might be an idea to wander past a number of lettings agencies and note how busy they are. If the workers inside are chatting to each other and there is nobody in the shop, the rental market, at least in that area, may not be all that good. But if, on the other hand, the premises are crowded with people and everybody looks extremely busy, you are likely to have hit on a location that has more people looking than properties available.

If you are new to the lettings market, it is probably not a good idea to buy a three-bedroom house, with professional sharers in mind. Although there is a demand here, it is much less than for the smaller units. The one exception to this, maybe, is if you are looking to buy accommodation for students to rent.

You may, if you have a lot of money, a lot of nerve, or both, wonder whether to buy a large dilapidated property which you then turn into flats. Such properties can certainly become excellent investments but I would advise leaving them alone until you have got your hand in by first buying studios and one-bed flats. Very often, the budget runs away with you when converting large houses into flats, and it may be a very long time before you see a return on your investment.

Although estate agents always remind clients that buying rental properties should be seen as a medium to long term investment, the fact is that by buying a small flat in reasonable condition, you can be receiving income on it within months of purchase. If you buy somewhere extremely dilapidated, it may be years before you come into profit. Also, unless you are a builder or have expertise here, you can find yourself paying through the nose. And if you add on fees for architects, surveyors and so on, you could find yourself with an extremely expensive liability.

The best advice is: start small and build up gradually, if you find it's working. It's easier to extricate yourself from a small studio flat than from a five-bedroom half-converted Victorian pile.

3

Working out the numbers

One reason why property can be such an attractive investment, apart from the fact that property is exciting in itself, is that you stand to get two bites of the profit cherry. There is the income you obtain month by month from rentals, and there is also, with any luck, the capital increase on your initial outlay.

For instance, if you buy an investment property for £80,000 and rent it out for £8,000 a year, you don't have to be a mathematical genius to work out that you are making a gross annual return of 10 per cent. This is far higher than you can get by any other relatively safe means. Three years later, that same property may be worth £120,000, meaning that your capital has increased by £40,000. Therefore, in three years, you could have made a whacking £64,000 on an initial investment of £80,000, which is not bad by anyone's standards.

Even though these figures are gross rather than net, this sort of return is still extremely handsome, and not at all unusual in the investment property market. If you take away as much as half for costs and taxes, you have still made a wonderful return on your initial investment.

A friend bought an investment property a few years ago for £43,000 and rented it out at £600 a month, the then market rent for that property. Within three years, the value of his flat

had shot up to £90,000, more than doubling his initial investment. He would have, therefore, made loads of money *even if
the property had remained empty for all that time* – a truth not
lost on commercial investors, for whom it may be more profitable to leave a building empty than to rent or lease it out.

However, such large percentage increases cannot be guaranteed or assumed. So, once you have sorted out a good location and have decided, by judicious research, on the type of
property you would like to buy, the next thing to do is to sit
down and work out all the figures as accurately as possible,
down to the last hundred pounds, *before* making any offer.

Cash buyers

We will assume for the moment that you are a cash buyer, as so
many people are these days. Once, when I was viewing a
potential property, I proudly reminded the estate agent that I
was, or would be, a cash buyer. He was unimpressed, saying:
'Everybody is a cash buyer nowadays.' Buy-to-Let schemes,
for those who are not cash buyers, will be explained later in
this chapter.

Rents and payback times

Let's say the asking price of the type of property you have in
mind is £80,000. Before making an offer, it's essential to have
a close idea of the kind of rent you are likely to achieve with
this kind of property in this particular area. You can do this by
asking a number of lettings agencies, or by looking in local
newspapers and agents' windows.

You then have to work out, before doing any other kind of
arithmetic, the optimum yearly gross rental. Most professional
landlords quickly work out the number of years it would take
for the property to pay for itself in rental income before decid-
ing whether to go ahead. Greg Shackleton, for instance, works
according to a 'rule of six': the properties he buys must have
paid for themselves within six years, otherwise he does not
make an offer.

If he buys a property for £60,000, say, the annual gross rental has to be £10,000. Greg, in common with many investment landlords, does not expect the kind of properties he buys to increase greatly in capital value. He does not buy with capital increase in mind, so he has to maximize the rental return.

If your property is likely to increase substantially in value (this must always be an inspired guess, of course, as nobody knows for sure what will happen in the future) then I would say you could go for a 10-year payback period – but not more. A property costing £80,000 has to be capable of earning back that amount in rent within 10 years, otherwise it is most probably not a wise rental investment.

In any case, the gross annual yield should be at least twice that of any savings or investment account at the bank. As there are very many unforeseen costs and circumstances in the property world, you need to make the investment as risk-free as possible.

When talking about payback times, we are assuming that the property will be fully let at all times, without any voids. And of course you never can assume this. Nor can you be absolutely certain that the high rental you get in one year will be achievable in another year. Many landlords have stories of how a particular property was let at an enormous rent for several years, and then could only be let at a dramatically reduced rent. If you discover you have bought in an oversubscribed area, you may not be able to get the rent you hoped for, or were led to believe you could get.

Any rule of thumb on payback times has to be a guesstimate, because none of us has a crystal ball to see into the future. It has been worked out that a void of just one month represents 8.3 per cent of yearly rental income. Letting is never an exact science, so when working out possible returns and costs, one must be as clear-sighted, not to say pessimistic, as possible.

The most you can hope to do is not to fall into obvious traps. If you are considering buying a property costing £200,000 or more, and you are told that the likely rental is £800 a month, or £10,400 a year, then you are most probably not making a wise investment, as it would take you 20 years, not 10, to get back your investment in rent. This is too long.

If, instead of renting, you invested that £200,000 at 4 per cent, you would be getting £8,000 a year, which is almost as much as from rentals, and without any of the hassle.

Other costs

The cost of purchasing the property, though, is by no means the only cost you have to take into account. If you are buying a leasehold flat, there will also be annual service charges on the property. These are charges for which you as a landlord are responsible. Service and maintenance can vary from as little as £200 a year, for an ex-council property, to £5,000 a year or more for a very smart mansion block.

And the charges can change from year to year. Before exchanging contracts you, or your solicitor, need to obtain from the freeholder or managing agents, accounts for the past three years and an estimation of likely charges in the near future. These charges will have to be deducted from any rent you might obtain, as they are not recoverable from the tenant. If the annual service charge is extremely high, you may not be able to recover this in extra rent.

Wily landlords rarely buy investment properties that have very high service charges, as they can substantially eat into your profits. For instance, I once viewed a potentially very nice one-bedroom seafront flat. The asking price was £59,950 and the property needed at least £5,000 spending on it to make it lettable. An agent advised me that I could get perhaps £400 a month for it in rent. At best, that meant an annual gross yield of around 8 per cent. A possibility, then.

But the service and maintenance charges on the property were £2,400 a year. On an income of £400 a month from the place, I would be paying half that just in service and maintenance charges. I'm no mathematician, but it didn't take even me long to work out that these figures didn't add up to a good investment at all.

Outgoings on the property don't necessarily stop with the annual service charges. There will almost certainly be extra levies from time to time to pay for external redecoration, rewiring, repair of the lift and so on. These could mean extra one-off payments of several thousand pounds; again, money you will be unable to recover in increased rentals. All blocks of flats, even those with low service charges, are liable to these levies.

There will also be annual buildings insurance to pay. Sometimes this is included in the annual service charge, sometimes it is an extra. Again, it is something you must find out before buying anywhere. Buildings insurance is compulsory, not optional, as without it you will not be covered should any damage occur to your property.

A corporate or celebrity tenant may not mind, within reason, how much rent they pay, as they will value convenience, smartness and a good postcode above financial considerations. But tenants of this type are not available in every area, and if your most likely tenants are office or bank workers, teachers or lecturers on fairly low incomes, rents cannot be sky high.

There will in addition, on leasehold properties, be an annual ground rent to pay. Usually this is not much, maybe £50 or £100 a year, but it all adds up.

Leases

It is important to know the length of lease, as this can affect the property's resale value. If your lease is 80 years or more, there is little to worry about, but if it is getting dangerously near 70 years or fewer (properties tend to get cheaper as leases shorten, and may therefore be tempting to the investor) you may be better off looking elsewhere. Mortgage providers are not keen to lend on properties where leases are 65 years or less, so you may have trouble reselling the property. Sometimes, though, leases can be extended.

If considering buying a property with a short lease, always ask about the possibility of extending the lease, as you may be lucky. A friend took a deep breath and bought an investment flat with a 60-year lease. As he was a cash buyer, he did not have to worry about satisfying a mortgage company. The short lease meant, though, that although the property was very cheap indeed for what it was, the possibility of reselling at a profit was low.

However, a couple of years later, the residents in the block decided to club together and buy the freehold. This meant another outlay of £3,000–£4,000 for my friend, but because the leases were now extended to 125 years, the value of each property in the block doubled overnight. But my friend was not aware of this when he bought; he just had a lucky strike. He was quite prepared to recover, eventually, his initial outlay in rental income, and was not looking for capital growth.

In some specific cases, though, it can be worth considering buying on a very short lease. Interior designer Linda Camp has bought a small London flat cheaply on a very short lease, for the sole purpose of financing her son's school fees. The lease finishes at just about the same time as her son's education and although there will be no value on the property when the lease runs out, she is able to let it at a high rent in the meantime.

Of course, as Linda is a professional designer, she has been able to make the flat look good on a very tight budget.

Making the property lettable

How much would you have to spend on the place to get into lettable condition? Although when letting privately you can rent it out in any condition at all, provided you can persuade somebody to pay rent for it, if you go through a letting agency, certain standards have to be maintained. There is also the consideration that the better the property, the better the tenant – as a general rule. Also, you are likely to get a higher rent when going through an agency, so it is probably worth refurbishing your property to current standards and regulations.

Reputable agencies will not accept any property where current regulations relating to fire, gas and furniture safety are not met. It is against the law, and no agency wants to be seen breaking the law. It is a risk they dare not take. Nor will agencies these days take on their books a property that does not have a telephone and television point and, if applicable, an entryphone system.

There must be a working shower and a usable kitchen. Agencies vastly prefer properties that have a washing machine and tumble drier, fridge–freezer and microwave. Although not all of these amenities are essential, the more there are the easier the property will be to let. All have to be bought, all have to be in good working order, and instructions and guarantees should be available with every appliance.

Your letting property does not have to be in good condition when you buy it, but it should look like a showhome by the time it is ready to let. Clearly, then, you have to assess not just how much money you would need to spend on it to make it habitable and attractive, but how long this work will take.

One investment landlord makes a point of buying vacant properties in bad condition, and allowing one month between exchange of contracts and completion. During this month, the workforce move in, install a new kitchen and bathroom, paint and decorate throughout, and rewire and re-plumb as necessary. Once contracts have been exchanged, he alerts his local letting agency that a new property will soon be available. They advertise it and, assuming all goes according to plan, on the very day the workforce move out, the new tenant moves in.

This particular landlord reckons to spend between £5,000 and £10,000 on the refurbishment of each property. This sum does not include furniture, as all of his properties are let out unfurnished.

If you are considering buying a property in bad condition, it is worth asking local agents how much extra rent you may be able to achieve if the place is done up superbly, rather than if it is just adequate. In some areas, such as South Kensington in London, for example, there may be a striking difference. In other areas there is a definite rental ceiling, however wonderful the condition of the place, and this cannot be exceeded. In such cases, it may not be worth going for the most expensive kitchen, bathroom and so on.

On the other hand, it is rarely worth going for the cheapest you can get, as you only want to install a kitchen and bathroom once. Bearing in mind that a place that is tenanted gets quite a lot of wear and tear, spending more money upfront may save you repair and renovation costs later. Second-hand appliances, such as a cooker, fridge, washing machine and so on, may be a false economy.

If you already know an excellent and not too pricey team of local builders, then it may be worth your while buying somewhere in bad condition. My South coast studio flat was in truly terrible condition when I bought it. Indeed, it had not been inhabited since 1972 and needed total gutting. But I already knew a good local builder, and so had the confidence to go ahead and buy the place. Small as it was, the renovation cost over £3,000 and it took a year for this to be recouped in rent.

If you do not have anybody reliable to call on, and have to take pot luck out of *Yellow Pages* or similar, you may be better off looking for a place which is more or less lettable as it stands, or simply needs redecorating. You may even consider buying somewhere already let. Estate agents Hamptons International have specialized in this area of the market, and are selling properties already tenanted. This has nothing to do with the grim spectre of the 'sitting tenant' paying a few pounds a week, but an entirely new section of the property market.

In this case, you as the buyer have to do nothing to the place except buy it. The tenant is already there and the appliances, furniture and so on are in place as well. George Humphreys, of Hamptons, said: 'We started doing this in 1997 when we realized that many investment landlords did not want the bother of doing somewhere up and finding tenants. Many of our landlords want somewhere already producing income, without having to wait.' Some examples: a property on the market for £700,000 is already producing £1,000 a week in rent. This represents a gross annual yield of 7.4 per cent. A two-bedroom, two-bathroom property on the market for £220,000 is producing £350 a week in rent, which is a gross yield of 8.3 per cent.

The advantage of this type of purchase is that you do not have to advertise for a tenant and there is no void period – the main terror of the investment landlord – to take into account. Another advantage of buying in this way is that, because the property is already producing income, tax relief will be claimable at once.

All the properties being sold in this way are rented out according to the strictures of the current Housing Act, on Assured Shorthold or company tenancies. Thus, the full market rent is already being obtained for the property.

Although the gross rental yields mentioned above might seem somewhat low to those living outside London, against this you have to remember that the value of the property is likely to rise more than in the provinces, so what you lose on the swings you gain on the roundabouts.

Hamptons confirmed that the cheaper the property was to buy, the higher, percentage-wise, was the gross annual yield in rent. This is almost always the case: the more expensive the property, the lower the percentage rental.

Although it is always tempting to buy a place cheaply and then do it up, as this represents a challenge to the property freak, it is not always a good idea. In some cases renovation can be so expensive that it takes years to recover the amount in rental income. If there is serious structural work to do, as may be the case with an older property, you may not be making a wise investment.

Once you have worked out the likely cost of refurbishment and any furnishings, plus theoretical length of time taken to complete everything (some sofas take three months to deliver), you must add it all to the cost of the property. One property I bought for £82,000 had cost me £85,000 in fees and costs by the time it was ready to let. Also, after completion, there was a month's gap before it was ready to let, meaning that I had a 'void' of one month to take into account.

Although you can claim repairs and refurbishment on tax once the property is let, you cannot do this while you are not receiving income, so you must add it to the capital cost of the investment. These costs can, however, be deducted from your capital gains tax liability when you sell.

Professional and legal costs

Solicitors' fees will be £400 at least; more if there are complications to work out on the lease. There may be other costs for local searches and surveys and you also have to remember to add on VAT for all prices quoted. In normal circumstances, you will not be able to recover the VAT which, at 17.5 per cent at the time of writing, can add considerably to your purchase costs.

If the property costs over £60,000 there will also be stamp duty to pay (again, at the time of writing). This sneaky government tax amounts to 1 per cent of the purchase price; 2.5 per cent if the property costs over £250,000. So, on a property of around £60,000, you would be paying stamp duty of £600. In investment terms, this is also money down the drain and unrecoverable, except when you come to sell.

What about surveys, also very expensive items? I have a personal confession here, which is that I never, ever spend money on a survey when paying cash for a property. Surveyors may say this is foolish (well, they would) but it seems to me that you can tell by looking and smelling whether a place has subsidence, damp, a leaky roof or unsafe wiring. I once viewed a one-bedroom flat, in bad condition, as a prospective investment. The price of the property was £24,000 and the attic flat was characterful and charming. With a little work and expertise, it could have made a wonderful renter, except for one thing: the roof was extremely dodgy, and there was a huge damp patch in one corner. Because of this, I decided against it.

But I didn't need an expensive survey to tell me this. It was possible to assess the condition of the roof just by looking. When surveys cost upwards of £300, doing without one can represent a considerable saving. Over the years I have bought very many properties, both for myself and as rental investments, and I have never once had a full structural survey, not even when buying a totally dilapidated Queen Anne property containing squatters. And I have never once regretted it.

Utilities and council tax

Suppose you have now bought your property. It has been refurbished, all the legal work has been done, and you are ready to let. There are still more costs to come. First of all, if the property contains a gas cooker or gas central heating, you must obtain a gas safety certificate from a fully qualified CORGI engineer, every year. There is a standard annual fee for this job, but it must be done. For this reason, many landlords renovating properties from scratch decide not to have gas. Instead, they go for electric cookers and storage heaters, thus avoiding the expense and organization of getting annual gas certificates. Small flats may not need central heating, and can be heated perfectly adequately with storage or Dimplex heaters.

Because of the need for a gas certificate, wherever I have a choice I won't buy a property with gas heating or gas cookers. Sometimes, though, the property is so perfect in other ways that I sigh and put up with the gas cooker and boiler, and the hassle and expense of obtaining the yearly gas certificate.

While your property is not let, you will be responsible for paying all utilities, including council tax. Gas, electricity and water rates do not stop coming just because you do not have a tenant. And although you may not have to pay council tax while the place is empty, unfurnished and uninhabited, you do have to start paying at least half the full amount as soon as it becomes lettable. In my experience, it is not worth trying to dodge these payments.

Finding a tenant

Whichever way you do it, it costs money to find a tenant. If you decide to go it alone rather than use a letting agency, you will have to factor in the cost of advertising in local or national newspapers, and time spent answering telephone calls and showing prospective tenants round. You will also have to obtain an Assured Shorthold Tenancy form from a stationer. These forms are perfectly legal, and absolutely essential to make the tenancy agreement viable.

Whether you let privately or through a letting agency, it is essential to take up references. Usually, these come from the prospective tenant's bank, current employer and previous landlord. You also have to take one month's rent plus one month's deposit in advance. The deposit is returnable to the tenants at the end of the tenancy, in full – so long as you are satisfied that they have left the place in the condition they found it.

Using an agency

You may well decide that it is safer and better to go through a letting agency than to risk renting out a property by yourself. Again, there are pluses and minuses. The minus is that you have to pay the agency at least 10 per cent plus VAT of the rent. The plus is that all the proper checks are made, tenants are properly vetted, and you may well get a higher rental than through private ads. You may also find that the cost of advertising the flat yourself comes to almost as much as six months' commission from the agency.

Although professional letting agencies can reduce many potential risks of a non-paying or otherwise unsatisfactory tenant, they cannot cut them out altogether. When I first became a landlord, I let my flat through an ad in a local newspaper. This proved so successful that I used the same method for three successive tenants. I came unstuck, however, when I tried to find a fourth tenant. Although many people came to view the property, none took it. Seeing an endless aching void opening up in front of me, I contacted a letting agency that found me a tenant straightaway.

They took up references, one month's rent and the deposit and the tenant moved in, professing herself 'delighted' with the clean white space of the flat. She proved to be my one and only tenant from hell. First she moved her boyfriend in. Then a little dog came. Then she refused to pay rent, complaining that the street outside the flat was 'noisy'. Finally she had to be evicted. She had, naturally, trashed the flat, and it took me two full weeks to get it back in lettable condition.

I chased her through the courts for unpaid rent but never got it, as she had been sent to prison for other offences. After her release, she left the country and I never saw or heard from her again. She left a trail of unpaid bills behind her – the telephone bill, water rates, electricity and council tax. All of which goes to show that, however careful you or the agency may be, it is impossible to be clever all the time.

A friend let a very nice flat, again through a long-established letting agency, to a tenant who apparently had a millionaire brother. This tenant had recently got divorced, and his ex-wife had been awarded the marital home. He had a good steady job, though, and a reliable income. None of this prevented him from losing his job not long after moving in and absconding after two months, leaving unpaid rent and quite a lot of damage in the newly refurbished flat.

If using an agency, you should make sure you go to one that is a member of ARLA, the Association of Residential Letting

Agents. ARLA was founded in 1981 as the professional and regulatory body for letting agents, and is regularly consulted on matters pertaining to the private rented sector by government, local authorities, housing interest groups and researchers.

In order to become a member of ARLA, an agency must have successfully run a lettings business for at least two years, hold and operate separate client accounts and carry professional indemnity insurance to a required standard. A copy of this insurance policy must be lodged with ARLA in order to comply with the requirements of the ARLA Fidelity Bond.

A firm that has been in business for less than two years may apply for intermediate membership until the Association is satisfied that all the criteria have been met. Letting agents who are members of ARLA usually display the logo prominently, and use it on all their advertising and company literature. There should also be a certificate of membership available for inspection in their offices.

This safeguard is designed to protect the landlord's rent and the tenant's deposit. There have been all too many cases of rogue letting agents using client's money to pay staff, rather than being kept in a separate, untouchable client account.

ARLA have produced a useful leaflet, *Trouble Free Letting,* which is available from their head office (see Chapter 10 for their address). This leaflet outlines all the main points landlords should bear in mind when considering letting their property through an ARLA member.

Agency fees and services

So, what about their fees? These may vary slightly from agency to agency, but in practice there seems little deviation. Most charge 10 per cent of the monthly rental, and this is payable upfront in its entirety for the length of the tenancy. So if your tenant signs on for a year, you will have to pay the agency a year's commission. Refunds are given when the tenancies end before this time.

Most agencies operate on a sliding scale, whereby the longer the same tenant is in place, the less commission you pay. An average commission would be 10 per cent for the first year, 7.5 per cent for the second year and 5 per cent for the third and successive years.

Landlords are often tempted to tell the agency that the tenant has now left, to avoid paying this commission. Some landlords feel that as the agency is now doing nothing to earn its commission, it should not be paid. But this is illegal. Should the agency discover that the same tenant is in place, they will be able to sue you for unpaid commission. And they will usually win.

Most letting agents have a complicated structure of fees charged, according to the service provided. There may, for instance, be a fixed sum, usually about three weeks' rent, charged for an 'introduction' to a suitable tenant. Once the tenant is in and the various checks completed, the agent withdraws and plays no more part in the transaction. This system works when you live nearby and can attend to your tenant's problems yourself.

Other services may include rent collection, responsibility for repairs and renovation, and attending to tenant's problems. Every extra service comes at extra cost. Fees for short-term lets, where the tenant stays for a shorter time than the standard six months, may go up to 20 per cent, although as you almost always get a much higher rent for short-term lets, you may still be well in pocket.

The standard 10 per cent that most agents charge includes advertising for and finding a suitable tenant, showing prospective tenants round, checking references and bank statements, taking a holding deposit (usually £200 or so, to secure the property for the tenant) and later, taking the full deposit and one month's rent in advance. Agents will also set up a standing order whereby the rent is paid monthly into your account. They will also draw up the tenancy agreement. Most agencies will also, at the same time, arrange for all utilities to be put in the tenant's name, telephone reconnection and council tax.

All this paperwork takes on average 10 working days. Agents will also introduce you to your tenant, but after the initial work has been completed, they do no more work apart from taking their commission when it becomes due. And don't think they will ever forget: letting agents have elephant-like memories when it comes to taking their commission.

For another 5 per cent, on average, you can have 'management'. This is a more comprehensive service and includes rent collection, holding the deposit, arranging repairs and calling out plumbers, for instance. If you go for 'management' this means that all the cares of being a landlord will be taken off your shoulders. But of course, for this luxury you pay an extra 5 per cent, plus, as ever, VAT.

Management is essential if you live abroad, or at a great distance, and simply cannot manage the place yourself. But if you live locally, I would say that management is a luxury that most landlords can do without. Management may make sense, though, if you have a very large or extremely valuable property to let.

Some agencies will also arrange to have your property furnished, and all the requisite appliances delivered and installed. Full management, which may include furnishing and kitting out a property, is probably only sensible with very expensive central London properties. It is a good idea in any case to go to several letting agencies and compare prices and services.

You can also have a professional inventory carried out. This will cost you another £100 or so, and only you can decide whether it is worth it or not. Again, if you are renting out an expensive property that contains valuable antiques and paintings, a professional inventory is a must. Letting agents can arrange these. Usually, inventory clerks do a very thorough job, but they are another luxury and another cost to be taken into account. If you have a very standard type of property, containing only the basics, you can perfectly well write out the inventory yourself. It's not a difficult job. An example of a typical inventory is given in the next chapter.

Some agents may prefer to hold your deposit and put it in their own bank accounts, whatever level of service you go for. In some countries, notably Australia, it is the law for agents to hold the tenant's deposit, or 'bond' as it is called. When using agents, I always prefer to hold the deposit myself, and also have the monthly rent paid straight into my account by direct debit. If deposits are held by an agency, you do not get any interest on the amount and neither does the tenant, however much it is or however long it is held. Administrative costs, I'm told, almost always exceed any interest payable.

Members of ARLA will also arrange insurance cover, although they are not allowed to tout for this kind of business. ARLA strongly advises landlords to go for legal expenses and rental insurance cover, usually calculated as a percentage of the monthly rental paid. Personally I never take out any insurance of this type as I don't think that on balance it's worth it. But again, if you are letting a very costly property, or one where non-payment of rent would cause your world to collapse, you may think it worth considering. But now that you can get tenants evicted in eight weeks, you are only talking about two months' rent at most. In fact, it usually comes to one month's rent in effect, as when tenants do not pay rent as agreed, their deposit is automatically withheld.

It is also possible to get contents insurance if you are letting out a furnished property. Again, this is probably only sensible if your property contains extremely valuable and not easily replaced items.

Here is a typical rundown of costs on a property costing £60,000 to buy. Say you obtain a rental of £600 pcm, amounting to £7,200 a year, you are making a gross annual return on your investment of 12 per cent:

Letting and management @ 15% plus VAT	£1,270
Documentary charge	£100
Ground rent pa	£150
Service charge/buildings insurance	£700
Contents insurance	£120
Repairs allowance	£300
Gas contract and safety report	£130
Total:	£2,770
Net revenue return before tax	£4,430
Net revenue return on capital	7.38% pa
Possible capital appreciation	5.00% pa
Total return before tax:	**12.38% pa**

(Figures courtesy of ARLA)

On a freehold house costing £100,000, the total return before tax is likely to be slightly lower, at 11.65 per cent pa gross.

These figures are for guidance only, and exclude any void periods. But it is important to bear in mind that the value of any investment, including property, may go down as well as up.

E-letting

Since the first edition of this book was published, e-letting, or online letting, has become a force to be reckoned with. E-letting sites are, in the main, smart, easily accessible, highly comprehensive and provide a valid alternative both to using a traditional high-street agency and to going it completely alone.

Online letting is a high-tech facility whereby landlords and tenants can find each other and, with any luck, meet each other's needs perfectly. Tenants key in what they want, landlords key in what they have to offer, and so long as all goes well, a perfect partnership results, thanks to the wonders of modern science.

Potential tenants can type in all their requirements, such as location, number of rooms, type of property sought, whether they are looking for something furnished or unfurnished, and the maximum rent payable. They can do this from anywhere in the world.

Landlords, for their part, can upload a set of photographs of their property onto the same site, together with a full written advertisement. For a fee, payable by credit card in advance, landlords can also download all the information and documentation required to create a legally valid tenancy.

There is also a large amount of advice available for both tenants and landlords to download. On e-letting sites, tenants tend to be known as 'home hunters', which is, perhaps, a more up-to-date and politically correct term than 'tenant', which can have pejorative connotations.

Most e-letting sites also have a freephone number that either party can call for advice on matters relating to the site. Letting advisers are available to speak to, although only on an advice basis. They do not act as agents.

E-letting sites are updated daily and are comprehensive enough to enable both landlord and tenant to bypass the traditional high-street agency completely. E-letting also has the distinct advantage of being far cheaper than an agency, while at the same time providing all the services needed, such as credit reference checks, inventories, gas safety check reminders, insurance, rent guarantee arrangements and document packs.

Some online letting companies can also arrange for gas and electricity checks, repairs and furnishings, for a suitable extra fee, of course.

All downloadable documentation and agreements have been carefully checked by lawyers conversant with the highly complicated landlord and tenant laws, and these are regularly updated as laws and requirements change.

When e-letting sites first began to appear on the Internet, there were fears from traditional voices in the industry that online letting would become an unregulated free-for-all whereby unscrupulous operators would offer poor or non-existent services at the same time as taking your credit card details for their own nefarious purposes.

ARLA also strongly advised against e-letting, on the basis that the personal touch was required for successful matching of landlord and tenant. It was feared that such a delicate and complex process as letting properties could not properly be accomplished purely by electronic means.

So far, though, these fears have proved unfounded, possibly because most, if not all, the companies that have set up online letting sites are run by people with many years' experience as letting agents. Successful letting is a many-step process, with a great deal that can go wrong at any stage, so it would probably put off get-rich-quick merchants and fly-by-night operators. Also, unless the service provided was both cost-effective and efficient, no landlord or tenant would use it for very long.

Further, there is the fact that because the service has to be vastly cheaper than high-street agencies in order to persuade anybody to use it, there are no instant dotcom fortunes to be made. Those who have established e-letting sites accept that, as with most property matters, the road to riches is likely to take years rather than months.

E-letting is pure e-commerce, in that you can do the whole thing via the computer. These days, most high-street agencies have a Web site on which they post properties to be let. But that is not e-letting, as after you have viewed the properties, you still have to go to the agency to register and physically view the properties. All the Web site does in these instances is to advertise properties on their books. With e-letting, the landlord is responsible for everything.

Once potential tenants have posted their requirements on the site, they have to sit back and wait for landlords with properties that meet these requirements to contact them. Usually, there is no charge whatsoever for the tenant aspect of the equation.

Most e-letting sites are getting a large number of hits from tenants from all over the world, though the uptake from landlords, who have more to do, more to spend and more to lose if anything goes wrong, is proving slower.

Landlords can usually advertise their properties for nothing, for a limited time at least, but they have to pay for any documentation they download. Reference checks, insurance, tenancy agreements, property management diaries and so on are usually priced individually, so it is up to each landlord to decide how much material it is necessary to download to create a legally valid and hopefully trouble-free tenancy.

So the important question must be: is e-letting for you?

The answer is that all depends. It is currently the case that about 50 per cent of private landlords prefer to go it alone rather than use an agency. These landlords advertise, draw up agreements, check references and show tenants round their properties themselves. The other 50 per cent of landlords prefer to have the neutral buffer zone of a professional agency.

E-letting operates as a kind of halfway house between these two options and, as with most halfway houses, you get a service that is better than going it alone, but not as good (or more trouble) than using a reputable agency.

The enormous advantage of e-letting is that it is cheap. At the time of writing, the most a landlord has to pay per property is about £100. This contrasts with about £1,000 to let a property via a high-street agency. But there is no quality control and there are no minimum standards. Property owners can post any kind of property they like on the site and it is up to the tenant to discover whether the kitchen is clean, whether the furniture meets safety requirements, or whether there is severe damp, for instance.

Landlords also have no quality control over tenants. One task of a high-street agency is to vet and filter tenants and weed out the undesirables. With e-letting, as the landlord you have personally to meet potential tenants at your property, and take the time and trouble to show them round. It is you who has to make a snap decision as to whether a particular person would be a good bet; agents do this all day and every day, and get to know the bag eggs.

E-letting is necessarily far more time-consuming and may be more frustrating than using an agent. With the former, as landlord you have to set the rent (though rental advice is available on some sites). By contrast, when instructing an agency you will be advised as to the likely rent your property would command. The standard advice from e-letting sites is that it's better to have a lower rent with the property permanently occupied than to demand an unrealistically high rent that might mean long void periods.

That's all very well, but if you are a novice landlord you may simply not have any idea of the kind of rent your property might command. Nor might you know whether the property is smart enough or renovated adequately to meet modern requirements, which are becoming more exacting all the time.

Another downside of e-letting is that landlords have to do their own management, such as organizing repairs, preparing inventories and giving tenants notice. None of this is done for you on the Web site. In fact, there is little or no human contact at all.

But e-letting is far cheaper than registering with an agency and has the added advantage that if you suffer from insomnia and wish to upload or download property details at three in the morning, then there is nothing to prevent you. There are no opening and closing hours, and if you are highly computer literate, you may even enjoy this means of finding your ideal property or your ideal landlord.

But you have to remember that, however carefully the e-letting site has been designed, at the end of the day it is up to you. All you download are pieces of paper, not a guarantee that this particular tenant or that particular property has been through any kind of screening.

Will e-letting make the high-street agency redundant? My own view is that this is unlikely for the foreseeable future. It is just another means of doing the job, that is all.

Although e-letting is certainly harder work for both landlord and tenant than going through an agency, it is – for the landlord at least – a considerable advance on going it entirely alone. When going it alone, you have to advertise your property in local or national newspapers, which can work out extremely expensive and does not guarantee results.

When I advertised a property in what used to be called the 'top people's' paper, the only responses I received were from lettings agencies. It is very easy to spend several hundred pounds on advertising, yet receive no suitable responses at all. And all the time you are advertising and waiting for replies, the void period is likely to be lengthening.

With e-letting, as a landlord you are far less likely to receive those frustrating responses from agencies. There is also the huge advantage that you can describe your property in detail, with pictures, for no extra cost. When you advertise in print, by contrast, the more space you take up, the greater the cost of the ad. Display ads, picture ads, wordy ads: all cost more and you are also operating in the dark.

I would say that e-letting is far cheaper, far more efficient and more effective than going it totally alone. All the information and advice you receive is up to date, whereas landlords who have gone it alone for a long time may not be fully conversant with all the current rules, regulations and legal requirements.

If you fully own your rental properties, then there is no reason why you should not use e-letting, if you so wish. But those landlords acquiring properties on a bank loan or Buy-to-Let mortgage may be required to use an ARLA-registered agency. It has to be remembered that Buy-to-Let mortgages were an ARLA initiative, and are organized under their auspices. You may be falling foul of your contract, therefore, to use an e-letting site to save the cost of a high-street agency. It is worth checking.

Two of the best-established e-letting sites are Froglet.com, and Lettingbrokers.com. Both of these comprehensive sites are operated by people with many years' experience in the lettings industry. The operators of both these sites also continue to operate high-street agencies, and see both running happily in tandem.

Jason Cliffe, marketing manager of Froglet.com, an offshoot of Leaders Rental Agents, says:

> Froglet is pure e-commerce, and bypasses the high-street agency completely. The two big advantages for the landlord are those of price and of fulfilment. It's a bit like online banking, where you can do it at a time to suit you rather than anybody else.
>
> We don't advise on pricing and receive very few direct enquiries. Everything is done through the Web site, although we do advise on how to present your property to its best advantage. The advantage for the tenant is that e-letting provides another, completely free access.

Many rental properties, adds Cliffe, are not available through high-street agents because so many landlords don't use agencies anyway.

> We have worked hard to make sure our site looks professional and functions efficiently. There are reference checks available at three levels, buildings and contents insurance and rent guarantees. Not all landlords use all the facilities available, but they are there.
>
> As we see it, the two markets – those of using an agency and going it alone – are very different, and never the twain shall meet. The advice we give to both landlord and tenant is very basic, but is geared to both new and experienced landlords.
>
> We have, of course, no control over the quality of properties posted on the site, whereas agents insist on minimum standards.

Froglet.com operates throughout England and Wales, whereas Lettingbrokers.com has decided to concentrate on London and Hertfordshire only. Co-founder Steven Constanti, also a lettings agent, says:

Our slogan is 'no agents, no commission', and that's exactly how e-letting works. We are slightly different from other sites in that one of our representatives will personally visit the property to be let, and advise the landlord accordingly. We can also provide smart-looking To Let boards.

People who have not let before can call us on our freephone number, and we will talk them through the letting process. We offer a fully comprehensive pack, and have a tie-up with Maras, the reference-checking company. What landlords require above all is a full credit reference check for a potential tenant. We advise landlords not to proceed with any tenant whose references are unsatisfactory.

Letting agencies carry out credit and other reference checks as a matter of course, but so far it has not been easy for go-it-alone landlords to access detailed credit checks. E-letting fills this important gap, as all sensible landlords will need to know that the tenant can pay the rent, and does not have any County Court Judgements or any other record of non-payment.

In common with Jason Cliffe, Steven Constanti believes there is room for both e-letting and the high-street agency to coexist peacefully. It is not a matter of the motor car replacing the horse and carriage, more that cars, motorbikes and push-bikes can all use the highway at the same time.

Constanti says:

At least 50 per cent of our landlords have also instructed an agency, and it's a matter of which comes up first. We started business early in 2001 and instantly had a phenomenal response from tenants. I predict that e-letting will grow slowly, but that it will take its place as a recognized facility within the letting industry.

As e-letting sites do not quality as agencies, they cannot be members of ARLA and as yet do not have their own profes-sional body. Some e-letting sites belong to the Which? Webtrader Code of Practice, and this sign is worth looking out for on an e-letting Web site.

It is true that there is nothing to prevent anyone starting up an e-letting site, whether or not they have the background expertise. But then the same can be said of letting agencies.

Although most reputable ones are members of ARLA, this is not a legal requirement for setting up an agency. The general advice with e-letting must be: if you feel at all nervous with using this facility, leave it alone and go for the traditional high-street agency.

But if you want to save yourself a four-figure sum, and are computer literate, there is no reason at all not to go for it.

Buying at auction

Very many investment properties are bought at auction. In fact, it is a fair bet that the majority of people at house auction sales will be there with a view to buying an investment property, either to rent, or to do up and sell on. Usually, estate agents arrange block viewings when properties are to be sold at auction, so at least you will get a preview of your fellow bidders.

You can now get whole books and reams of advice on buying at auction. As with any other form of purchase, there are pros and cons.

Prices at auction sales often seem to be very low, but properties are usually sold at auction for a very good reason – they are unsaleable by other means. They may be in terrible condition, there may be outstanding service or other charges on them, they may have had squatters in for many years. There may be legal problems, there may be serious subsidence, or a major road may be planned to run right past the property.

Auctioneers and estate agents have a duty to point out the defects of each property coming up at auction, but otherwise it is a case of *caveat emptor* – let the buyer beware. At auction sales, you will be up against hard-nosed experienced property developers and investors. However, you can certainly pick up a bargain, or what seems like a bargain.

One property developer bought a totally dilapidated London house for £230,000 at auction. At the time, similar houses in the street were going for around £500,000, if in impeccable condition. His house took over a year and cost £150,000 to renovate. It looked good when finished, and went on the market for £600,000. But – it didn't sell, and in the end the buyer was forced to rent it out for £800 a week. This represented an extremely slow way of getting his money back. The problem was that houses in that particular street simply would not sell for the high price this buyer needed, because they did not have gardens. Nor could he get more than £800 a week in rent, in that particular area. So in the end, that house was hardly the bargain it first seemed.

Buying at auction assumes all the preliminaries have been made, because when the hammer comes down, the property becomes yours. The knock of the hammer signals that contracts have been exchanged. Therefore, solicitors must have been instructed, mortgage valuations made (if appropriate) and surveys and searches undertaken well in advance of the auction date. You must be financially ready to take possession of the property on the very day of the sale.

If you do not manage to secure the property at auction, you will lose all the money incurred in instructing solicitors, carrying out local searches and so on. You will have to put it down to experience, as there will be no way of recovering your money. So far I have never dared to buy a property at auction, although as I get bolder, that day may come. Many investment landlords I know have done extremely well with auctioned properties, although most, it must be said, are able to call on a reliable team of builders to renovate the property.

Buy-to-Let

So far, all figures have been worked out on the assumption that you are a cash buyer who does not need to borrow money to buy your investment property. Until 1996, the great majority of private landlords were people who had paid cash for their letting properties, simply because it was extremely difficult to rent out any other type of property. As a rule, you were not allowed to rent out a property on which you had an outstanding mortgage, although some mortgage lenders gave permission for this if certain conditions were satisfied. However, the now famous Buy-to-Let scheme then came in, and has proved

The natural choice in Kent for mortgages and savings.

Call freephone **0800 783 4248** or call in at any branch.

Advertisement feature

THREE STEPS TO
LETTING HEAVEN

The rapid and substantial growth in the buy to let market has provided a welcome source of income and capital growth for a new breed of small private landlords at a time when the returns on more traditional forms of investments such as equities and bank and building society deposits have been falling

However, there are very few types of investment which are without risk, even with long established and reputable firms, as policy holders with Equitable Life have recently discovered.

Landlords who have considered the potential risks and taken the appropriate steps to minimise their effects will be better prepared than those who have only looked at the rental income available.

Step One: Choose the right property

Estate agents will tell you that the three most important things to consider when buying a property are location, location and location. This applies whether you are purchasing a new home to live in or as an investment to let out.

Ideally the property should be in a sought after residential area popular with owner occupiers. If there is then any fall in demand for rented properties, a suitable property could be sold for owner occupation.

The cheapest property may appear to provide the highest return on capital invested, but is there any scope for capital growth? If a property rises in value, not only does this provide a potential nest egg but it also provides the opportunity to trade, i.e sell the property, realise the profit and reinvest in cheaper property.

Avoid properties in estates of largely ex local authority properties, flats in high rise blocks, poorly converted flats and houses in multiple occupation. Although gross rents may appear attractive, maintenance and management costs are also likely to be high resulting in lower net income and less scope for capital appreciation.

Step Two: Choose the right lender

Your choice of lender is as important as your choice of property. The lender should not be looked upon simply as a means to an end, but as an important partner in making the deal work. A good lender will effectively be looking for the same things as you, i.e. a good property at the right price in the right location; a good tenant who looks after the property and pays the rent when due; sufficient rent to cover the mortgage with something to spare and the likelihood that the value of the property will increase rather than fall.

Choose a lender who understands the buy to let market and is able to adapt to individual circumstances, some of the new "specialist" lenders are in fact very rigid with limits on the numbers of properties you can buy, minimum loans and only one form of acceptable tenancy agreement: the assured shorthold. A good lender will allow you to choose the number of properties you buy, will not have a minimum loan, will consider controlled tenancies, fair rents and other forms of agreement. A very good lender will offer repayment or interest only mortgages, fixed or variable interest rates and will charge interest on a daily or monthly basis, rather than the old fashioned and expensive annual basis still charged by some lenders.

Some lenders will also insist that the property is professionally managed. Whilst this should give peace of mind, it may be too restrictive if you are capable of managing the property yourself thereby avoiding management fees. If you know the area, have plumbers, electricians, glaziers etc on call, adequate insurance and the time to look after your property and tenants, then there is no reason why your lender should not let you manage your own properties.

Step Three: Choose the right tenant

Interview prospective tenants and obtain meaningful references. A good tenant is worth looking after and holding on to. A bad tenant may damage your property, not pay the rent on time and take up so much of your time and money that you wish that you had never bought the property. If you have a good tenant, then charge a realistic rent. It is better to receive £300 per month every month than ask £325 and have the property empty for four weeks.

Whilst nothing is fail safe, choosing the right property, lender and tenant will give you the best chance of making a success and avoiding problems

Rob Procter BA FCIB
Head of Lending
Kent Reliance Building Society

UNTANGLING BUY TO LET

The property market has been the salvation for many a shrewd investor in recent months. It is little wonder therefore, that so many people wanting to break into this market do so without much thought or preparation and frequently get their fingers burnt. In this article Pauline Roessler from Leek United Building Society, looks at the buy to let market and points out both the pitfalls and the opportunities open to investors with excess capital in their pockets.

The buy to let market is increasing at a rapid rate. Bricks and mortar are seen as a more shrewd investment than invisible stocks and shares and potential buyers can see what they are getting for their money. However, there are some key considerations that need to be taken into account before plunging into the market.

Number One – Choose you area carefully
You need to work out where you want to buy a property and then consider the type of tenant you would like to have. Overall you want an area which is not saturated with rented property but has a good mix of owned and rented accommodation.

Number Two – Work out your budget and stick to it
Buying a second house is no different to buying your first. Get a budget in mind and stick to it. There is no point in finding what you think will be an excellent property to let only to find that it is £20,000 out of your price range and in order to afford the repayments.

Number Three – Ensure you have the right insurance cover
Make sure you have adequate insurance cover. You should guard yourself with insurance against non-payment of the rent by your tenants, this will help you to ensure that the house remains your property.

Number Four – Be aware of forthcoming changes in government legislation
Changes in legislation means that areas that were previously considered taxable are no longer covered. Work carried out on your property that could be classed as improvement can no longer be offset against the rent.

Number Five – Be a good landlord
Lettings agents are all very well and good but if you only have one property and you live close enough to it, do the job yourself and help to ensure a strong and cordial relationship with your tenants. You can save yourself money by checking meter readings, doing minor repair work around the house and keep the gardens in shape.

One of the most competitive products on the market is currently being offered by Leek United Building Society at 1% discounted for the first three years (assuming a base rate of 5.69%). Established for 139 years and known as the Friendlier Face of Finance, Leek United Building Society is well renowned for its personal approach to customer service. Customers don't necessarily have to live in an area where there is a Leek United branch … they even have customers who have bought from the comfort of their home in Calgary, Canada. If you are interested in buy to let as a way of investing, contact Leek United on freephone 0800 093 0004 for details on its rates for buy to let products.

extremely successful. This was an ARLA initiative, and has completely transformed the private rented sector.

Previously, those who wished to buy investment properties were either surcharged or forced to borrow at commercial bank rates. In these cases, potential rental income was not taken into account for servicing the loans. From 1996, however, a number of mortgage lenders have brought their interest rates in line with rates for owner-occupied properties, and also take rental income into account. These changes came about, says ARLA, because of the new confidence with which mortgage providers regarded ARLA members. If professional letting and property management agents were involved then, the thinking went, the risk to lenders would be very slight indeed.

Here is a typical Buy-to-Let scheme, as offered by Mortgage Express. Note: other lenders' figures and conditions may vary slightly, but are unlikely to differ dramatically from this information given.

You can buy an unlimited number of properties, either privately or at auction, up to a maximum total of £500,000. In order to be eligible for an investment mortgage you must have a guaranteed income (earned from sources other than letting property) of not less than £20,000 if you are a single person, or £30,000 joint income when buying with a spouse or partner. If you are self-employed the mortgage lender will need to see three years' audited accounts.

The ability to repay the mortgage is not based, however, on your income, but on the rent received from the property or properties. This must be between 130 and 150 per cent of the monthly mortgage payment. For instance, if your mortgage repayment works out at £100 a week, your income from rent must be at least £130 a week. The minimum age for eligibility for an investment mortgage is 25, and the maximum age 75. The minimum term for borrowing is five years and the maximum term is 25 years' repayment.

Once you have bought your property with an investment mortgage, you must let it out on an Assured Shorthold Tenancy agreement (known as 'Short Assured' in Scotland) within three months of purchase. It must be let, or be available to let, for the whole duration of the mortgage. You cannot live in it yourself.

Interested in
Buy to Let?

Call us to talk about our range of highly competitive flexible mortgages, designed to adapt with your needs and lifestyle. You can overpay, underpay, borrow back or take payment holidays.**

You could even save thousands of pounds over the life of your mortgage.

Let's talk

0500 666 555*

Legal &
General

Advertisement feature

Multiple tenancies and DSS or diplomatic immunity lets are not usually allowed, and properties must have one kitchen and not more than five bedrooms. Rooming houses, or houses where facilities such as kitchen and bathrooms are shared, are not suitable for Buy-to-Let schemes. Under certain circumstances though, it may be allowable to let to local authorities.

The rate of interest payable is linked to the Bank of England base rate, so is liable to change as interest rates fluctuate. You can borrow up to 75 per cent of the purchase price of the property, provided always that the rental is at least 130 per cent of the mortgage repayments.

Some part of the loan may be available for repairs and renovation, or as a deposit for a new investment property. Usually, you will not be required to purchase insurance cover, and the standard mortgage arrangement will be straight repayment or interest-only repayment. Most Buy-to-Let mortgages are quite flexible, and it is advisable to discuss the possibility very thoroughly with a mortgage provider so that you are aware of all the pros and cons before taking the plunge.

In fact, it is quite difficult to buy a pig in a poke on a Buy-to-Let scheme, as you are required to have an inspection and valuation of the property you are interested in buying. The valuer will also advise you on the suitability of the particular property for rental purposes. The valuation fee is based on the value of the property and can vary (at the time of writing) between £117 and £205, or thereabouts. There is also a fee of around £250 for setting up the mortgage and this will be added to your loan on completion of the deal.

You can make capital repayments to reduce your loan at any time, but if the mortgage is redeemed within three years, a redemption fee of three months' interest will be payable.

Here are some typical figures: if you borrow £30,000 to buy a property valued at £50,000, repayable monthly over 25 years on a repayment basis, the total amount payable will come to just over £73,000. With any luck your investment property will be worth at least that after 25 years. If you are paying back £100 a week on your investment property and you achieve £130 a week in rent, that leaves you with just £30 a week pocket money – hardly a billionaire's income. 'It provides a holiday for you,' said one mortgage company, 'but that's about all.'

Advertisement feature

THE PROFIT OF A
BUY-TO-LET INVESTMENT
IS IN THE BUYING . . .

There is some conjecture that TV's Rigsby delayed the growth of the Buy-to-Let market single-handedly for many years. The rather seedy live-in landlord, the dilapidated building and its rather archaic decoration, the hands-on attitude to rent collection offered little to the aspiring entrepreneur or investor.

However, 30 years on, the business of letting property has changed radically. Greater awareness of its potential, dramatically growing demand for property, a legal framework that protects the parties involved set the scene. These together with the increasingly flexible financial products have brought about a metamorphosis in the image of the traditional landlord, suggesting that perhaps Leonard Rossiter's portrayal of the character exploited the weakness of that individual.

Buy-to-Let has become a popular and fashionable investment. It is built on the dynamic growth of UK residential property values, growing awareness that property is, in the medium to long term, a "safe" investment and, perhaps most importantly, on the wealth inherited from the property boom of the seventies and eighties. For many, this will have provided the first financial cushion ever.

Now, choosing a lender is not a question of just going down the High Street, or calling an existing lender. True, many address the market, and almost all can adapt a standard residential mortgage to suit Buy-to-Let criteria, but if you are true to the disciplines of calculating the return on your investment, the Buy-to-Let Landlord must buy financial products professionally to maximise the investment opportunity.

It is not so much choosing a lender, but choosing a broker that is the important task facing the investor. Buying privately from lenders can be a repetitive, and time-consuming - ultimately a wasteful process. Choosing a reputable broker may not be easy at first glance, however a little research will point you in the right direction.

Look for a broker who is an active member of the National Association of Commercial Finance Brokers, an organisation set up to safeguard consumers' interests, to establish a code of practice and to market the industry by providing introductions to reputable specialists in the commercial finance industry.

One such broker Mortgages for Business Ltd, a recognised market leader, has embraced the internet and provides a quick and easy introduction to a host of commercial mortgages through its web site **www.mortgagesforbusiness.co.uk**. The company has built its business on the back of the growth in the buy-to-let market, working with a panel of lenders to develop exclusive and unique products which it markets to discerning customers.

"Our customers have become increasingly professional as the market has grown," said David Whittaker the company's managing director. "We have been able to communicate their needs to our lenders and package special products that enable Landlords to create and develop portfolios quickly and efficiently."

A buy-to-let investment is rarely a one off purchase. The dynamics of Buy-to-Let appreciating capital values, regular conversations with letting agents and mortgage brokers, and expenses covered by rental payments all highlight opportunities to extend from one property to two and then to a portfolio with remarkable ease.

"When a landlord is looking to improve the financial performance of an investment or a portfolio," comments David Whittaker, "we are often able to take a proactive approach that will be different to many 'first choice' lenders. For example we have negotiated an exclusive mortgage with a higher loan to value of 85% and interest rates from 0.95% over LIBOR. The investor can then be sure that his rate will remain consistently competitive with interest rates for the term of the mortgage but can also increase his ability to extend his portfolio by borrowing a larger amount on new or existing properties, to maximise his potential to invest further."

Taking care and professional advice is the cornerstone of any investment strategy; in Buy-to-Let it is no different.

For more information visit
www.mortgagesforbusiness.co.uk
or call 0845 345 67 88

Investment mortgages are aimed at the small-ι.
for those who have savings on deposit they are ι.
increase. Investment properties, provided the right cheι.
carried out, are relatively safe, and Buy-to-Let schemes are ι.
for what one agent termed the 'pork belly speculator' interested in high risk and high returns. They are not aimed at
people with a gambling mentality, but rather, the more timid
type of investor.

Feedback from those who have taken advantage of Buy-to-
Let schemes shows that they tend to be cautious people who
are attracted by the idea of something tangible as an investment, 'something you can walk past', rather than an abstract
share portfolio.

ARLA gives some useful tips for Buy-to-Letters:

- *Do* think of it as a medium to long term investment.
- *Do* make sure the rent covers borrowings and costs, after
  allowing for void periods of between one and two months a
  year.
- *Don't* purchase anything with serious maintenance problems, such as a thatched roof or a very large garden. These
  add nothing to the rental value and cost a lot in upkeep.
- *Don't* imagine that investment properties can be left to
  friends or relatives to look after. Professional services are
  essential.

Tax

Now we come to the thorny but unavoidable subject of tax.
Net rental income is subject to income tax at the marginal rate
(22 or 40 per cent, whichever is applicable). 'Net' income
means that amount of income left over when all expenses
incurred in letting, including loan interest payments, are
taken into account. Insurance cover and any VAT incurred are
also allowable. A wear and tear allowance of 10 per cent of the
rent is available where properties are furnished. All income
from letting is subject to tax, and this applies whether you are
letting rooms in your home, you are an investment landlord, or

are letting your home while you are abroad. UK landlords living abroad are subject to UK tax on their rented properties.

If you carry out any refurbishment while the place is let, you can claim this. But in order to set costs against income tax you must be receiving income, however small. One friend got round the refurbishment problem by allowing a relative to live in her flat at a peppercorn rent, while she refurbished it with a view to letting it.

Your accountant, if you have one, will work out the figures for you. Some of the larger letting agencies can also give information on your tax situation. Although novice landlords are understandably frightened of having to pay huge taxes on investment properties, especially when there are so many other costs to consider, in fact there are very many items you can set against tax.

When you come to sell your investment property you will most probably incur Capital Gains Tax, set at 40 per cent of any profit made, or the capital gain. For instance, if you bought an investment property for £50,000 and sold it for £75,000 you would be liable for Capital Gains Tax on the £25,000. Forty per cent of this comes to £10,000, which is your tax liability.

Capital Gains Tax is commonly seen as a terrible bogey, but it is not always as bad as it seems. When you sell, although not when you let, you are allowed to set against tax all the costs incurred in the purchase, such as legal fees, stamp duty, cost of renovating and furnishing, carpeting, accountancy fees and so on. That tax liability could easily come down to £3,000 or £4,000 – far less painful. There is also, when calculating Capital Gains Tax, an added complication known as indexation. This means that inflation is taken into account. For example, if in 1976 you bought an investment property at £50,000 and it is now worth £250,000, a significant proportion of that increase will be due to inflation. The amount of Capital Gains Tax paid also depends on how long you have had the property, as this tax was only introduced in 1982.

If you have been renting out rooms in your own home, the situation gets even more complicated. If you have a lodger with her own bedroom, you are not liable for Capital Gains Tax when you sell. But if you have been letting, say, a self-contained basement flat you could be liable for a proportion of the gain on your home. This proportion will depend on how much of your home you have let out, and the length of time for which it has been let.

As Capital Gains Tax is extremely complicated, you should talk to your accountant or tax adviser before selling any investment property, as you may gain or lose according to when the tax year falls. To take a personal example, in one single tax year I sold two investment properties, and so had to pay Capital Gains Tax on both. But if I'd waited just three days to complete on the second property, I would have been liable to pay for this in the following tax year. I shan't make such a mistake again.

Inland Revenue staff these days are extremely helpful, and can give you chapter and verse on Capital Gains and other tax liabilities relating to furnished and unfurnished lettings. As the tax position can be complicated, and vary according to other circumstances in your life, each case has to be assessed individually. What we can say is that income derived from lettings is subject to tax: nothing is more certain than that.

There is one notable exception, however. Under the Government's Rent-a-Room scheme, you do not have to pay tax on rent from a lodger in your home if the gross annual amount of rent is less than a specified amount. Obviously this is liable to constant change, but in 2001, the first £4,250 could be tax free. To find out more, you can obtain the Inland Revenue leaflet, *Letting and Your Home* (IR87) from any tax office. The Rent-a-Room scheme was designed to encourage more people to provide accommodation by letting spare rooms in their home. Previously, fear of tax liability put people off doing this.

Generally speaking, expenses that are 'wholly and necessarily' incurred in letting out property can be set against tax. Food, if provided (as with a lodger or B&B guests) is an allowable expense.

It's worth it!

Although initially the figures on the debit side may look daunting, as there seem to be so very many costs to set against gross rental income, the fact is that most people who let properties find they do very nicely, and the extra dollop of income received every month from rent is very welcome indeed.

When I have gone through lean times in my 'day job', that guaranteed income, provided the tenant pays up of course (and the vast majority do, I'm glad to say) has helped through many a crisis. In fact, if you have some savings, an inheritance or redundancy money, it's hard to think of any better way to use it.

The late newspaper columnist Auberon Waugh once wrote an article asking whatever do you do with a sum such as £90,000 – an amount he had received from selling an antique at auction. He complained that it was an awkward amount of money, too much just to spend and not enough to invest with any reasonable return. But clearly, the best thing to do would have been to buy an investment property and let it out to somebody who would be grateful for a decent roof over their head.

In fact, it's hard to imagine a better way of using spare cash than to provide somebody with a desirable home in return for rent. You gain, and somebody else gains. If it all works out well, it's a win–win situation.

Hodgkinson's Law of Landlord and Tenant

A sum of money which seems large for the tenant to pay is not much for the landlord to receive.

BEAUTIFUL HARDWOOD FLOORING

Make your floor an object of desire. It's what it's made of that makes the difference. Insist on 100% genuine timber, fitted by Timberland, the UK's leading hardwood flooring company.

- Beautiful, natural and enduring
- Free nationwide Home Design Service
- Easy to clean and non-allergenic
- Europe's largest choice of timbers
- Installed by Timberland craftsmen
- 10 year independent guarantee

FREEPHONE TODAY
0800 980 2468
FOR YOUR FREE DESIGN SERVICE AND COLOUR BROCHURE
OPEN 24 HOURS A DAY, 7 DAYS A WEEK
www.timberland.co.uk

 Timberland Flooring Co. Ltd

THE ORIGINAL AND STILL THE BEST

Décor and renovation

How 'desirable' does the property have to be to attract good tenants? And what constitutes a desirable property in today's terms? There is little doubt that standards of rental flats are getting higher all the time, and that clean, smart flats and houses are fast becoming the norm rather than the exception.

It must be said that the success of the Buy-to-Let scheme and the increased professionalism of letting agencies since the formation of ARLA have pushed up the standard of much rented accommodation, including even student accommodation.

Furniture stores selling mainly to landlords report that since letting became a middle-class, professional activity, there has been a new insistence on chic, matching furniture, plain carpets and neutral coloured walls. The days of swirly carpets fighting with mildewed, faded-rose-patterned wallpaper and grim, brown, uncut moquette three-piece suites are, if not over, rapidly passing, thank goodness.

Hamptons International, which has produced a *Lettings Handbook,* makes the following recommendations for investment property:

- Carpets and walls should be in a neutral colour. Whites and pale creams make the freshest, cleanest impression.

A most desirable residence

Making the decision to let a property often comes after careful consideration. With so many things to sort out, security for your rented property may not be at the top of your list – until your tenants have a break in. It is a sad fact, but most burglar alarms are only installed after a burglary. As desirable as your property is to the prospective tenant, wouldn't a safe and secure home make it even better?

If you have already made the wise investment of a burglar alarm, can you be certain that the Police will know that your property has been broken into? The only way you can be sure, is to have an intruder alarm that is monitored. What's more, a monitored alarm can not only look after your property and tenant's possessions but their personal safety as well.

The Myth of ringing bells

A traditional burglar alarm tries to scare off intruders by the noise of a ringing bell or siren. But did you know that these traditional ringing alarms cannot ensure a response from the Police? If you were lucky, a neighbour might phone them to report the alarm, but the Police may only respond if someone can actually tell them there has been a burglary or an attempted burglary at your property.

Monitoring means a guaranteed response

A monitored alarm can help protect your property and your tenants around the clock. If the alarm is activated, they can be assured of the right help – quickly.

Your property is connected 24 hours a day to a fully manned Alarm Receiving Centre via the phone line and if the system is activated, the Centre will know about it straight away. Within seconds they will call your property to verify the alarm (to help filter out false alarms) and where appropriate, will summon help immediately.

Good news for neighbours

Monitored alarms don't always need a loud external siren, so there's no noise to annoy the neighbours. An internal siren is used as a deterrent to intruders to let them know that the alarm has been activated.

Twice as good

Monitored alarms can also help guard against personal attack and fire, or even obtain emergency support from a designated friend or neighbour who has keys to the property.

Panic buttons can be added enabling your tenants to summon help if you they are attacked at their rented home. Some systems could let them send a secret signal if an intruder forced them to switch off the alarm against their will.

Many people use battery-powered smoke detectors at home as a warning against fire, but all too often the batteries are dead. Adding monitored smoke or fire detectors to a system can help protect your property and tenants from the threat of fire 24 hours a day, even if the intruder alarm is not switched on.

Reducing False Alarms

In England, Wales and Northern Ireland, Police Policy states that new monitored alarm systems have to be 'confirmed'. This means an Alarm Receiving Centre can only report a break-in to the Police if they receive a signal from two separate detectors, which 'confirms' the break-in. This was introduced to cut down the number of false calls that the Police attend, so they can deploy their resources more effectively.

How do I get a monitored alarm?

Most security companies will visit your property to conduct a free no-obligation survey, to find out your specific security needs and design a system to suit you. Once you have had a survey, the company will give you a quote for their recommended system. Choose a reputable company, which is independently regulated (look out for ones that are approved by NACOSS or SSAIB). This will ensure that your installation is of the highest quality and that your monitored alarm will qualify for Police response. Some companies have their own Alarm Receiving Centres whereas others use a third party, so be sure to check.

Having a monitored alarm will require you to have keyholders – people whom you have designated to hold keys to the property. When the alarm is activated (and if the tenants cannot be contacted) one of the keyholders will be asked to provide access for the emergency services - they do not have to put themselves in harm's way. Keyholders should live nearby to your premises and know how to operate your alarm system! As the owner of the property, and if possible, it would make sense for you to be one of the keyholders.

How much?

For a monitored alarm system you will usually pay an up-front installation cost and an ongoing monthly charge for monitoring and maintenance. Prices will vary according to the amount of detection equipment that is installed.

Having an approved monitored alarm may entitle you to a discount on house insurance and your insurer can advise you on this.

A monitored security system is capable of fending off more than just burglars and can summon help when it is needed it most. It can look after your property whether rented or vacant, as well as making your tenants more safe and secure. A monitored security system can help turn your 'To Let' into a most desirable residence.

This property was more appealing for them to rent, it had a monitored security system installed

ADT MONITORING • ADVANCED SECURITY • RIGHT DOWN THE LINE

When you're letting a property, you need to be sure that your property and your tenants are fully protected. With a monitored security system from ADT Fire and Security your property is connected 24 hours a day to a fully manned Alarm Receiving Centre via the phone line. If your alarm is activated, we will know about it, and where appropriate, can get the right help quickly. We can also help protect against the threat of fire 24 hours a day. ADT is the UK's leading security systems company protecting homes and businesses nation-wide.

Call ADT now and find out how you can make your rental property even more appealing with ADT monitored security.

Phone free on 0800 010 999

Please quote reference "KP Letting" to book your free no-obligation security survey

- Paint finishes are easier than wallpaper to maintain, although wallpaper may be expected in very high-value properties.
- Good-quality curtains and carpets are essential. They are particularly important in unfurnished property where they are highly visible.
- Kitchens should be well equipped, and this ideally means a dishwasher, large fridge-freezer, washing-machine, separate tumble-drier and microwave.
- Bathrooms should have high-quality fittings and be well lit. Power showers and fully tiled floors and walls are expected by corporate clients.
- Bedrooms should have ample wardrobe space.
- If letting to corporate clients, high standards are expected. Woodstrip floors, low voltage lighting, granite work surfaces will all impress premium clients.

To furnish or not?

If you have recently bought, or are considering buying an investment property, you will at some stage have to make a decision as to whether to furnish it. There is little, nowadays, to choose in rent, and the days when unfurnished lettings gave tenants more security of tenure are over. At one time, unfurnished premises were considered more 'permanent' than furnished, as tenants could not be so easily evicted. For this reason, most landlords preferred to 'furnish' their property, even if the furniture consisted of broken chairs and collapsed beds. These days, both furnished and unfurnished lettings are governed by the same laws and tenancy agreements, so there is little advantage either financially or in terms of security of tenure either way. Tenants in unfurnished accommodation can be evicted as swiftly as those in furnished lettings. A landlord enjoys the same legal protection, whether the property is furnished or unfurnished.

Generally speaking, the majority of properties in central London are let furnished, whereas country properties are more likely to be let unfurnished. Greg Shackleton, our super landlord, always lets his properties unfurnished as, on the scale he operates, it is simply not practical to keep buying sofas and washing machines. By contrast, the former actress Fiona Fullerton, now a property magnate, says that she always lets her properties furnished, wherever they are, simply because they look so much nicer that way. It is certainly true that unfurnished flats can look bleak, bare and uninviting. They may not 'show' as well as furnished properties.

This is something all landlords must take into account: first impressions. It is not a scientifically proven observation that I am about to make, but it seems to me that women prefer to let places furnished, whereas men tend to let them unfurnished. This may be because female property investors can't bear to leave a place unfinished, and just love putting in little touches. I always put a vase of flowers, a plant or some ornaments in my flats, simply because I prefer them that way when showing tenants round. At the risk of seeming sexist, it also seems to me that women naturally tend to make a home of an invest- ment property, whereas men, with a beady eye on maximizing profit, will be content to leave them as bleak and unhomely looking as possible.

So in a sense, the decision to furnish or not depends on your temperament, as there is little to choose either in legal protec- tion or in achievable rent. Agents do point out, though, that unfurnished properties may take longer to let, so there is an increased risk of void periods. Against this, it has to be remem- bered that furnishing a place will cost something, so it may be a matter of balancing possible void periods against the expense of furnishing a property.

Many agents report that unfurnished properties take longer to let than furnished ones, because they tend to look bleak without furniture. In fact, one agent said: 'If you want to let a flat unfurnished – furnish it first, even if you take the furniture out before the tenant moves in.'

Two friends of mine bought dingy, dated flats, renovated them to a high standard, then waited – and waited – for a suit- able tenant to move in. One waited nine months, the other waited five months, before the flats were let. The reason? They were completely unfurnished and so had little 'eye appeal', even though they were clean, smart and modern.

In fact, when one of the owners put in a bed, table, sofa and chairs, his flat was let instantly. When considering whether or not to furnish, one has to ask oneself: why do property developers always have show homes? Simply so that prospective buyers can see for themselves how wonderful the place could look.

Most tenants, it has to be said, have decidedly undeveloped powers of visualization when they are shown an unfurnished flat. They can't imagine how it could look. Another important factor is that rooms look far larger and more impressive when furnished than when empty. An empty room is just uninviting.

Also, it may be difficult for potential tenants, giving the place a cursory glance, to see how a double bed, sofa, wardrobe, computer desk and so on could fit into the space available. Many properties that are let unfurnished do have furniture in them, of course, which belongs to the outgoing tenant. It's the completely bare flat or house that can be hard to let, even to those who are actually looking for an unfurnished property.

Another option for those who do not want to be landed with dozens of tables, chairs and beds is to hire all furniture. This is a solution adopted by property developer David Humphreys, who buys properties to let both for himself and on behalf of clients.

He says: 'If you hire furniture, you can replace anything which is broken or past its best with a matching item. This may not be possible if you buy at sales or at places like Ikea or Habitat, which have a fast, unrepeatable turnover of styles.

'There is also the advantage that furniture on hire is tax-deductible, which is not the case when you furnish before letting.' An average price for hiring a whole flat full of furniture is around £175 per month.

The essentials

Whether a property is let furnished or unfurnished, it should *always* have a fully fitted kitchen which contains a cooker, washing-machine and dryer, fridge-freezer, and if the property is a three-bedroom house or flat, a dishwasher is recommended as well. There is no need to put a dishwasher into a studio or one-bedroom flat; indeed, it is most probably a waste

The sensor electronics and technical innovations in the Bosch Maxx iT deliver faster wash times across all programmes with no loss of performance.

The new Bosch Maxx iT washes up to 40% faster.

BOSCH
Excellence comes as standard

www.boschmaxxit.co.uk
Brochure line 0870 727 0446

"It's just up the stairs and into the attic"

space
you've more in an ideal world

Ideal-Standard www.ideal-standard.co.uk e-mail: ideal-standard@aseur.com Tel: 0800 228476 Fax: 01482 445886

Ideal Standard

More Rooms, Less Space?

Not with Ideal-Standard, who took 'the smallest room' in the house and combined it with design excellence to produce a market leading award-winner.

Today tenants want more rooms in their rented properties. En-suite bathrooms, walk-in wardrobes and studies, are high on the 'hit-list'. Although these 'additional spaces' are being added, overall the sizes of properties is not getting any larger. As a result, rooms are small so landlords need to make the most of the space available. The bathroom – 'the smallest room' in the house - is no exception to this.

Research has found that the average family bathroom is no larger than a king-sized bed. En-suites and even second family bathrooms are increasingly popular in new-build properties. The latest Building Regulations make an additional downstairs cloakroom an essential requirement. With this in mind, Britain's best known bathroom manufacturer, Ideal-Standard produced a bathroom suite that was both designed to fit neatly and purposely into small bathrooms and best of all make use of every inch of available space.

Ideal-Standard then carried out a survey in which one hundred of Ideal-Standard's customers supplied drawings and dimensions of their bathrooms, of which the six smallest and most awkward were recreated using full-scale models, in what became known as the 'Space Lab'. Prototype products designed by Royal Designer for Industry Robin Levien, were then installed, tested and altered accordingly within these model bathrooms until the perfect product was produced.

The result was the award winning Space range

Space is not only designed to make the most of every available inch of space in the home. The sloping rooms and awkward corners of additional bathrooms are brought into use with products that help to fill 'dead' spaces.

When fitting the Space suite into a family bathroom, typical installation challenges such as the basin overhanging the bath are solved. In this instance with the Space narrow basin. Short-projection basins prevent un-necessary intrusion into the rest of the bathroom and in return make the bathroom appear larger.

The Space offset shower bath, available in both left and right hand versions, is shorter and wider than the standard size bath and has an extra wide 'foot' end which becomes the showering space. Co-ordinated with the specially designed shower screen, a shower fitting over the Space bath eliminates the need for a separate shower cubical, once seen as an essential addition to a bathroom.

Space WC suites incorporate a number of innovative designs. Corner WCs fit neatly into un-used corners demonstrating Space's philosophy of making the most of every available space. All Space WCs come with the option of having the seat at a 45° angle. With the seat angled in this way, the WC suite can be fitted closer to the wall or to other sanitary ware. The Space WC can be fitted as close-coupled suite, corner close-coupled suite or as a back-to-wall suite.

The latest addition to Space is a range of fully fitted bathroom furniture. Space furniture neatly optimises living space and conceals plumbing, as well as saving space. The short projection of Space Furniture, just 20cm, is the smallest footprint of any furniture on the market and is crucial to its space-maximising properties. The 60cm wide washbasin unit can be used in a wall-mounted or floor-standing configuration with an optional plinth. Storage space is created under the basin hidden by two decorative doors.

The high-pressure laminate fascias and doors are available in three finishes; gloss white, maple effect or lavender.

The unique WC unit is 45cm wide and when installed side by side with the washbasin unit they provide WC and full size basin facilities in a width of only 150cm.

For the past four years, since its launch in 1998, the Space range has won many awards for its innovative design. Included amongst them are: the FX International Design Award for Best Residential Fitting; The Design Council Millennium Product status, a scheme recognising innovation, creativity and design; and the 1999 D&AD Silver Award for Most Outstanding Product for the Home, beating off strong competition, which included the iMac Apple Computer. This year Space added the Your Home/Daily Mail Ideal Home Show award for Best Bathroom Product.

For stockist information or to order a Space brochure call Ideal-Standard on Tel: 01482 346461 or visit www.ideal-standard.co.uk

For additional press information please contact:
Cathryn Brannan, DRA Communications
Tel: 01296 670178 Fax: 01296 670179 Email: cathryn@dracommunications.com

of money, as tenants usually consider them too much of a hassle to use. Also, it's yet another possible thing to go wrong.

If putting in a new kitchen, I would always go for white units in tenanted properties. As kitchen units are basically all much the same, and it's only the doors that add the style or otherwise, there's nothing wrong with going for the cheapest units available. I have found that Wickes kitchen units work perfectly well. Tenants can add their own touches of colour. Also make sure all 'white goods' are white. Colours date a place.

There should also be in all rental properties a good working heating system, a power shower, curtains and carpets. Also, service contracts, guarantees and useful phone numbers should be provided and left in the tenant's file.

Many landlords do not pay enough attention to the important matter of the tenant's file. From experience, I have learnt that it is essential to have important information in a readily accessible, durable file that remains in the property.

All guarantees and instructions that are likely to get wet, such as those for the shower and washing-machine, should be laminated. Also, take a photocopy for yourself, as it can be difficult to replace instructions once lost.

You should also give your tenant details of any peculiarities pertaining to the lease or the building, such as whether washing can be hung on the balcony, or relating to noise or pets. Some managing agents now prepare cut-down versions of leases especially for landlords to give their tenants. Ask your managing agents whether they do this.

Tenants often complain that landlords never leave sets of instructions or, if they do, they are in a tatty, unreadable pile hidden away in a cupboard. Leaving a smart file shows that you care – and this encourages the tenant to care as well.

All letting agencies say that properties should be 'in good decorative order' – but what exactly does that mean? There are certain golden rules which must be obeyed, the first of which is not to decorate in your own personal taste, if this is in any way eccentric or idiosyncratic, as the more individual the property, the fewer tenants it is likely to attract. The safest option is to go for white or, preferably, very pale cream, ivory or buttermilk. Magnolia now looks rather dated, and in any case, has a rather nasty pink tinge. Paint all doors and woodwork in eggshell gloss. Use good-quality paint and if you can bear it, put on three coats. Then the property won't have to be repainted for several years. In flats without picture rails or coving, I always paint the ceiling the same colour as the walls, thus avoiding the inevitably wobbly demarcation line. You could alternatively put up a wallpaper border or polystyrene coving, but both require quite a lot of expertise and are expensive in labour.

Wooden floors are extremely popular with tenants, and some tenants even request them when going to letting agencies. Before going to the expense of laying a wooden floor, however, check that it is allowed if the property is leasehold. Some leases stipulate that floors must be covered in fitted carpet, for the sake of the residents below. Wooden floors tend to be noisy.

Carpets are more hardwearing than wooden floors, and don't show up stilettos or scuff marks so much. Also, wooden floors ideally need sanding every two to three years – another expense. Ikea-type simulated wooden floors are not particularly hard wearing and probably not ideal for tenanted properties. Carpets should be the same throughout the property, as this makes the flat look more spacious and streamlined. Don't use cheap off-cuts and bits of carpet; do it properly. The best colour is beige, not too light and not too dark. Light carpet shows the dirt, and dark carpet shows up all the bits. A beige carpet with a darker fleck in it is probably the most practical of all.

Some landlords maintain that it's essential to put down good-quality carpet. I'm not so sure. I have found, over the years, that cheap cord carpet works perfectly well for rented flats. Whatever you do, though, don't ever put carpets in bathrooms and kitchens. Tenants coming from the Continent are often horrified to find carpet in UK bathrooms. Instead, put down vinyl, properly fitted, in any room where there is likely to be wet, or spillages. Even the very best tenants cannot always avoid spilling bleach, washing-up liquid, red wine or tomato ketchup on kitchen floors.

Curtains are a potential problem. Professional inventory clerk Jennifer Reigate, who visits several properties a week to check inventories, said: 'Even these days, I rarely see nice curtains yet these, more than anything else, absolutely make a property.' My number one rule is: if you can't afford, or don't feel inclined to buy, expensive furniture, don't economize on

BEAUTIFUL HARDWOOD FLOORING

Beautiful hardwood flooring

Real wood. It's a living, breathing natural material that will last a lifetime. Little wonder it's become the most popular natural floor covering – nothing else can compete. Unlike thin plastic laminates, hardwood flooring is warm and extremely durable, and with just a little basic care, will last for decades.

Don't compromise – get the very best

With Timberland you get the very best in hardwood flooring – 100% genuine timber. **Beautiful, natural and enduring – today, tomorrow and for a lifetime.**

Easy to clean, hygienic and non-allergenic

The ultimate choice in timbers sourced from every corner of the globe

Complete peace of mind with our 10 year no-quibble guarantee

Professional installations by our trained expert craftsmen

Comfort and practicability – warm in winter, cool in summer

Simple, trouble-free maintenance

The Timberland Home Design Service – FREE

To ensure you get the floor that's perfect for you, Timberland offer a free, no obligation Home Design Service. One of their trained Flooring designers will visit you in your home with samples of our floors to discuss your requirements. Décor and furnishings may change over the

years, so the timber species should be chosen with this in mind. Timberland only work with real wood, so their designers understand the various species, grains and finishes available and will work with you to ensure that you get the perfect floor for your individual needs.

Complete peace of mind

Once you have placed your order, one of Timberland's qualified surveyors will visit your home and undertake a thorough pre-installation floor survey, noting any particular little quirks or peculiarities individual to your job. Every home is different, and the Timberland survey ensures that once fitted your floor will be durable and beautiful for many years to come.

All Timberland floors are installed by skilled craftsmen working only for Timberland. And you get complete peace of mind with their no-quibble guarantee. Installation is normally completed in just one to two days with minimal fuss, mess or dust.

The end result is a complete transformation – the very best in hardwood flooring – beautiful, natural and enduring.

It's easy to get a floor with more

Timberland is committed to offering unbeatable value and unrivalled service. They make getting your hardwood floor easy. If you'd like to get a floor with more, call Timberland today for more information or to arrange your free Home Design Service consultation.

FREEPHONE
0800 980 2468
or visit their website at www.timberland.co.uk

THE ORIGINAL AND STILL THE BEST

curtains. This doesn't mean you have to go for the most expensive curtains you can find, but it is a good idea to have them specially made, in fabric thick enough to hang well, floor-length, with rope tiebacks, lined and interlined. You only have to curtain a place once, as curtains get very little wear at all, and can look as good as new many years later.

A number of my flats have been enthusiastically snapped up purely because of the luxurious-looking curtains. They can be in cream or off-white thick cotton, and they add a definite touch of luxury to even the simplest flat. Second-hand designer curtain shops are good places to look if the prospect of paying for specially commissioned curtains makes your eyes water.

Many younger tenants like wooden and Venetian blinds, and these may be a good idea where floor-length curtains might cut out too much light, or look too 'staid' for younger tenants. These blinds look trendy and are extremely versatile in the amount of light they let in, but they can get sticky and dusty and be difficult to clean. Also, they can get stuck or become difficult to operate in time. There is virtually nothing to go wrong with curtains once they are up, which is another major factor in their favour.

Bathrooms and kitchens should have roller blinds rather than curtains, which can get in the way of sinks and washing up, for instance. Slatted blinds in kitchens, whether of metal or wood, can get very greasy and in any case are difficult to clean.

If you're putting in a new bathroom, this should be white. As with kitchens, tenants can add their own touches of colour with towels, soap and toiletries.

If you have decided to let your investment property unfurnished, then that's about all you have to do.

Furnishings

If furnishing your property, then more decisions have to be made. I personally always furnish my flats, providing at least the basics. Apart from the fact that furniture makes a place look immediately like a home rather than a daunting white space, it also means that people are not humping double beds, huge sofas, sideboards and dining tables in and out every six months, thus risking damage to carpets and walls and increasing wear and tear on the fabric.

To be adequately furnished, a flat or house must have:

- a sofa;
- at least one easy chair;
- a coffee table;
- standard and table lamps;
- bedside lamps;
- a double bed;
- a chest of drawers;
- a wardrobe;
- a bedside cabinet or table;
- coat hangers;
- dining or kitchen table; and
- kitchen chairs.

This is the minimum. It should be smart and, if not new, at least looking like new when you first furnish the place.

In the kitchen, you should provide cutlery and crockery, glasses, saucepans, kettle, toaster, iron and ironing board, cleaning materials, buckets, mops and tea towels. In fact, the kitchen should have everything needed to cook, eat and clean. Ever more landlords are providing microwaves, as so many tenants these days want to just pick up their microwave meal on the way home, then heat and eat. But a microwave is not absolutely essential. After all, tenants can provide their own if they are that keen.

Some agents maintain that, in order for a property to be presented fully furnished, it must contain bed linen and two spare sets for each bed. This is certainly the case when letting to short-term or corporate clients, but in my experience, most ordinary tenants prefer to bring their own bedding, including pillow-cases and duvets. I always provide just one set of bed linen, a duvet and pillows, in case of emergency, but not a spare set. If tenants staying for a year do not have their own bed linen when they arrive, my feeling is that they can go out

morphy richards

PARTS & LABOUR
2 year guarantee

Sanitises the bathroom

Leaves windows and mirrors sparkling

Removes grease from cookers and worktops

Refreshes upholstery, curtains and garments

Cleans carpets and floors

Wallpaper stripper
(optional accessory)

Professional steam iron
(optional accessory)

GRIME BUSTER

Super heated dry steam at 140°C kills germs, bacteria and dustmites, neutralising their allergens making the GrimeBuster ideal for allergy sufferers. It maintains high steam pressure for more powerful cleaning and saves yourself pounds on cleaning materials and dry cleaning.

The power of steam to do more than just clean

For further information call our helpline on 08450 777700

STEAM YOUR WAY UP
THE PROPERTY LADDER!

Having decided to rent out your property you will obviously want it to look as pristine as possible to ensure that you get the maximum rent. It may be that you have short-term lets in which case the chore of a true spring clean will be a frequent occurrence or if you have long-term tenants it may be an annual event. Whichever, you will want to make the whole process as easy as possible. With a steam cleaner you can tackle a multitude of tasks simply and effectively.

A steam cleaner works by producing dry steam at a temperature of around 140°C. The cleaning performance is determined by the power of the boiler, a powerful boiler ensures faster heat-up time and sustained steam pressure. At such high temperatures stains and grease are removed and also germs, bacteria and dust mites killed - making a steam cleaner ideal for allergy sufferers and those wanting a truly deep clean. Plus it can save pounds on cleaning materials and services like window cleaners and dry cleaners as it can perform such an extensive range of tasks.

Walk into any house or flat and one of the first things you notice is the carpet. Carpet stains, especially in an unfurnished or sparsely furnished room, stand out a mile. A steam cleaner combined with a carpet nozzle attachment makes getting a deep down clean a breeze, be it on dirt or stains in the deepest pile carpets, stone and hard floors.

One of the most unpleasant jobs has to be tackling the bathroom. With a steam cleaner all you need do is attach a jet nozzle and you can spray away any limescale or unpleasant stains with ease. The same nozzle is also extremely effective at removing mildew from around a bath and even can be used to clean grouting that has become discoloured.

In the kitchen you can forget hours with a scouring pad and oven cleaner. The power of the steam combined with the dry heat of the steam cleaner easily shifts grease stains from on the hob and also inside the oven. Plus, with a long nozzle, there is no need to be a contortionist as you try to reach into the back of the oven.

Most steam cleaners also come with a squeegee which is ideal for cleaning windows and mirrors producing smear free results every time. Many also have an upholstery nozzle that can quickly inject a new lease of life into the oldest curtains and mattresses and the most sat upon sofa.

Several top of the range steam cleaners come with a professional iron attachment which, when combined with the 4 bar pressure of steam output, makes for faster easier ironing of traditionally difficult items such as curtains, dry cotton and denim. And a few also have a wallpaper stripper, so, if between tenants you feel like a touch of decorating removing the old wallpaper is far less strenuous and quicker with the power of steam.

And it's not just inside where steam can be put to good use. Steam cleaners are also a huge benefit outside cleaning slimy algae off patio furniture or cleaning patio stones. In the workshop too they can be used to ensure that worksurfaces are really clean from oil and dust and finally, as if that is not enough, they can be used to give the inside of the car a quick valet!

and buy it. After all, you can get new linen extremely cheaply from seconds shops and sales these days.

I have cheap white or off-white Indian cotton throwovers on the beds, as they make the beds look neater and more welcoming, and they are easily washable. I can't resist the temptation to scatter matching and coordinating cushions around, and often have a few made up in the curtain fabric, while I'm at it. But that's a personal quirk, not an essential. As a landlord, I feel I am somewhere between a cynical investor and a compulsive homemaker. Although a matching, specially made cushion may not be a very clever idea from an income-producing point of view, I have to have one if it absolutely makes the place.

A word on sofas and upholstered chairs: these must conform to the 1988 safety regulations. Sofas manufactured before this date are considered a fire hazard, and should not be used in furnished accommodation. Letting agencies, which have to abide by the law, won't allow these sofas. But sofas and couches manufactured before 1950 are safe, as these are upholstered in horsehair rather than foam.

Sofas should either have loose, washable covers, or be in materials and designs that do not show the dirt. A white sofa in a tenanted flat is asking for trouble: what if they spill red wine or Ribena on it? I once saw a lovely white sofa in a junk shop at an amazing price, £90. The only thing was, it was rather dirty. By some weird chance, a couple of friends of mine who run a carpet-cleaning business happened to be passing by as I was looking at the sofa. They inspected it and advised me not to buy, even though it seemed such a bargain, because it was not possible to clean the type of fabric that covered the item. Therefore, it would have been the opposite of a bargain and, thanks to their miraculous intervention, I avoided a nasty mistake. Loose covers on sofas, if you have to buy them, can cost as much as buying a new piece of furniture, so the best advice is not to buy any furniture for your investment properties which is not absolutely perfect at the moment of purchase. It is simply not worth it.

There are so many furniture bargains and sales around that you would do far better to shop at places like The Pier, Carpenter's, John Lewis First Furniture and Habitat than go

Classic lines finished in sleek silver, our new Satin collection is the ultimate in kitchen cool. And behind the looks lie some smart features... the kettle boasts a powerful 3kw concealed element, 360° easy fit power base and a sensible, wide angled spout, while the toaster can reheat, defrost, as well of course, make perfect toast...

start your day in style

KENWOOD

MAKING GREAT FOOD SIMPLE

The new Kenwood Satin range is available from most good electrical retail outlets now. Call Kenwood on 023 9239 2333 for stockist details.
www.kenwood.co.uk

Advertisement feature

Contemporary style for a modern kitchen

The kitchen is often the most important room in any home - a focal point for much of a household's daily activity from cooking, washing, ironing to chatting over morning coffee at the table, painting with the kids and so on. Traditionally, it is also a room that requires a large financial investment to ensure kitchen equipment and appliances that not only appeal to the eye, but also are durable and fully functional.

Kitchens can have a huge impact upon a prospective tenant's decision to rent; it is make or break, so it's worth investing the time to project a fresh, contemporary space. As a tenant searching for a dream that is to become a home for the next year or so there is nothing worse than walking into a shabby, dated kitchen that leaves a tired, flat impression of dirt and grime. Minds are made up on the spot and the tenants you want to attract to your property will go elsewhere.

There are a few simple tricks that can achieve an impression of modern living for maximum appeal for a relatively low-cost. A lick of paint in a neutral colour will brighten up a room and always ensure the room is tidy. Kitchens are pivotal in the decision process so include a nice vase of fresh cut flowers and brew coffee - or bake bread - to invoke a feel-good factor when prospective tenants walk through the door.

Kitchen trends are heavily influenced by the interiors world and currently chrome, brushed nickel and wood finishes are en vogue.

By simply placing a few modern kitchen appliances in fashionable styles on the worktop, landlords can instantly transform dated kitchens and create a positive first impression of a kitchen.

Kenwood, a name long associated with quality kitchen electrical appliances, offers a range of stylish and affordable products to complement the kitchen. The recently launched Kenwood Satin range, which includes a stylish brushed stainless steel finished toaster and kettle combo and matching silver finished espresso maker, really does give a slice of style to even the plainest of kitchens. And the espresso maker recreates the café culture experience at home with its unique facility for thick, creamy coffee and perfect cappuccinos. Not only do they look great but they are built to last too and project a lasting impression of modern living to prospective tenants.

Paint, kitchen appliances and common sense are a quick and easy solution to bring contemporary style to your kitchen at an affordable cost. Such suggestions are easy and cheap to implement and will make the difference between an empty and a rented property.

to junk shops or auctions. Also, I've discovered that auction and junk-shop furniture is *just as expensive* as buying new sofas in sales and on special offers.

For small rooms, wicker furniture can look smart, informal and welcoming although it is not always particularly hard wearing. A few stackable chairs are a good idea as they enable your tenants to have the facility to entertain guests without the rooms being totally bunged up with furniture all the time.

Flatpack furniture is fine for rental accommodation, and present-day designs are sleek, streamlined and functional. Do not ever be tempted to put your old cast-offs into an investment flat. It should look, if anything, even smarter than your own home.

If you have inherited a property that you are interested in letting out, it's a good idea to ask a letting agent to come round and inspect it, then advise on what renovation or refurnishing needs to be done to bring it up to present-day letting standards. Properties that have been lived in by very old people are unlikely to be considered safe or desirable by present-day standards, even though the old people concerned probably lived in them extremely safely for decades. But we are living in a nannying age, and rules and regulations are likely to increase, rather than decrease, in future.

Hamptons says that you should expect to spend around 5 to 6 per cent of the purchase price of the property on furnishings. On a £60,000 property, that would come to around £3,000. I've found that it's hard to spend less than this, at least if you want to take a pride in the place. It's amazing how a trip to Ikea adds up.

To sum up, whether you are letting furnished, unfurnished, or 'part furnished' to use a new phrase now creeping into agents' jargon, your rental property should be decorated in neutral colours, have a clean, crisp overall look, be professionally cleaned and well aired. Hamptons recommend using glass table tops rather than wood as this reduces staining and scuffing. Glass table tops are not recommended in Feng Shui, as wood is supposed to create better vibes in the place, but with rental investments you have to be practical.

While we're on the subject, is it, or might it be, worth having a rental property Feng Shui'd to maximize the rent and 'luck' coming into the place? Although this Eastern-originating art of correct placement and clutter avoidance is now extremely popular, I would not imagine it is worth going to the time and trouble of arranging a Feng Shui consultation for investment properties. Most tenants are fairly transient creatures, by their nature, and it may be that the demands of the current market are very different from advice likely to be given by Feng Shui experts. Save that for your own, more permanent, home.

Letting out your own home

There may be a number of reasons why you want to let out your own home. It may be that you or your family are relocated to another country for a year or two, and want to return to your home at some future date. It may be that you are in negative equity, and can get more money from letting out your home to tenants and renting a cheaper place yourself. In this case, the mortgage provider's permission will have to be sought, and the lender may well want to see any tenancy agreement.

It may be that you are temporarily relocated to another part of the country, have accepted a contract for a few months which takes you away from home, or work part of the year in another country anyway. During this time, you do not want your home to be empty and a temptation to squatters and burglars. It may be that you are in a new relationship and living with a partner, but do not at this stage want to give up your own home.

Whatever the reason, it is unlikely that your own home will meet, in every aspect, the current demands of letting agents. You may have pre-1988 sofas, for example. As with an inherited property, the best thing here is to ask an agent round to inspect the place and give advice. If you are locating abroad for a year or more, you should have your property professionally managed.

ARLA's advice here is never to leave property management to well-meaning friends and relatives, as this invites disaster. Such a disaster happened next door to me. The owners of the house were relocated to Hong Kong and wanted to let their property for two years. An agent found them tenants, but the property was managed by the owner's sister. Clearly, the young owners did this to save money, but as it turned out, it cost them dear. The tenants, four young men, paid no rent, trashed the place, held noisy, smoky barbecues until 4 in the morning, dealt in drugs, were rude and offensive to neighbours and had drunken parties every few days. The owner's sister, who I contacted many times, soon decided she could not manage the tenants, and washed her hands of the matter. It took the owner two months to get the place habitable once again, when the tenants were finally evicted. Every piece of furniture in the place was ruined, and the owner had to start again from scratch.

It is not advisable to try to let your own home on the cheap, or rent it to friends or relatives to avoid having to have gas certificates, fireproof sofas and safe installations. Have an agent round and do the whole thing professionally from the start.

By far the worst problems occur in landlord–tenant relationships, according to agents, when the owner's own house is let out. Tenants find themselves accused of stealing antiques, slashing paintings and ruining priceless pieces of furniture. A common complaint from tenants is that sideboards and cupboards are so stuffed full of the owner's items that tenants have nowhere to put their own things. An owner's house is also very likely to be over-furnished, leaving no room for the tenant to add personal bits and pieces.

When letting out your own home, you should clear all cupboards and bookcases, and put it all into store until you return. Don't expect tenants to be impressed by lots of ornaments, thousands of flower vases and kitchen cupboards full of years-old herbs and spices. As far as possible, your own home should be scoured of personal stuff. Remove all personal and important documents, such as birth, marriage and divorce certificates, wills, pension schemes, deeds of the house and so on and either put them in a bank vault or place them with your solicitor.

What if your home is full of priceless antiques, yet you want to let it out? What if you have fine Persian rugs on the floor, designer furniture, paintings by artists whose work is now worth thousands of pounds, then you are posted abroad for a year or two? Should you let such a home, bearing in mind that in central London you could get up to £2,500 a week for such a place?

Barry Manners, director of Chard, a London estate agent which deals with this kind of problem, advised: 'If you have a property full of expensive goods, my advice is to seek the opinion of an insurer, telling him all your circumstances.' It is important to keep up insurance cover during the letting period, especially if the value of the contents runs into six figures. The insurance company would need an extremely detailed inventory and valuations on file. With any insurance policy, you should make sure you are covered for damage by the tenant. If the unthinkable happens, and the tenant allows the bath to overflow, thus water-damaging priceless antiques, you may not have a claim unless this eventuality is specified.

But Barry Manners advises that, where possible, the most valuable goods should be put into storage and fakes substituted. 'Few tenants will be able to tell the difference between a Matisse and a Monet, or even a Monet original and a copy,' he said, 'So do what hotels do and hang fakes.'

Preparing for corporate or company lets

Although by far the commonest form of tenancy agreement these days is the Assured Shorthold, which lets the property out in six-monthly renewable dollops, in some cases you may want, or be in a position to let your home or investment property for shorter periods than this.

Short lets are becoming increasingly common in large cities, and can range from a few weeks to a few months. In some boroughs, landlords are not allowed to let properties for less than three months, as the local authority does not want a large transient population. Also, very short stay tenants can take away from the area's hotel trade.

Short lets tend to command a far higher rent than standard tenancies. They usually achieve between 20 to 50 per cent more rent than standard lets, and this rent is almost always paid by a company or corporation, rarely the individual.

Because of this, short-let flats must be fully furnished and decorated to a much higher standard than ordinary lets, and must be absolutely ready for the tenant to move in and start living.

Flats intended for use as short lets must have several sets of bed linen, towels, tea towels, good-quality ranges of glasses, crockery and cutlery and a full complement of cooking utensils. The flat should be welcoming, with pictures on the walls, rugs on the floor, green plants, and plenty of table lamps for subdued lighting. With short lets, it is unlikely that tenants will be wanting to add their own touches, as they are looking for a place they can already call home, without further additions.

Kitchens in such flats should have dishwashers and always, washing-machines with tumble-dryers. Tenants of these flats are buying comfort and convenience and they, or at least their company, are prepared to pay a high rent for such convenience. In these flats, you can keep a few antiques or valuable paintings, as these tenants are usually the kind of people who would take great care of them. When accidents do happen, tenants are usually mortified, as they realize they are living in a privileged and comfortable temporary home.

The better taste you have, and the more 'designer' your flat and furniture, the higher rent a short-let tenant is likely to be prepared to pay. Corporate tenants, which the majority of short-let tenants will be, nowadays also expect cable and satellite TV as well as terrestrial channels. The best kind of furniture for upmarket short-term tenants is very modern, very clean, very streamlined, without being too minimalist. A very minimalist flat can make tenants feel uncomfortable.

Don't put in very personal, quirky touches. An agent told me he found one particular short-term flat difficult to let, even though it was in the right location, had all the right furniture and fittings and was an ideal size and shape. 'But', said the agent, 'in the hall there was a row of very grainy, stark black and white pictures of naked men. Many corporate clients would be embarrassed to entertain in such a place, and would feel they had to apologize for the artwork on the walls. The advice we always give is: never make very personal statements in an investment flat, but make sure your décor and pictures appeal to the widest possible range of tastes.'

Students

At the other end of the scale we have the dreaded students.

Ever since Chaucer's time, students have had a bad reputation. They are commonly supposed to be dirty, noisy, uncaring of other people's property, drunken, druggy louts who get up at noon (at the earliest), leave the place in a filthy mess, with the sink perpetually piled high with washing-up.

For these reasons, few landlords are happy with the idea of letting to students. It is also a common belief that students never have any money, and that any student flat will at all times be littered with 'friends' sleeping on the floor.

Nowadays, my ex-husband is the cleanest, tidiest person imaginable. But when he was a student, his flat well surpassed that of *Withnail and I* in the famous film. I had to put newspaper down on the sofa before sitting on it, as otherwise my clothes would be filthy. The floor was littered with cigarette ends and ash, there were (literally) hundreds of unwashed milk bottles in the disgusting kitchen, and I don't think the sheets were changed once. His three flatmates lived in similar squalor, yet all had come from impeccably clean middle-class homes. My ex's view was that everybody should have at least a year or two of seedy squalor, as it is all part of life's rich tapestry. When my elder son became a student, I'm afraid he followed in his father's squalid footsteps.

Because of the propensity of male students at least to turn every place into a chaotic tip, it is popularly imagined that, for students, any old accommodation will do. (And before I get accused of sexism, yes, I am aware that the female of the species can be deadlier and dirtier than the male. But as a generalization, student squalor seems a standard rite of passage for many young men.) However, nowadays, even students can be fussy.

Joel Lazarus from the Black-Katz agency, one of the few letting agencies to handle student accommodation, said: 'Nowadays students are not impressed with squalid tips. Although the standards need not be as high as when letting to professionals, kitchens should be well equipped with washing-machines and working cookers. There should be a television point and also a telephone point as nowadays most students are working at computers. For this reason, there should be desks in each room.'

All student accommodation should be furnished with the basics, although it is usual to expect students to bring their own bed linen and towels. They will most probably not take good care of that provided by the landlord.

I don't think I would put up bespoke interlined curtains in a student flat, or matching scatter cushions. But even if you are prepared to consider students, it is still the case that the better presented the accommodation when the student moves in, the better it is likely to be looked after.

Whenever letting to students, or people without a regular income, it is essential to sign up a guarantor (usually a parent) who will guarantee the rent in the event of non-payment by the tenant. It is possible to arrange a guarantor via e-letting, and a lettings agent will certainly insist on such a signature for student lets.

Some general points on letting

Whether you are considering letting to high-paying short-let tenants, students, young professionals, families or company executives, the following strictures apply in each case.

Electrical equipment

The more electrical and electronic equipment you have in your property, the more there is to go wrong, and the more guarantees and instructions you must provide. Unless concentrating on short lets, it is not a good idea for the landlord to provide a television set, stereo, hairdryer or any other type of electrical equipment. These are up to the tenant to supply, if required.

In any case, you should always aim at the absolute minimum of electrical equipment necessary for modern living. Complicated kitchen gadgets (again, you can make an exception for short lets) such as food mixers, ice-cream makers, cappuccino makers, sandwich makers and the like, are not recommended.

Inventory

Whether you are letting a furnished or unfurnished flat, you must prepare a detailed inventory. Most landlords start off with extremely amateurish inventories (I did myself) and get more professional as they go along.

You can, if you prefer, have an inventory prepared for you by a professional, and there are advantages to this. Professionals check not only the moveable items, but the condition of the walls and ceilings, noting any cracks in tiles, the number of knobs and shelves on the cooker, the condition of the bath, taps, shower and sink in the bathroom. They also test cookers, washing-machines and so on to see whether they work, and they also test the shower. Showers are frequently a bone of contention between landlord and tenant, and a professional inventory clerk will be able to assess the power and pressure capacity of the shower when the tenant moves in, in case of arguments later.

Clerks make a note of everything to do with the property's condition and equipment before the tenant moves in, and hand a completed copy to the landlord and tenant to sign. This means there can be no arguments about the number of items or the condition of the property.

Professional inventory clerk Jennifer Reigate said: 'When I check a property, the fabric is as important as the contents. Replacing a bath, for instance, can be far more expensive than getting a new sofa.'

Major things to check, advises Jennifer, are cracks in baths and sinks and whether anything is wrong with the cooker. 'I find that having a very detailed inventory makes tenants more responsible,' she said. 'If they know that the condition of the walls, for example, is being taken into account, they're more careful about what they put on them. Also, having a professional inventory provides valuable distance between the tenant and the landlord. And the check-out is just as valuable as the check-in.'

As disputes about the condition of the flat and its contents can cause terrible disputes between landlords and tenants, very often ending up in bitter court battles, the more thorough the inventory, the less likely this is to occur. Here is a typical simple yet detailed inventory.

Living room
1 pr damask curtains, full length
1 large cream rug
1 large white coffee table. Condition: new
1 yellow upholstered easy chair. Condition: new
1 two-seater sofa, yellow upholstered. Condition: new
1 cream table lamp. Condition: 10 years old
3 scatter cushions, newly cleaned
Walls: newly painted: doors, newly painted. Immaculate
1 central halogen light, new
1 dimmer switch

Bedroom
1 pine double bed. Condition: as new
1 pr Indian cotton curtains, cream. Full-length. New
1 white dining chair, Ikea
1 wicker waste paper basket
1 blue under-blanket
1 white Indian double bedspread
1 king-size duvet (not new)
2 pillows
1 set bed linen: duvet cover, sheet, pillowcases
1 table lamp, cream
2 bedside tables
1 white chest of drawers, good condition. All handles
Overall condition: newly painted

Kitchen
1 round dining table. New
2 dining chairs. New
2 fold-up chairs, aluminium
8 glass tumblers
4 white dining plates
4 white side plates
2 white soup bowls
4 mugs

5-piece cutlery set for 4: teaspoons, dessert spoons, butter knives, large knives, forks; wooden handles: new
2 wooden spoons
1 wooden spatula
1 fish slice
1 colander
1 plastic bowl
1 vacuum cleaner
1 corkscrew
1 bottle opener
1 white microwave cooker: new
1 toaster
1 large cafetière
1 iron
1 ironing board
4 cream tea towels
1 brush and dustpan
1 grater
3 saucepans with lids
1 frying pan
1 milk saucepan
1 electric kettle
1 venetian blind at window
1 plastic bucket with mop
1 fridge-freezer
1 integrated dishwasher
1 integrated washing-machine
1 gas cooker, good condition. No parts missing
Condition of kitchen units: perfect. All handles present, no scratches. All drawers working

Bathroom

1 venetian blind at window: new
1 lavatory brush
1 bucket
1 mirror
2 pine cupboards
1 power shower: new
Condition of bath: immaculate
Condition of toilet: immaculate. Pine seat
Condition of sink: immaculate
Condition of taps: clean, working perfectly
Wall tiles: all perfect
Floor: no missing or cracked tiles
Paintwork: immaculate

Hallway
1 long mirror
1 rag rug
Condition of carpets: slight stain on living-room carpet near window: otherwise perfect

Signed:

Landlord:

Tenant:

Date:

The inventory should also contain a schedule of condition, noting overall condition and anything stained, broken or damaged.

Complying with regulations

There are many safety regulations to be borne in mind when letting property. All furniture and fittings must be covered by the 1988 Fire and Safety Regulations. This means that it is an offence to let out any property that contains furniture and fittings that do not comply with these regulations. If any property is found not to comply, the landlord could face up to six months' imprisonment or a fine of up to £5,000.

From March 1993, it became an offence to supply furniture in rented property which did not comply with standards contained in Regulation 14 of the 1988 Regulations. This only applies to furniture first supplied after 1 March 1993. Furniture manufactured before 1950 is exempt from the regulations.

These regulations apply to investment landlords, although the situation is less clear regarding owner–occupiers letting their own home. These people, letting their own homes on a 'one-off short-term' basis, are less likely to be deemed as acting 'in the course of business' and may be exempt from the regulations.

Items covered by the regulations include:

- furniture intended for private use in a dwelling, including children's furniture;
- beds, headboards, mattresses;
- sofabeds, futons and other convertibles;
- nursery furniture;
- scatter cushions and seat pads;
- pillows;
- loose and stretch covers for furniture.

These items are exempt:

- sleeping bags;
- bedlinen;
- loose covers for mattresses;
- pillowcases;
- curtains;
- carpets;
- furniture made before 1950 and re-upholstered furniture made before that date.

Most furniture purchases since March 1990 should automatically comply.

Other regulations include:

- *The Gas Safety (Installation and Use) Regulations, 1994.* Under these regulations, all landlords have a duty to maintain gas appliances in their property through annual inspections and safety checks. These must be carried out by a registered CORGI engineer. Failure to comply with these regulations could result in a fine or imprisonment.
- *The Electrical Equipment (Safety) Regulations, 1994.* These regulations require that electrical equipment between 50 and 100 volts a/c should be safe and tested regularly.
- *Smoke Detectors Act, 1991.* Any building built after June 1992 must have smoke detectors installed on each floor.

It should be said that the details on décor outlined in this chapter apply to smart self-contained properties on which you are seeking an optimum rent. Cheaper flats and rooms that are advertised in local papers and in newsagents' windows, for instance, may not conform to all these regulations, and are unlikely to be nicely equipped with sparkling, shining cookers, washing-machines and fridges.

We are talking here about a gold standard of rental properties, and one to which not all landlords, unfortunately, conform. But to my mind, everybody benefits from a chic, harmonious interior, including the landlord who gets a better class of tenant and more rent. The thing is, as always, to bear in mind the needs and pocket of the market you are hoping to attract.

contracts & design
PART OF ROOMSERVICE GROUP

As specialists in residential investment furnishing, Roomservice Group know that intelligent and efficient furnishing solutions ensure excellent returns on property investments. By creating the right, desirable lifestyle appearance within your property, you will not only increase its rentability but will subsequently also reduce unwelcome rental voids.

Whether you are furnishing one or hundreds of properties throughout the UK, Roomservice Group's comprehensive understanding of the marketplace combined with innovative design flair, enables them to provide you with stylish, fit for purpose furnishing solutions, ideal for achieving your desired market rent.

Their services are tailored to your individual needs and budgets and range from refurbishment programmes and pre-designed furnishing collections through to a full interior design service. They also supply, fit and install fine quality curtain and carpet products as well a vast range of household and lifestyle accessories to suit.

Available on a rental, purchase or rent-to-own basis, Roomservice Group provide *total* furnishing solutions to the UK property investment market.

TRADING INTERIORS
QUALITY EX SHOWHOME FURNITURE FROM ROOMSERVICE GROUP

As an alternative to buying new furniture, or renting, **Trading Interiors**, sells quality, ex-showhome furniture direct to the public. Ideally suited to Landlords who want to create a certain look but are restricted by tight budgets, Trading Interiors offers savings of between 30-70% against new retail prices on a whole host of home-related items. The reason you save more is simply because it's been rented before!

For more information on Roomservice Group *and how they can help you create better returns on your property investment, please contact them directly on:*
Tel: 020 8397 9344
www.roomservicegroup.com

28 Barwell Business Park, Leatherhead Road, Chessington, Surrey KT9 2NY

furnishing solutions
from roomservice group

providing landlords and tenants with flexible furnishing solutions throughout the UK

- Furniture
- Housewares
- Curtains
- Carpets

- Lighting
- Linens
- Accessories

Services are available on a purchase and rental basis which guarantees to maximise your investment

contracts & design
28 Barwell Business Park, Leatherhead Road
Chessington, Surrey KT9 2NY

tel 020 8397 9344   fax 020 8974 1440
website www.roomservicegroup.com
email info@roomservicegroup.com

contracts & design
PART OF ROOMSERVICE GROUP

THE NATIONAL FEDERATION OF
ROOFING CONTRACTORS (NFRC)

The National Federation of Roofing Contractors (NFRC) (0207 436 0387) is the largest roofing trade association in the UK whose members include some 740 contractor companies and 125 manufacturers and service providers. Every contractor member is carefully vetted to ensure that they comply with the NFRC's Code of Practice, are suitably qualified to lay products to specification, have sound Health and Safety policies in place and are covered by third party and public liability insurance.

The Federation has a variety of tailor-made insurance packages which members can offer to the clients, since investing in independent insurance is an important consideration when thinking about getting any kind of construction work done. These independent guarantees give the client added peace of mind for up to 10 years for domestic work and 15 years for commercial work. A typical domestic insurance guarantee costs £20 for the whole 10 years.

You can also get free and help and advice in the unlikely event of any disputes between you and your contractor or make use of the NFRC's technical advisory service.

To get a free list of NFRC registered member contractors in your area visit the website at www.nfrc.co.uk or call 0207 436 0387. So if you find yourself in any doubt over who to trust, remember that the NFRC have already done the checking for you!

Advertisement feature

5

Finding suitable tenants

All landlords, without exception, want clean, smart, tidy tenants who will pay the rent on time, never bother them, never have any complaints, and who leave the property in exactly the same condition as they found it. Ideal tenants never have noisy parties, never sublet, never bother the neighbours and never cause any trouble of any kind whatsoever.

But how do you find such paragons? There is no guaranteed way of finding perfect tenants, but there are a number of safeguards you can take to minimize the risk.

In their *Lettings Handbook*, Hamptons estate agents admit: 'Letting out a property can be an anxious time for a landlord. There will naturally be concerns that will arise and fears that need allaying.'

One way of minimizing the risk is to make sure that the property is absolutely immaculate and in the right location to attract professionals in high-paying jobs. If you as the landlord feel proud of the flat, and know that the location is good, there will be that much more confidence about the place, a confidence which will be instantly relayed to the tenant.

Advertising

If you decide to go it alone rather than using a lettings agency, once the flat is ready the next thing to do is to advertise the property in the places that your ideal kind of tenant is likely to look. E-letting has been described in Chapter 3.

As most of my rental flats have been near White City, where the BBC studios are, I have often advertised in *Ariel,* the BBC staff magazine, and this has produced several excellent tenants. You could also try local gyms and health clubs, language schools, personnel departments of large companies and supermarket notice boards, for example. Local newspapers can be a good idea, although you are very likely to get calls from agents, even when stipulating 'No Agents'. Advertising in national newspapers can be very expensive, and I have never had a good response by this means. Newspapers such as *Loot* can work but again, you are very liable to get calls from agents. One flat I advertised in *Loot* produced nothing but calls from agents.

Advertising in magazines such as *The Lady* and *The Spectator* will usually guarantee an upmarket tenant, and often produce a good response. Shop window ads can also work well, although response is not guaranteed. The advantage here is that this type of advertising is very cheap. The disadvantage is that it is very local indeed.

Deciding on the sort of tenant you want

Most landlords, myself included, are paranoid about rent not being paid. The Hamptons booklet states: 'Whilst all landlords will have worries specific to their own circumstances, there is a concern and fear common to the majority – that the tenant may default on their rental payments.'

There is no absolute way of preventing this, whatever checks are carried out, but it's possible to reduce the risk greatly by choosing your tenants with care. I have a personal rule that all my tenants must be people in full-time paid employment. No freelances, thank you. Now, obviously I know that freelance people must find accommodation, but for me at least, people without a steady income are too worrying to have as tenants.

I do not let my flats to freelance graphic artists or struggling writers, for instance, however nice they may be, and *absolutely never* to musicians of any kind, as I do not want complaints about noise from residents above and below my flat. Other landlords I know make a point of never letting to doctors or nurses, on the grounds that they smoke like chimneys and never look after the place, and some landlords will not, on any account, let to lawyers, as these people find ways, apparently, of dodging their responsibilities. Legally trained tenants know how far they can go without paying rent, withholding rent and other such anti-landlord behaviour, so I'm told.

Although one is not allowed to discriminate on racial grounds, I'm afraid I discriminate extremely forcefully against potential tenants with tattoos, men with ponytails, and anyone with lots of body piercing. I also discriminate violently against would-be tenants who can't be bothered to turn up for appointments on time, or who are always cancelling at the last minute. Such sloppiness does not augur well for good tenancies. I like my tenants to look clean, neat and tidy, and I use my gut reaction here. I always ask myself: would I want this person to live in my house? After all, your investment property is the next thing to your own home.

I also discriminate against children and pets, as my particular flats are not suitable for either. Some landlords don't mind these, and it certainly does widen the scope of the tenant pool to choose from. There is nothing I can do, of course, to prevent female tenants getting pregnant, and this has happened. The tenant in question, an extremely neat, smart Japanese woman, moved out before she had the baby, and then found a larger flat.

I do not discriminate on grounds of gender. Experience has taught me that there is no automatic difference between male and female tenants. They are equally likely to be neat or slobby, equally likely to pay rent on time or try to wriggle out of their obligations. The two male tenants I have had have both been immaculately clean and tidy, and one female tenant, although otherwise fine, turned out to be the world's untidiest woman.

If going it alone, which I often do, I never, ever bargain with the tenant over the rent. If they offer less, they can look elsewhere. I would rather wait for a full-paying tenant than grab at somebody who wants to negotiate me down. Some agencies advise against this, saying that it is better to have a lower-paying tenant than no tenant. But in my experience agencies want, above all, 'bums on seats', and are inclined to grab to get their commission. My rents are non-negotiable because they are always the exact market rent for that particular property. Allowing yourself to be bargained down just causes resentment against the tenant later, and feelings that if you'd waited just that bit longer, you could have got the full asking price.

When looking for suitable tenants, there is one absolute, unbreakable rule to bear in mind: *never, ever let your property to friends or relatives* – at least, not if your main concern is to run a business. One friend of mine has a tenant in a beautiful flat she owns, who is not paying the full rent. 'She simply can't afford it,' my friend explains – but underneath the pity for the poverty-stricken tenant, there is seething resentment.

Although it can be tempting to let to somebody you know rather than a complete stranger, the arrangement is almost guaranteed to break up the friendship or relationship, and will virtually always end in tears. My next-door neighbours, a young couple, had a loft room with bathroom at the top of their house. It was not self-contained, but surplus to their immediate requirements. They kindly let a friend crash there for four weeks while she found herself somewhere to live. Ten months later, the friend was still in residence (she was fast becoming an ex-friend) and my neighbours were tearing their hair out wondering how on earth to get rid of her.

Although she was paying the market rent and there was no problem with this, she also expected to join them every night for supper, and at weekends. When she finally left, my neighbours celebrated by buying a very expensive sofa and chairs with the rent money. In this way, they felt at least that they had something to show for all the months they had endured in purgatory.

Another acquaintance once let a couple of rooms in her house to a friend who lived in the country, but who was doing a course in London and wanted somewhere to bed down during the week. Everything went fine and she was a perfect tenant, paying her rent on time, leaving the bathroom and kitchen immaculate, and being away every weekend. In the evenings, she was very careful to keep herself to herself. But then the owner decided to put her house on the market, and the tenant went spare. 'Where does that leave me?' she asked. The tenant had come to expect that her friend would provide a cheap, comfortable roof over her head for the whole three years of her course, although there had been no agreement that this would be the case. The owner duly sold her house, and lost a friend. They have not spoken since she moved out, now several years ago.

I hope the moral is now clear. Don't let to friends or relatives or, I might add, to student or 20-something children of friends. This can also ruin a long-standing friendship.

Before they move in

Once you believe you have found a suitable tenant – and if the property, the price and the location are good, it shouldn't take more than two weeks, at most – the next thing is to ask for, and take up, references. Typical references are from the current place of employment, the bank, and the previous landlord.

Once these references have been received, the next thing is to check them out as far as possible. This is most important, as it is all too easy for a wily person simply to make them up. A 'previous landlord' reference I received from one tenant turned out to have been written by her boyfriend, also a shyster and criminal, as we later discovered. One letting agent said: 'However much you check references, they could always have been written by the tenant's sister, or aunt, or somebody. It's easy enough for somebody to pretend to have been a previous landlord, and no real way of checking up on this.'

Once you are satisfied that the references are genuine, you must take one month's rent and one month's deposit in full before handing over the keys. At the same time as taking the rent, you and the tenant should sign the tenancy agreement – legal forms for this purpose are available from most stationers – and set up a direct debit whereby future rents will be paid directly into your account.

If there are any problems over this, or if the potential tenant wants to pay a smaller deposit, be on your guard. If the tenant does not have the deposit ready then there is every likelihood you will have problems with the rent, or difficulties with the tenant in other ways.

It is easy enough to instruct the bank to stop a direct debit, and dishonest tenants know this. One potential tenant of mine really loved the flat, she loved it to death and wanted it like crazy. The only thing was, she didn't have the full deposit. She would have it next week, she assured me, once she had received her salary. I was suspicious. She might have been completely genuine, but I decided against her anyway. It seemed to me too much like starting out on the wrong foot. My own belief is that you should make it an absolute rule that you do not let the tenant in unless and until the entire deposit is paid, and in your account, or your agent's.

Next, you and the tenant should go over the inventory together, and both sign it as correct. You give a copy of the rental agreement and the signed inventory to your tenant to keep in a file along with instructions and guarantees for electrical goods, central heating and so on.

Finally, you must make sure all utilities such as gas, electricity and water rates are now in the tenant's name. The tenant is also responsible for paying council tax, and for organizing the telephone and television licence. All you as the landlord have to do here is to provide a telephone point and television point. It is then up to the tenant whether she wants to reconnect the telephone, or have a television. Some tenants don't watch TV and just use a mobile phone.

It cannot be said too often that you must never, ever allow a new tenant into your property until all these preliminaries have been completed. One landlord friend, Mike, did this, with disastrous results. He had just spent over £10,000 on refurbishing his one-bedroom flat and on completion of the renovation, advertised it in a local paper. Instantly, a potential tenant came along. Mike let him in without going through the proper checks, for two reasons. One was that he was desperate for the flat to be let after a void of several months during the refurbishment period, and the other was that he was about to go on holiday.

The incoming tenant assured Mike that the deposit and rent would be paid into his bank without delay, and he took possession of the property. But when Mike returned from his holiday, no rent or deposit had been paid. When the tenant was questioned, he started to wriggle and shift and say that he'd had a bit of bad luck lately, and some money he was expecting had been delayed, but he would pay as soon as possible... Mike had to understand the tenant's position and be patient. The weeks went by and yes, you've guessed it, no rent appeared. In the end, Mike took direct action and, when his tenant was out one day, changed the locks.

An understandable action, you might think, but a crime, and so completely against the law. The tenant sued the landlord – *and won*! Mike had put himself completely in the wrong by locking his tenant out, and emerged from this terrible experience a sadder and wiser (and much poorer) man. He never did get any rent or any deposit. But such an eventuality could happen to any of us. It is easy to become desperate for a tenant when you have spent months, maybe, on redecoration of your property. 'If I'd carried out the proper checks and insisted on one month's deposit and one month's rent, this would never have happened,' Mike said. 'I learnt a very hard lesson, one which I will never repeat.'

One letting agency told me: 'We've all heard about terrible landlords, but in our experience, it's usually the tenants, if anything, who are terrible.' There is a very good reason why this is so. Tenants, by their nature, are transient creatures, living in the same property for perhaps six months, perhaps a year, but rarely longer. They move on and have no involvement with the property other than paying the rent, nor do they particularly care about the property, as they have no sense of responsibility towards it. The landlord, by contrast, has invested many thousands of pounds in the property, sometimes hundreds of thousands of pounds. He is responsible for it, and he is the one who stands to lose serious money if he has a bad tenant. The most that the tenant will lose, if she is unlucky enough to sign up with a bad landlord, is a few hundred pounds' deposit.

The landlord is also the one who has to carry out repairs, pay tax, pay service charges and buy furniture and fittings. So there is more onus, these days at least, to be a good landlord than to be a good tenant.

Using an agency

If you find tenants by yourself, you will keep all the rent they pay you. But if you go to a letting agency, they will take at least 10 per cent, plus VAT, of the agreed rental in commission.

Most lettings agencies, although not all, will only agree to handle self-contained flats. If you wish to let a room or rooms in your house, then you may find that you have no choice but to go it alone. Any worries about the legality of the arrangement, though, can be solved by having agreements drawn up by a solicitor. This will incur a one-off fee, but not commission as such.

The major advantages of using a letting agency are:

1. they put some distance between yourself and your tenant;
2. they handle references, inventories, deposits, direct debits, every single working day, so are well geared up to it; and
3. they can intervene on your behalf if disputes arise.

The disadvantages are that they take away some of your hard-earned rent, and that they will not take your property onto their books unless it meets every one of the current fire and safety regulations.

Also, it must be said that no agent can magically produce a suitable tenant for you. I have sometimes had flats with agents for three or four weeks before a tenant has appeared. Sometimes a potential tenant seems very keen and then changes her mind – as when you are going it alone. Agencies can do their best, but they cannot create tenants for you where a market does not exist. They cannot guarantee that there will be no void periods, or that your property will be let for 365 days of the year, every year.

Choose your agent with care

If you do decide to use an agency, it is imperative to do some homework first. Although they may all seem much the same, in fact they vary widely. You should always use an agency that is a member of ARLA. Although some non-ARLA agencies may be perfectly reputable, there have been stories where letting agencies have used clients' money to pay their staff. Any lettings agency you use should have a separate client account that can't be raided to keep the business going. In fact, one agency that went bankrupt and was discovered to be raiding client accounts, *was* a member of ARLA. So, there are never any absolute guarantees.

In addition, I would always recommend using a specialist letting agency, rather than an estate agent that buys and sells property as well. If you do go to a general estate agent, make sure they have a separate well-established lettings department. The advantage of specialist agencies is that where lettings is their only concern, they have to work harder on your behalf, otherwise they have no business.

I once asked a major high street estate agent to find a tenant for one of my flats. I was unable to keep a check on them as I was going away for three weeks. On my return, I was extremely disappointed to discover that they had failed to let the property. I immediately went to a specialist lettings agency a few yards up the road, and within hours they had found an ideal tenant. I now don't think the big agents could be bothered – there wasn't enough money in it for them.

Always make sure you match the agency to the type of property you are letting. So, if you want to let to students, use an agency that specializes in this type of letting. If you are interested in short lets to corporate clients, choose a market leader for this kind of rental. Upmarket properties need upmarket agencies and vice versa. No agency is all things to all people, so look in the windows first, to discover the speciality of a particular agent.

It makes sense to use an agency if you live a long way from your property, if you are very busy, if you are away a lot, and if your property is likely to command a very high rental.

Company lets

Where the tenant is a company rather than an individual, the tenancy agreement will be similar to an Assured Shorthold, but will not be bound by the six-month rule. (See Chapter 6 for details of Assured Shorthold agreements.) Company lets can be of any length of time, from a week to several years, or as long as you like.

The major difference between contracts and standard AS agreements is that the contract will be tailored to individual needs, and the agreement is bound by the provisions of contract law. Company tenancies are governed by contract law and are not regulated by the Housing Act 1988. Note: if you are considering letting to a company, you *must* use a letting agent or solicitor. In fact, most companies will insist on it.

The advantages to the landlord of letting to a company are:

- A company or embassy has no security of tenure and therefore cannot become a sitting tenant.
- A company tenant cannot seek to reduce the rent by statutory interventions.
- Rental payments are often made quarterly or six-monthly in advance.
- The financial status of a company is usually more secure than that of an individual.
- Company tenants often require long-term lets to accommodate staff relocating on contracts of between one and five years.

The main disadvantages of company lets are:

- A company tenancy can only be to a bona fide company or embassy, not to a private individual.
- A tenancy to a partnership would not count as a company let and may have some security of tenure.

- If the tenant is a foreign government, the diplomatic status of the occupant must be ascertained as courts cannot enforce breaches of contract with somebody who possesses diplomatic immunity.
- A tenancy to a foreign company not registered in the UK may prove time-consuming and costly if it became necessary to pursue claims for unpaid rent or damage through foreign courts.

Short lets

Although company lets can be of any length, it is becoming increasingly popular for companies to rent flats from private landlords on short lets.

A short let is any let of less than six months. But here, it is essential to check the rules with the borough concerned. Some boroughs will not allow lets of less than three months as they do not want to encourage transient people in the neighbourhood.

Generally speaking, short lets are only applicable in large cities where there is a substantial shifting population. Business executives on temporary relocation, actors and others involved in film or TV production, contract workers and visiting academics are examples of people who might require a short let.

From a landlord's point of view, short lets are an excellent idea if you have to leave your own home for seven or eight months, say, and do not want to leave it empty for that time. Short-let tenants provide useful extra income as well as keeping an eye on the place. Or, if you are buying a new property and have not yet sold the old one, it can make good business and financial sense to let it to a short-term tenant.

Short-let tenants are usually, from a landlord's point of view, excellent, blue-chip occupants. They are busy professionals, high earners, out all day and used to high standards. You may also get a celebrity tenant, as these people also provide a big market here. You could have Leonardo Di Caprio or Sharon Stone staying in your flat, while they are filming on location.

As the rent is paid by the company, there are no worries for the landlord on this score, either. Sometimes the company pays the deposit, but very often the deposit is paid by the tenant, as a safeguard for the landlord. The thinking is, that if the tenant pays the returnable deposit, there will be that much more incentive to keep the place in pristine condition. Also, a large company may not want dollops of deposit money sitting doing nothing in other people's accounts.

If a company has a hundred employees in short-term accommodation, this could mean that at any one time £100,000 is out of use. To counteract this, some firms offer 'letters of guarantee' rather than cash deposits to the landlords, where they guarantee to replace any lost, stolen or damaged goods. In practice, this does not always work out as planned, and landlords are strongly advised not to accept letters of guarantee instead of deposits. There have been several cases where companies have simply refused to pay up where goods are damaged.

A major plus of short lets is that they command between 20 and 50 per cent more than the optimum market rent for that type of property. The greatest demand is for studios and one-bed flats, as mostly, short-let tenants are single people rather than families. The days when whole families were relocated from one country to another are fading fast.

The one downside of short lets from the landlord's point of view is that no agency can guarantee permanent occupancy. Most agencies operate on a 75 per cent average occupancy in a year. The tenants are great when you've got them, but you may not always have them.

Upmarket estate agents Foxtons have pioneered short lets in central London. Director Arnaud Cheung said: 'We started when there was a need for short-term accommodation for the entire cast of "Riverdance". They wanted accommodation for four and a half months, and there was nothing available. It was felt there was a huge gap in the market, and since 1993 we have tried to fill it. The demand is fantastic, and increasing all the time. In one sense, short-term accommodation is similar to a hotel, but there are very many pluses. For the company which is paying, private flats are much cheaper than hotels, and better too, as few people like living in hotels for months on end.

'Multinational companies have multinational staff and it's a nightmare to try to put 15 important employees in hotels or serviced accommodation when working out budgets. Also, with a hotel, you are paying for services you may not require, such as room service, reception, restaurants. There are so many outside costs, yet in a self-contained flat, the tenant can feel much more a part of the city. It's more tranquil than a hotel.'

Although a number of short-let landlords are people letting their own property temporarily, by far the biggest number of owners are investment landlords, owning perhaps whole blocks of flats. 'Very often, investment landlords buy show flats for this purpose,' said Arnaud Cheung. 'They buy the entire stock – furniture, curtains, kitchen appliances, the lot.

'The short lets that go fastest are those where the landlord is prepared to go that bit further than the absolute basics, and provide magazines, coffee makers, a few touches of luxury which will be appreciated by the tenants.'

Students

Very many letting agencies will not consider students and a lot of now-prosperous, clean and tidy landlords are not keen, either, remembering how they themselves treated flats in their student days.

Joel Lazarus, whose agency Black-Katz is one of the few that will consider student lets, said: 'Over the years, we have developed a good relationship with universities and colleges, and at about the middle of August every year, we turn our mind to student accommodation.

'Nowadays, student accommodation – at least, the kind we handle – works on exactly the same basis as any other Assured Shorthold Tenancy. Although students only want to take places for nine months, which is a landlord's nightmare, we make them sign for a year. Then it is up to them to sublet to friends during the long vacation. They have to pay for the whole year, including short vacations. Student flats are not like Halls of Residence, but owned by private landlords who want their rent like any other landlord.

'Rent is guaranteed by confirmation that this person is a genuine student, and references from parents, who act as guarantors. This is the only basis on which we can let to students.

'Unlike young professionals who may want to be single occupants, students are always sharing flats or houses, and these must be self-contained. Although student accommodation is less classy than that offered to professionals, it still has to offer the basics. Most students, or their parents at least, prefer purpose-built blocks to conversions as they usually have porters, and are seen as safe.'

As with other self-contained flats, students themselves are responsible for paying the utilities. 'They seem to have a lot of money often,' said Joel, 'as they all have overdrafts, and the banks look kindly on them, while they are bona fide students, at least.

'There is a lot of money to be made from letting to students and these days, landlords should not automatically exclude them. The accommodation need not be classy, just adequate.'

It's all a far cry from my 1960s student days, where I first shared a bedsit with another student, then later upgraded with the same student to a two-room attic flat. We shared a bathroom with the tenants downstairs, we had no fridge, and the 'kitchen' consisted of a cooker and sink on the landing. There was no telephone or television point, and for heating, we had a hissing gas fire in each room into which we had to constantly feed shillings. We took our washing to the launderette up the road, and thought we were in heaven.

During August and September, many local papers carry advertisements from colleges and universities inviting landlords to let to students, and asking them to get in touch with the college housing officer. If you go through the official channels, you have a statutory body to complain to if anything goes wrong with the tenancy.

Not long after I left university, I became a university landlord. All my tenants, who lived in a two-roomed flat at the top of my house, were found for me by the university's lodgings officer, and all were absolutely fine. All paid their rent on time, all were polite, courteous and clean and there was the distinct advantage that the rent they paid also paid my mortgage at the time. The students also came in handy for babysitting.

But it's salutary to think that such accommodation as I provided, which earned the undying gratitude of my student tenants, would probably be considered unfit for human habitation today. The student flat was not self-contained, and the tenants had to share our bathroom. Nor did the flat possess a washing-machine or fridge.

The DSS and Housing Benefit

Very few letting agencies will touch DSS or Housing Benefit (HB) tenants. Agencies often say it's a nightmare they don't need, and very few landlords welcome the prospect of HB tenants either. But before you dismiss the whole idea of accepting HB tenants, you may like to consider the other side of the equation.

Letting agents Wyatt and Son of Worthing have accepted HB tenants for many years, provided certain criteria are met. Robert Wearing of Wyatts said: 'Obviously it's up to the landlord, and some landlords won't consider HB tenants under any circumstances. It is essential for the tenant to have a guarantor, who must be a homeowner in full-time employment. This person, very often a parent or relative, will guarantee payment of rent in case anything goes wrong.

'The prospective tenant goes through a predetermination process, where an HB officer comes round and estimates the rental value of the property. Then the Benefit will be a proportion of the market rent. In our experience, the rent is usually estimated at the current market price.

'We insist on a proper deposit and we also insist, with HB tenants, that the rent is paid directly to us at the agency by direct debit. We will not accept any other conditions, and will not let the Benefit go directly to the tenant.

'We don't have problems with arrears, and find that on the whole, HB tenants are in that position through no fault of their own. Very few are determined scroungers. One landlady we took onto our books recently said she was perfectly happy with an HB tenant as, years ago, she had been in that position herself and knew what it was like.'

Mostly, it is the inner-city and more rundown properties that are likely to be available to HB tenants. 'If a landlord has a nice house in an upmarket neighbourhood, he is unlikely to want HB tenants, as these might upset the neighbours. But always, it depends on the landlord,' Robert Wearing added.

Eileen Daniels and Geoff Sadler, who between them let a number of properties in the south of England, have been mainly very happy indeed with DSS and HB tenants. Eileen said: 'Geoff and I often let to DSS tenants and I must say that we have had very few problems of any kind. In fact, all of our problems have come from private tenants with a lot of money. It's the upper-class types, in our experience, who spill wine and trash the place, rather than those on Housing Benefit. For one thing, HB tenants are often extremely grateful to have a nice flat, with good carpets and curtains.' However, added Eileen, it's essential to make sure certain safeguards are carried out.

'We always make sure the HB money is paid directly into our accounts or to the agent, and does not go to the tenant. When it goes to the tenant, there can be problems as they tend to get behind. We have not experienced problems in getting the money direct from the council. In fact, it goes straight into your account and you don't know anything about it.

'You get exactly the same rent as with a private tenant and we have never found HB tenants to leave the place in a slummy mess. You do have to take a deposit, and we would never ever rent out a place to anybody, whether private or HB tenant, where a month's deposit was not available. HB tenants have to find some money for the deposit, as that is not paid by the council. Also, it's another safeguard for the landlord.

'Again, we have found that it's often the private tenants, rather than the HB people, who make out they can't find the deposit. One tenant I had, who was a model earning good money, said she could not find the deposit money. Eventually she borrowed it from her grandmother, and when it came to the end of the tenancy, it was eaten up in its entirety by the mess she made. An ordinary person would not have made that mess.'

If you have a tenant who suddenly becomes unemployed through no fault of her own, and has to go onto Housing Benefit, you may not even know, if the rent continues to be paid in the usual way by direct debit. In such cases, the Housing Benefit will go directly to the tenant.

If you feel you might be prepared to accept a tenant on Housing Benefit, you absolutely *must* make sure all the checks are carried out; do not allow them in otherwise.

Here is a cautionary tale from a landlord who looked too kindly on an HB tenant: 'A young woman had been sent by an agency to look at a flat I was letting, and she fell in love with it right away. She said that unfortunately she could not find the deposit, as she had been out of work for some time and simply didn't have any money.

'She promised faithfully to pay the rent, however, and pleaded to be let in. Eventually, I let her in – and regretted it ever since. Once in, she never paid any rent and on top of that started complaining about the place. She complained that the shower didn't work, that the carpets were filthy and disgusting and that the cooker had broken. The rent money came to her and was not paid directly into my account, and of course she spent it on living.

'As it happens, I take out insurance against non-payment of rent, so I got the money back eventually, and she was finally evicted. But not before she'd had a wonderful free run. She never did pay rent, because she alleged she never had any money.'

To me, that particular experience speaks of an extremely dangerous type of potential tenant: the conwoman. Once you get to know them, they are easy enough to spot, as they are extremely plausible and they always over-praise the place. In fact, if any potential tenant over-praises your flat, be very much on your guard. Another ploy of the practised fraudster is that they tell you over and over again how honest they are, they make extravagant claims about paying rent, yet often they mysteriously don't have the deposit. These people are well practised in exploiting every positive quality that you as the landlord might possess, and flatter you into the bargain. Then, once safely in, they start to slag off your property, your furniture and your appliances, claiming they are unsafe or faulty.

Their pattern of behaviour never varies. Sometimes you need more than one example of a fraudster before you get to know the warning signs. *But they are always the same.* Scroungers and fraudsters run to a well-defined pattern, and they are most definitely not confined to the DSS and Housing Benefit range of tenants.

Although some landlords say they can make good money from DSS and HB tenants, they are perhaps best avoided by the novice or nervous landlord. After all, if the flat is in a prime location, is smart, clean and fully equipped, you most probably do not need to go down this route. The other aspect is that Housing Benefit itself is extremely complicated – there are several thick volumes in existence on this subject alone – and difficult for the amateur to wade through and understand. If you have any doubts or misgivings, leave it alone.

Some landlords have horror stories concerning tenants they allowed in because they were single parents, perhaps, and the landlord felt sorry for them. As a general rule, it is a grave mistake to mix business with philanthropy. Unless you are a Rowntree or a Guinness and in a position to provide philanthropic housing, you should treat your investment as a business proposition and leave sentiment out of it.

In an article entitled 'Landlords follow conscience or take risk', published in *The Guardian,* lawyer Richard Colbey advised all landlords to find out as much as possible about their tenants, but added that insisting on employer references, a large deposit and surety is going to make it all but impossible to let to any but relatively well-off tenants.

He wrote:

> The Housing Benefits system offers little solace for landlords who think it socially undesirable to impose such a means test. The Benefit, which helps tenants pay some or all of their rent, is paid to the tenant, unless they request it to go to the landlord.
>
> Only if there is eight weeks' arrears can the authority pay it to the landlord without their agreement. Once such a level of arrears exists, it is irrecoverable.
>
> Many landlords are faced with a stark choice between ignoring their consciences and risking their money.

My own advice is simple: ignore your conscience, unless you can take losing your money in your stride with complete equanimity.

Holiday lets

Before the Housing Act of 1988 became law, many landlords advertised their properties as 'holiday lets' to bypass the then rules regarding security of tenure. Strictly speaking, a 'holiday let' is a property let to one tenant for no more than a month. If the same tenant renews for another month, the landlord is breaking the law. Nowadays holiday lets must be just that – let for a genuine holiday.

If you have a flat or cottage that you wish to let for holiday purposes, whether or not you live in it yourself for part of the year, you are entering quite another type of landlord–tenant arrangement.

Holiday lets are not covered by the Housing Act. The contract is finalized by exchange of letters with the tenants where they place a deposit and the owner confirms the booking. If the let is not for a genuine holiday, you may have problems in evicting the tenant as the whole point of a holiday let is that it is for a fixed period of no more than a month.

Generally speaking, certain services must be provided for the property to count as a holiday let. Cleaning services and changes of bed linen are examples. The amount paid by the holiday-maker will normally include utilities such as gas, electricity, water and council tax, but would exclude use of telephone, fax machines and so on.

Magazines such as *The Lady* have dozens of pages of holiday lets, but you can if you like go through an agency specializing in holiday cottages, which undertakes to find you suitable tenants. But beware – some holiday cottage companies are extremely fussy, and insist on gas, electricity and furniture safety regulations being met. If the equipment and fittings are not 'compliant' the company may refuse to take your cottage onto its books.

Neil Collins wished to let his idyllic cottage on the South Downs. He contacted a well-known agency, but soon found himself hemmed in by red tape. A representative of the agency called and inspected the place. She told him that the carpet would have to go, she demanded a washing-machine, a heated towel rail in the bathroom and redecoration of the kitchen. She also suggested redecoration of the hall and landing and replacement of the cooker. Two of the beds were deemed 'non-compliant', and the wiring appeared suspect. A stair gate should be put at the top of the stairs in case of small children falling down, Mr Collins was advised.

Tenants eventually arrived and paid a very high rent, a quarter of which was deducted by the agency. But there were yet more inspections and regulations, so Neil Collins decided to pull out of the country cottage scheme. 'Full compliance is virtually impossible for any normal mortal who is trying to let a home that is not built and equipped specifically for the task,' he wrote. 'Like your beds, your house is bound to be non-compliant: look round at that slightly frayed carpet, that cup with the handle stuck back on, that dodgy banister you always meant to fix...'.

Robert Brew, who recently converted all his former Assured Shorthold Tenancy flats into holiday lets, said: 'Holiday lets bring you in three times the money of six-monthly rentals, but for six times the work. You have to clean the place completely before each tenant arrives, and they may be only there a week. Also, you have to change the sheets and have everything ready for occupation – literally down to the last teaspoon.'

Holiday lets, it goes without saying – or should do – will only be popular in holiday resorts. As such, the demand may be seasonal, although some holiday-let landlords report that even in resort towns, there are often people coming for conferences or on short-term jobs who prefer a fully equipped 'home' to a hotel.

Letting rooms in your home

Lodgers, paying guests, tenants, call them what you will – from earliest times home-owners have let rooms or bedsits in their own houses for which they receive rent. If you are currently living in a house that has become too large for your needs, but are reluctant to sell it and move to a smaller one, then letting out rooms could be a good way of generating extra income.

There are special laws relating to running a bed and breakfast business, but generally speaking, there are very few laws relating to letting out rooms in your own home. Be careful to heed the warning above: do not be tempted to rent out rooms in your own home to friends or relatives, as it may not be such an easy matter to obtain a proper rent, or to get rid of them when you've had enough of them.

If you have a house with spare rooms and are considering letting some of them out for extra cash, make sure you embark on a business arrangement right away so that both of you know where you stand as regards use of the bathroom and kitchen, having guests in, access to your living room, television, telephone, washing-machine and so on.

Also bear in mind that having other people living in your house and sharing facilities is an intimate arrangement, and subtly alters the atmosphere in your home. At various times when I have had temporary lodgers in my home, I could always sense whether they were in residence. Although the vibes may be difficult to pin down, they are always there.

It is a far better idea, if at all possible, to create a self-contained unit where lodgers and tenants can have the place all to themselves. For this you will need planning permission. It may not be feasible to create a separate entrance, but if tenants have their own bathroom and kitchen facilities, and a separate telephone and television point, you are less likely to get on each other's nerves.

Some home-owners create granny flats out of their basement or other part of their home. There are special rules relating to dependent relatives, and if you are interested in letting out part of your home in this way, you should contact a council tax official, and ask for advice on whether the let part constitutes a separate entity or not. There are many grey areas here and it is not always easy to decide, but generally speaking a flatlet or bedsit may count as a separate self-contained entity if it has a proper cooker point. 'The provision of a microwave oven does not constitute a kitchen,' I was told by one council tax officer. If, however, a part of your house is designated a separate self-contained flat, you may be eligible for a different council tax banding.

Bedsits

Bedsits, or bedsitting rooms, to give them their proper name, were created in large numbers just after the Second World War, when many soldiers and others returning from service found themselves homeless. The idea of the bedsit was to give some privacy both to the tenant, or lodger, and the resident landlord. Very few, if any, letting agencies handle bedsits as they do not constitute self-contained accommodation, and for the novice or potential landlord, they are best left alone.

For many years, the trend has been towards creating self-contained accommodation that will be subject to the Assured Shorthold Tenancy agreement. The days of the seedy landlord presiding over an assorted jumble of bedsits and ever-complaining tenants, like Rigsby in the TV sitcom *Rising Damp*, are numbered.

Now that even students require self-contained accommodation, there seems little future, at least for the private landlord, in providing non-self-contained bedsits.

Buying a property with existing occupants

If you buy a property already tenanted, in a sense the search for tenants will be unnecessary. Mostly, existing tenants in an upmarket property being sold as a rental investment will be corporate or professional tenants who should not create problems.

Properties sold with protected or regulated tenants paying perhaps £10 a week rent are virtually non-existent nowadays. In any case, these cannot be considered as an investment as the sitting tenant is a liability, not an asset. Some seaside properties, for instance, are sold with existing tenants, and these are most often houses that have been divided up into four or more units, where the freeholder wants to offload the property. Very often, such properties are extremely run down and suitable only for the serious property developer.

Your relationship with your tenant(s)

Whether or not you decide to use a letting agency or e-letting, you will still have to decide on what kind of relationship, if any, to have with your tenants. Agencies are acting on your behalf and will take their instructions from you. If you stipulate that you do not want children or pets, then agencies must abide by this.

Mostly, children and pets are looked upon with horror by landlords, but not all landlords object. Greg Shackleton, for instance, is quite happy to have tenants with either, and says that in some flats he has even provided a cat-flap. The main objection to children and pets, especially in blocks of flats, is that they disturb the other residents. Also, there may be a clause in the lease excluding domestic animals.

Unless you opt for full management from a letting agency, you will have at least some relationship with your tenant. I have discovered that the best kind of relationship is one where you remain friendly and polite but never interfere, and you do not mix your tenant with your social life. Once my tenants are in place, I leave them completely alone to get on with their own lives. They leave me alone as well. However, if we meet in the street, or by chance, we have a friendly chat. We emphatically do not socialize together, though. It is simply not appropriate when you are taking money off people, and can make the relationship unclear. Agents and inventory clerks always throw their hands up in horror when either the tenant or the landlord says they have become great friends. 'The friendlier they are, the greater the problems at the end of the tenancy,' said inventory clerk Jennifer Reigate. 'Just about all the legal disputes happen when landlord and tenant have got too friendly with each other.'

Nowadays, first-name terms are indicated. My tenants refer to me as 'Liz' and I call them by their first names. So do all other landlords and tenants I know. Estate agents long ago stopped using surnames, and will always introduce your potential tenant to you as 'Clare' or 'Alex' or whatever.

If a tenant contacts you with a problem it must be attended to right away. A good landlord is one who sends out a plumber, or electrician, or washing-machine engineer, on the same day as the complaint is received, when at all possible.

One difficult problem with a good, long-standing tenant, is when or whether to put the rent up. Although you are legally allowed to put the rent up every year, some landlords waive this for an exceptional tenant. A landlord friend, with a single tenant of three years' standing, put it like this: 'When my tenant last renewed, I wondered about putting up the rent, especially as the agents mentioned it. I thought about it, but decided that although the increase would mean little to me, it might make a lot of difference to her.

'When I contacted her about renewing the agreement, I said that I would not put up the rent and she was profoundly grateful. She would have found the extra money, I'm sure, but I felt that three years without a single void was a good record, and also the agent's commission had been reduced after that length of time. Even one month's void during that time would have cancelled out the extra rent I might have got.' When this tenant leaves and a new one takes her place, then this landlord will of course put up the rent.

As to whether couples or single people make better tenants, I don't think you can generalize. Some landlords prefer single occupants on the grounds that one against one is better than two against one, but I have never had any problems with the couples who have rented my properties.

As with any business, establishing exactly the right relationship with your tenant is a matter of trial and error, and we all make mistakes. The thing is, though, not to make the same mistake twice, if you can help it.

There are few resentments stronger, or greater feelings of hate, than when a once-good landlord and tenant relationship goes sour. It can be compared to a once-loving couple squabbling bitterly over their divorce. And, like a bitter divorce, the ill-feeling can remain for very many years, on either side.

Checklist for assessing the suitability of tenants

1. Have a clear idea of your ideal type of tenant.
2. Is your prospective tenant clean, tidy and punctual?
3. Make sure the deposit is paid in full upfront.
4. Be on your guard if your tenant withholds necessary information, such as previous employer, previous landlord, etc.
5. Make sure they are in a financial position to pay the rent.
6. Do not accept a tenant who tries to bargain you down over rent. Rents should be non-negotiable, unless stated otherwise when the flat is advertised.
7. Be clear about whether you will accept pets or children and be firm about your decision.
8. Never panic over possible voids to such an extent that you accept a tenant about whom you have misgivings.
9. As with any other business transaction, use logic and common sense – and then go with your gut reaction. If there seems something odd about a potential tenant you can't quite determine, follow your intuition. You will rarely be wrong.

6

Rights and obligations

The main fear of landlords is that tenants won't pay the rent, and the main fear of tenants is that they won't get their deposit back. In theory, these twin financial fears, integral to all residential letting arrangements, should cancel each other out and make sure both sides are on their best behaviour at all times. However, it doesn't always work out like that, and in order to protect both parties, there exists a huge amount of legislation relating to landlord and tenant.

The Landlord and Tenant Acts, 1985 and 1987, are the main pieces of extant legislation governing the rights and obligations of landlord and tenant. They are extremely complicated documents, not readily understood by the layperson. Also, when disputes arise, there are many grey areas that often only a solicitor or judge can decide, taking all aspects of the dispute into consideration. No piece of legislation, however comprehensive, can foresee all eventualities.

Most of the basics covering the majority of eventualities are set out in the modern Assured Shorthold Tenancy agreement. (The main points of the tenancy agreement are set out below.) When the first Housing Act came into force on 15 January 1989, there were two distinct types of tenancy covered by the Act: Assured, and Assured Shorthold. The terms of each were similar, but the Assured Tenancy gave more security of tenure, as it was not for a fixed contractual term. Since 28 February 1997 however, all tenancies for self-contained properties are automatically Assured Shorthold, unless both parties wish to enter into an Assured Tenancy, for a longer term, or if the Assured Shorthold type of tenancy does not apply, as with a company let or where the annual rent exceeds £25,000.

Assured Shorthold Tenancy agreements state that, basically, the landlord has a duty to maintain the property in good repair and not to hassle or otherwise annoy the tenant. The law also recognizes that, while the tenant is paying rent, she is entitled to the same amount of peace and privacy she would have if she owned the property. The 1988 Housing Act states:

> Once a tenant has a market rent tenancy and is occupying the property as his or her home it is right that he or she should have a reasonable degree of security of tenure.

The tenant's main obligation is to pay the agreed rent on time and in full. So long as the landlord is fulfilling his part of the bargain there can be no deviation from this. Even if the landlord does not instantly carry out repairs, the tenant is not allowed to withhold rent. No part of the tenancy agreement makes any provision for withholding rent and if a tenant does so, she automatically puts herself in the wrong.

All landlords should remember this if and when a dispute arises. But even here there are grey areas, as in the following case. A landlord wrote to a newspaper legal advice column:

> I have let out a flat at a rental of £700 a month on a 12-month lease. The tenants have now decided to withhold £100 rent every month until I fix a so-called faulty shower. Two plumbers have looked at it and both say it's not faulty. The tenants also want a new washing machine because they claim that the present one does not work to their satisfaction. My tenancy agreement says that I can end the tenancy if they have not paid rent 14 days after it is due. Does withholding £100 a month constitute not paying rent?

The answer to this query, by *Evening Standard* lawyer Fenton Bresler, went thus:

Withholding a part of the total rent because of a genuine dispute is not the same as the non-payment of rent that entitles a landlord to end a tenancy legally. In fact, at times it can be a tenant's only weapon with which to force a landlord to honour his obligations, especially where the tenant has spent his own money in doing repairs which the landlord should have undertaken.

You would not, in my mind, be justified in ending this tenancy merely because one-seventh of the monthly rent is withheld. Indeed, your letter in its entirety indicates such a tense situation that I think you should discuss it calmly with a solicitor.

In this case, I can understand how the landlord feels, as in my own experience showers are a very common cause of complaint, and an easy one with which to berate the landlord. Hamptons' *Lettings Handbook* addresses the vexed issue of the shower, pointing out that although modern investment properties require power showers, water pressure varies and in the UK, what passes for a perfectly working shower may not be as powerful as one in the USA or in Australia, for instance.

Although it may seem trivial, I would say that around 90 per cent of tenants' complaints are about showers. In one of my present flats, both tenants have rung to complain about the shower. In the first instance, the complaint was justified – the shower had broken down. In the other, the tenant, an Australian, had just not worked out how to use it. 'These showers are different from the ones at home,' she said, after the manufacturers had carefully explained its workings to her.

Some wily tenants use the excuse of a non-working shower to withhold all or part of the rent. Every landlord I know has had a complaint at some time about the shower, but as it is essential to have one, it's difficult to see how this can be addressed in advance. My advice would be the same as Fenton Bresler's: where a dispute seems incapable of settlement by ordinary means, seek the advice of a solicitor.

For most of the time, the rules and regulations set out in the tenancy agreement are upheld by both parties, as both have a vested interest in the arrangement working smoothly. However, as in all human endeavours, things (even apart from the shower!) do sometimes go wrong, and it may not always be obvious what the landlord or the tenant should do. If in doubt, you go to your nearest Citizen's Advice Bureau, check with your lettings agency, if using one, or ask your solicitor.

Tenancy agreements

The usual type of tenancy agreement these days is the Assured Shorthold. This was originally devised in 1988 and amended by the Housing Act 1996. It was designed to make the letting of property to private individuals more attractive by making it easier to let property at a market rent, and to recover possession. Originally, these proposals were made to encourage the growth of the private rented sector and in this, it has been extremely successful.

Assured Shorthold Tenancies last for six months at a time, and apply to all dwellings rented since January 1989, with certain exceptions. Nowadays, the Assured Shorthold is a standardized form, and all lettings agencies have these as a matter of course. These agreements are legally binding between landlord and tenant although, like most contracts, they can be difficult to enforce if one or other party is determined not to abide by its strictures.

This is a fairly standard tenancy agreement under the Assured Shorthold legislation:

The agreement is called ASSURED SHORTHOLD TENANCY AGREEMENT for letting a residential dwelling house.

On the first page, the agreement contains this caveat:

This tenancy agreement is for letting furnished or unfurnished residential accommodation on an assured shorthold tenancy within the provisions of the Housing Act 1988 as amended by Part 111 of the Housing Act 1996. As such, this is a legal document and should not be used without adequate knowledge of the law of landlord and tenant.

The next page of the agreement sets out all relevant dates, the name of the tenant, address of the flat, term of tenancy, the monthly rental paid, and the amount of the deposit.

The rest of the agreement, every page of which should be signed or initialled by both landlord and tenant, sets out the terms of the tenancy. Again, they are standard items.

Here are the main points of the tenancy agreement, couched in appropriate legalese:

The Tenant agrees with the Landlord

To Pay the Rent on the days and in the manner specified to the Landlord.

To pay promptly to the authorities to whom they are due, council tax and outgoings (including gas, electricity, water, light and telephone if any relating to the Property, including any which are imposed after the date of this Agreement), and to pay the total cost of any reconnection fee relating to the supply of gas, electricity and telephone if the same is disconnected.

Not to damage or injure the Property or make any alteration or addition to it. Any redecoration is to be made only with the prior written consent of the Landlord.

Not to leave the Property vacant for more than 30 consecutive days and to properly secure all locks and bolts to the doors, windows and other openings when leaving the Property unattended.

To keep the interior of the Property and the Contents in good and clean condition and complete repair (damage by accidental fire and reasonable wear and tear excepted) and to keep property at all times well and sufficiently aired and warmed during the tenancy.

To immediately pay the Landlord the value of replacement of any furniture or effects lost, damaged or destroyed or at the option of the Landlord, replace immediately any furniture or effects lost, damaged or destroyed, and not to remove or permit to remove any furniture or effects from the property.

To yield up the Property and Contents at the expiration or sooner determination of the tenancy in the same clean state or condition as they shall be at the commencement of the tenancy.

To pay for any cleaning services that may be required to reinstate the Property to the same order that it was provided at the commencement of the tenancy, including the washing and cleaning of all linen, bedding, carpets and curtains which shall have been soiled during the tenancy.

To leave the Contents at the end of the tenancy in the same places in which they were positioned at the commencement of the tenancy.

That the Landlord or any person authorized by the Landlord may at reasonable times of the day on giving 24 hours' notice (unless in the case of an emergency) enter the Property for the purpose of viewing, inspecting its condition and state of repair or for the purpose of repair or repainting.

Not to assign, or sublet, part with possession of the Property, or let any other person live at the Property.

To use the Property as a single private dwelling and not to use it or any part of it for any other purpose or allow anyone else to do so.

Not to receive paying guests or carry on or permit to be carried on any business, trade or profession on or from the Property.

Not to permit or suffer to be done in or on the Property any act or thing which may be a nuisance, damage or annoyance to the Landlord or to the occupiers of the neighbouring premises, or which may void any insurance of the Property or cause the premiums to increase.

Not to keep any animals or birds on the Property without the Landlord's written consent, such consent if granted to be revocable at will by the Landlord.

To keep the gardens if any neat and tidy at all times and not to remove any trees or plants.

The Landlord agrees with the Tenant that provided the Tenant shall pay the Rent and perform the agreements on his part already referred to, the Landlord shall permit the Tenant to have quiet enjoyment of the Property without interruption by the Landlord.

The Landlord may re-enter the Property and immediately thereupon the tenancy shall absolutely determine without prejudice to the other rights and remedies of the Landlord if the Tenant has not complied with any obligation in this Agreement, or should the rent be in arrears by more than 14 days whether formally demanded or not.

The Landlord agrees to carry out any repairing obligations as required by sections 11–16 of the Landlord and Tenant Act 1985.

The agreement should also include a definition of what is meant by a Landlord, what is meant by a tenant, and on which grounds a tenancy may be brought to an end. It should also state the notice period necessary to be served by either party (one month by the tenant; two months by the Landlord) also stating that the tenancy must run for at least six months.

The tenant(s) and landlord must then sign the agreement in the presence of witnesses, and the contract then becomes legally binding on both sides.

The Assured Shorthold (AS) has become a user-friendly agreement, and the one most often used. The Assured Tenancy, originally designed for people who wanted longer tenancies, and offering more protection, and the AS became one and the same thing on 28 February 1997. The 1997 Housing Act amendment also stated that all tenancies should be AS unless otherwise stated.

In order to create an AS tenancy, the following points have to be addressed:

- The tenant must be an individual, not a company.

- The tenant must occupy the property as his or her own home, or main home. It is not possible to do an AS tenancy for a pied-à-terre, or a second home.
- The yearly rent must not exceed £25,000 a year or £480 a week. Where this is the case, the tenant is a non-Housing Act tenant, and the law of contract applies.
- The landlord must not be resident. If a property was built as one house and has been divided up, with the landlord occupying a part, then an AS cannot be created. However, most agencies say that where all flats are self-contained and the landlord, say, lives in the basement with a separate entrance and front door, then AS tenancies can be created, as with any other self-contained flat.

Note: the terms of the tenancy under the Law of Contract may be the same as with Housing Act tenants, but the agreement must be covered by contract law. In practice, this may not make all that much difference, but if you are renting out a property that comes outside these categories, legal advice must be sought. Letting agencies are geared up to deal with these eventualities.

Common problems

Here are the answers to the most vexing and frequent landlord and tenant problems.

Q: There appears to be a leak in the bathroom of one of my flats, and as a consequence the ceiling of the flat downstairs has fallen down. The owner threatens to sue me for damage. Meanwhile, the other tenant (not mine) is refusing to pay rent. There is no damage to my flat. What should I do?

A: Water damage occurs frequently in blocks of flats. Before admitting any liability, get a plumber to check the source of the leak; in blocks of flats, water can travel from all kinds of places. If the leak is traced to your bathroom your first job, after getting in a plumber to repair the damage, is to check with the freeholder or managing agent of the block to see whether you are covered by buildings insurance. You should be. If this is the case, the insurance company will pick up the bill for the damage to the downstairs flat. You should also make sure your tenant is not using the bathroom in such a way as to damage the downstairs flat.

If you do everything possible the owner of the downstairs flat would have no grounds to sue you. The downstairs tenant must not withhold rent and, in any case, this is a matter for the downstairs owner and tenant to sort out between themselves. For all you know, there may be long-running problems on other issues between these two people.

Q: My tenant is going away for two months and wants to sublet her flat in the meantime. Can she do this?

A: The person (or people) named in the tenancy agreement is the only one allowed to occupy the premises. If your tenant wishes to sublet she should ask you first. Should you agree, the new tenant's name can be added to the tenancy agreement, with the amount of time she will be staying there. Never let in a new person, though, without first checking references and taking a deposit. Do not ever admit somebody into your property on the say-so of the existing tenant, but always make sure all the same checks are applied as with the original tenant. All references must come from the previous landlord or employer, and not be provided by the tenant, as she could easily have faked them.

A common variation of this situation is that your tenant wishes to move in a boyfriend or girlfriend – permanently. Again, the same thing applies. If you are happy in principle with another person on the premises, take references and a deposit and increase the rent slightly, to accommodate the other person. There will be extra wear and tear on the property, and if damage is caused by a person not named on the agreement, you could be in trouble.

Lettings agencies say that the decision to grant permission to include another person rests with the landlord. If your tenant sublets or brings in another person without your permission, this is grounds for eviction, as they have broken the tenancy agreement. Many landlords do not mind having an extra tenant, but permission must always be obtained first.

One of my own tenants wished to move in his girlfriend. I checked with the lettings agency, and they took up references, an extra deposit and extra rent. My tenant was happy with this, the girlfriend proved no trouble at all, and the arrangement worked out perfectly well. It's where tenants sneak in other people, and you just happen to find out, that you should be on your guard.

Q: I have let my three-bedroom house with garden to young professionals sharing. Although they have looked after the house fairly well, they have let the garden – my pride and joy – go. It looks terrible, and I am bitterly disappointed, as gardening is my hobby. Do I have any redress?

A: This depends on what was stated in the tenancy agreement. If the tenants agreed specifically to look after the garden, then they are liable. But in general terms, you cannot expect tenants to be keen gardeners. The usual advice given where you are letting a house with a garden is that the tenants agree to keep it neat and tidy, mow the lawn and so on, but if you as the landlord want it kept as a wonderful garden, it's up to you to arrange to have a gardener.

Similarly, you cannot expect tenants to have green fingers when it comes to window boxes, houseplants and so on. If plants form part of the inventory, you should expect that they are in the same condition as when you left the property, either by the tenants looking after them or buying new ones, but in general, it's safest not to have loads of plants and window boxes. Leave it up to the tenants as to whether they want to be bothered. The best advice is to have any lawn paved over and a few low-maintenance shrubs.

Q: My long-term tenants have redecorated the flat in colours that I hate. Can I do anything about it?

A: Most tenancy agreements specifically state that tenants are not allowed to redecorate. If they wish to do this, they must get your written permission. Otherwise, you could make them decorate the flat back in the original colours.

Q: My tenant wants to leave after six weeks as her mother has become seriously ill, and she says she is needed at home. Yet she signed a six-month agreement. Can she just break the agreement like this?

A: Strictly speaking, she has broken the terms of her tenancy agreement, and is liable for the six months, whether she is there or not. However, unforeseen circumstances do arise, and you have to decide how flexible or rigid to be. Most decent landlords will let a tenant leave after a shorter length of time if (a) the tenant finds another suitable tenant or (b) the landlord or agency manage to find another tenant.

If this cannot be done immediately, you may be able to come to an arrangement whereby she agrees to pay you until a tenant is found. Then you can both sign off when the new tenant moves in.

Q: I hate smoking, and have a clause written into my tenancy agreements that only non-smokers will be considered as tenants. My current tenants signed the agreement, but they are smokers. I know this for a fact because my investment flat is just below my own flat. Can I turn them out?

A: If you hate smoking so much, and it's certainly up to you to decide whether or not to let smokers in, then yes, you can. To some, smoking seems a trivial reason for eviction, but allowing smokers in can be very expensive, as it means the property needs constant redecoration. In one flat of mine inhabited by smokers, the walls and ceiling needed repainting each year. Also, with heavy smokers, it is difficult to get the smell out of curtains and carpets. As smoking can be a serious addiction, it may not be feasible to order your tenants to stop, so you may have no option but to bring the tenancy to the speediest legal conclusion. If your tenants are smokers, it is in order to increase the deposit

Q: My tenant, who has been in residence for a year, wants to extend her tenancy for another year. Can I put up the rent?

A: Yes. Most tenancy agreements state that the rent will remain the same for a year. You are perfectly entitled to ask for more rent after a year, although not before. When extending tenancies, always make sure a new agreement, duly signed and witnessed, is drawn up. Never, ever leave anything to chance.

If your tenant wishes to extend her tenancy for another few months, this can be done under an arrangement known as a 'periodic tenancy', whereby the tenant continues to reside in the property from month to month, with a month's notice given in writing on either side.

Q: Although Assured Shorthold Tenancies seem to work quite well, six months is an awfully short time to live in a place. Surely longer tenancies are a better bet, for both sides?

A: It is true that some lettings experts are beginning to chafe at the restrictions of the Assured Shorthold Tenancy agreement. Frances Burkinshaw, chairman of the Association of Residential Lettings Agents said: 'Agents should stop dribbling out rental agreements in six-month doses, like Scrooge in a counting house. It suits everyone to arrange tenancies for as long as possible.'

Yet the experience of some landlords is that long lets can actually increase the problems, particularly when tenants prove unsatisfactory. One landlord let out his two-bedroom house to a childless couple who seemed perfect. All went well for a year, then the tenants asked for a three-year tenancy, during which time they agreed to replace the kitchen units. The landlord complied with this arrangement. But soon, neighbours complained about dogs barking, even though the agreement had a 'no pets' clause. Before long, there were 9 dogs and 18 cats on the premises, and rent payments became erratic. Eventually, the rent stopped altogether, and the landlord eventually obtained a possession order from the County Court. Still the tenants did not move out. Finally, a bailiff appeared, but by this time the tenants had disappeared, leaving the place filthy and uninhabitable. None of this would have happened, he said, if he had stuck to six-month agreements. 'My advice to other landlords is to insist on six-monthly terms with options for extensions. As it was, it took me two years to get the tenants out, and I had to employ industrial cleaners in the place.'

Although this story may seem extreme, something similar happened in the three-bedroom terrace house next to me. Non-paying tenants stayed in the place for several years, terrifying the neighbours, trashing the place and allowing all kinds of people to stay there.

From a letting agent's point of view, the longer the let, the greater the commission. Often, the whole of the commission is taken upfront, and the agent does not have to bother to find new tenants.

The best advice is to stick to the six-monthly agreements, and extend them if the tenant proves to be good.

Q: My outgoing tenant has left the place very untidy and dirty, although nothing has actually been broken or stolen. The fridge and cooker, for instance, have not been cleaned. Can I withhold the deposit?

A: The tenancy agreement specifically states that the property should be left in exactly the same condition as found, allowing for normal wear and tear. I should charge your tenant for professional cleaning, present her with the bill, and deduct this from her deposit.

Here is a common problem relating to owner–occupiers living in the same building as tenanted flats:

Q: We live in a well-maintained and very pleasant block where, until last year, all the flats were owner-occupied. We residents are mainly middle-aged or retired, but the owner of the flat adjoining ours moved out last year. The new owner rents it out to a succession of young foreign students, who presumably pay him a high rent, but are the most appalling neighbours. They seem to change every two months, but our leases all contain a clause saying that the minimum sublet is six months. We have complained to the managing agents, but they seem strangely unconcerned. Is there anything we can do about it?

A: Clauses limiting the length of permitted subletting are quite common. They are meant to ensure that good-class residential blocks retain their individual character, and it is in everyone's interest – including managing agents and freeholders – to do all they can to achieve this.

There are two ways of dealing with the problem. One is to remind the managing agents of the landmark 1997 Appeal Court decision in *Chartered Trust plc v Davies*. In that case, Lord Justice Henry ruled that the freeholder himself can be sued by an unhappy flat owner, where the freeholder's failure to enforce the terms of another flat owner's lease in the same block had materially damaged his enjoyment of his own flat. Lawyers are still working out all the ramifications of this judgment.

Secondly, all residential leases say that flat owners must not allow their property to become a nuisance or annoyance to the other residents. So you should ask the managing agents to enforce this clause. If they refuse, you can threaten, as a last resort, to report them to their clients, the freeholder, or apply direct to the local leasehold valuation tribunal to have them removed as managing agents. It would help you considerably in this to obtain support from the other flat owners in the block. (Advice given by Fenton Bresler in the *Evening Standard*.)

Q: How soon should the deposit be returned?

A: Some rogue landlords have attempted to retain the deposit, and this has led to a spate of court cases. It has also led to landlords getting themselves a bad name for non-return of deposits. Some tenants have said ruefully, 'Holes in walls (from putting up pictures) equal no deposit returned.' It is true that some landlords are looking for any excuse not to return the deposit. But beware – the tenant can take you to court for this, and may well win.

Some tenancy agreements state that the deposit will be returned within a week of the outgoing tenant departing. This gives the landlord time to note whether anything previously unseen, such as the cooker not working, for instance, shows up.

My own procedure is simple: on the day the tenant is due to leave, I go over the inventory, note the condition of the property and contents, and if I am satisfied, I hand over the deposit without further delay, that minute. Outgoing tenants usually need the deposit to put down on their next flat, and in my experience are almost always desperate for it. Because of this, I don't keep them waiting. As they hand over the keys, I hand back the deposit, in full.

It is important to remember that the deposit continues to belong to the tenant, and is not part of the landlord's income. You should ideally pay any interest due on the deposit as well as the initial sum but after six months or a year, interest due on a deposit of £1,000 or less will only amount to a few pounds. Where there is a large deposit, there may be a case for paying interest as well, but I think most tenants are more than happy for their deposit to be returned in full at the end of the tenancy.

Where there are disputes over the inventory or return of deposit, arbitration may be involved. The bigger the deposit, the grander the property, the more likelihood there is of this. *Moral:* never, if you can possibly avoid it, leave anything of sentimental or actual value in your property when letting it to others.

ARLA, the Association of Residential Letting Agencies, has an arbitration service whereby both landlord and tenant pay to apply, in cases of deposit disputes. The more professional and detailed the inventory at the beginning of the tenancy, the less likelihood there is of a dispute, but the possibility can never be entirely ruled out. If your tenant has been obtained through an ARLA agent, ARLA will appoint an arbitrator who will decide what deductions, if any, should be made, and a fee for this is charged according to the rentable value of the property. In 1999, a fee of around £350 plus VAT is standard for this procedure, on top of any deductions. The arbitrator will decide whether the landlord or the tenant is liable for this fee.

As arbitration can be an expensive and time-consuming procedure – inventory clerk Jennifer Reigate says some of her disputes last for three months or more – this is an avenue best avoided. Also, once an arbitrator has been appointed, the relationship between the landlord and tenant is effectively dead, and usually ends with the parties never speaking to each other again.

All disputes cause stress, to both landlord and tenant, but the stress is usually greater for the landlord, as he has a large investment at stake.

Q: The tenancy agreement states quite clearly that the landlord is responsible for repairs of appliances. But what happens when damage has been caused by the tenant's misuse? My last tenant ruined the microwave, which now won't work but which was in perfect order when she started the tenancy. It was an accident, and she is very sorry, but surely she is liable?

A: If damage is caused by the tenant misusing an appliance, then the tenant is responsible. Tenants can get insurance cover for this kind of eventuality, obtainable from most agents. I would deduct the cost of providing a new microwave from her deposit.

Q: If a tenant breaks a few cups and glasses, should I make her pay for them?

A: My inclination here is not to worry about such low-cost items, and not to deduct them from the deposit if you are otherwise happy with your tenant's occupancy.

Q: My tenant has Blu-tacked and Sellotaped pictures on the walls, even though this went expressly against the agreement, and now there are nasty gaps in the emulsion. Can I ask her to pay for redecoration?

A: Technically, yes. But bearing in mind that most tenants will want to put up pictures, why not hammer in picture hooks (the white ones with three nails in them) to prevent this possibility? Then tell them they can only put up pictures on these hooks. If a tenant leaves gashes in the walls where her pictures have been, and you did not provide masonry-type picture hooks, I think you have only yourself to blame. Unless of course, this is only one example of wider desecration, in which case you should withhold enough deposit to pay for redecoration of the affected areas.

Q: My tenant, although otherwise satisfactory, has just become pregnant. I do not want a baby or child in my flat. Should I give her notice?

A: If you have stipulated no children or pets, then yes of course, as the presence of a child alters the tenancy agreement.

Q: My tenant is impeccably clean and tidy, always pays the rent on time and I have no complaints about her except that she appears to have moved her mother in. How can I find out whether her mother is a permanent fixture, or only a temporary guest?

A: It seems, for some strange reason I have not been able to fathom, extremely common for tenants' mothers to move in. If the situation bothers you, you should confront your tenant and ask whether she would like her mother's name added to the tenancy agreement. You could point out that only one person has signed the agreement and that technically her mother cannot move in permanently. My own inclination, however, is to leave well alone. Mothers, in my experience, rarely cause trouble and often ensure the place is extremely clean and tidy.

Q: If I wish to put the rent up for my current tenant, what is the best way to do it? And by how much can I increase the amount?

A: There is a standard procedure for this. Renewal clauses in tenancy agreements usually link increases to the Retail Price Index (RPI). If there is no such clause, you should not increase the rent beyond this limit, or beyond the current market rate. To do so would inevitably sour the relationship between you and your tenant. Whenever rents are increased, paperwork is involved, and plenty of time should be left to give your tenant notice of an increase, and to complete the paperwork.

Q: I understand that as a landlord, I can legally make a slight profit on the electricity charges. Is this fair to the tenant?

A: It is true that electricity companies make allowances for this. To me, though, this is mean and underhand, and tends to complicate landlord–tenant relationships. In situations where I have custody of the electricity meter, I always charge the tenant the current price for the amount of electricity used and no more. Other landlords may feel they have a right to make a slight profit: it depends, really, where your conscience lies. In general, I feel that those landlords who can 'give a bit' tend to have better tenants, a stress-free life, and a more comfortable relationship with the tenant.

And now to the landlord's greatest fear: non-payment of rent.

Q: What if it all goes wrong and my tenant will neither pay rent owed, nor leave?

A: It must be said that, thankfully, these situations are extremely rare. When they do happen, though, you must abide by the law. You are not allowed to evict your tenant yourself, change the locks or use force to get her out – however sorely you may be tempted to do this.

Laws on eviction are always subject to change, but the present law (2001) states that non-paying or otherwise unsatisfactory tenants can be evicted after eight weeks of behaviour that directly contravenes the agreement. In order to evict a tenant, solicitors must be instructed. You can instruct your own solicitor, or your agent's solicitor can be instructed. Either way, you will have to pay, and you may not recover this money.

The solicitor will serve an eviction notice on your tenant, and make arrangements to hand this to her in person. If she does not leave or pay up of her own accord, the next thing is to take her to court, if you consider it worthwhile.

There is now what is called an 'accelerated possession procedure' whereby tenants can be evicted without the need for a court hearing. This particular procedure does not include a claim for arrears of rent – it is simply a means whereby bad tenants can be speedily evicted. You can use this procedure directly where the tenancy is an Assured Shorthold, and you claim possession under Section 21 of the Housing Act 1998, or where there is an Assured Tenancy dating back to before 1997, under Section 8 of the Housing Act. In this case, 'grounds', or reasons, must be supplied. Under Section 21, accelerated possession can be claimed if:

- The tenancy was for a fixed period and that period has expired.
- The existing tenancy, and any agreement covering it, is for an unspecified period.
- You as the landlord have given at least two months' written notice under Section 21, saying that possession was required.

Making a claim under Section 8 of the Housing Act 1988 is more complicated. 'Grounds' include: the property is your main home and you wish to reclaim it; you intend to live in it as your main home; the tenancy was a holiday let, let to students, or is now needed as a residence by a minister of religion. Where these grounds apply, you must have given your tenant notice at least four months before the end of the tenancy.

After you have filed your application to the court, and given the court all the papers required, including a copy of the tenancy agreement, the defendant has 14 days to reply. If an order for possession is made, the defendant will normally be told to leave the property within 14 days. Should the defendant be able to show that this will cause exceptional hardship, the court can extend this period for up to six weeks, but not longer.

Note: the best thing to do, if you think you may be able to use this procedure, is to go to your nearest County Court and ask to see an official. Nowadays, court officials are extremely helpful and will explain everything to you in person. They are not allowed to give actual legal advice, but can certainly explain what the procedure is all about.

Once rent gets into arrears, you should waste no time, but write to your tenant immediately, saying that this month's rent does not appear to have shown up in your account. It may be that there has been an oversight of some kind, so tenants should be given the benefit of the doubt initially. If the money still does not show up, or if the tenant does not reply to your original polite letter, you should write again, saying that if the money is not paid in full within 14 days, court proceedings will be instigated without delay. Then act on that threat immediately. If tenants know that there is no substance to your threats, they will just bin the letter and carry on.

Where it comes to getting rent paid, you should write out the amount owed in arrears, plus any damage to the property or goods stolen, on a form available from the County Court. You will also have to pay a court fee on a sliding scale, depending on the amount owed. This is recoverable from the defendant, should you win your case. The court will send this form to the defendant who will either pay up there and then, counter-claim, or let the judge decide the matter at a court hearing.

The procedure is now quick, simple and straightforward, and you should never be nervous of taking anybody to court when you are owed money. A High Court Judge friend of mine pointed out when I was dithering over whether to take a bad tenant to court: 'You owe it to future landlords' – and he's right. Bad tenants should be stopped in their tracks as quickly as possible – and taught that they can't hope to get away with it.

I have taken two people to court for non-payment of rent. The first was not successful, not because the claim was disputed, but because I was unable to serve papers on the defendant. She had left her job by the time the court summons was received, as she had been sent to prison for other offences. By the time I knew this, and sent the papers to prison, she had served her sentence and gone. I never did catch up with her, and she got away with owing two months' rent. However, when she eventually left my flat, taking the vacuum cleaner and some other items, I reported the theft to the police and managed to get the items returned.

On the second occasion, I got a form from the County Court and wrote out the amounts owed. The defendant counter-claimed, alleging that only some of the amount was owed. Eventually the case came to court and, before a district judge, we settled for the full amount minus interest.

In many cases, the threat of court action is enough to make the defaulter pay up, if for no other reason than if the judgement goes against them, they will find it extremely difficult ever to rent another flat. Also, with a County Court Judgement (CCJ) it can be extremely difficult to get any kind of credit. Defaulting tenants will usually do all they can to avoid a CCJ, although it must be said that some are so far gone that they no longer care.

But all relevant court leaflets make the point that there is little purpose in taking somebody to court if they absolutely do not have the money to pay you. Although the judge can order the money to be paid, it is up to you to enforce this. Leaflets advising plaintiffs on ways to enforce CCJs are freely available from County Courts, and many have been awarded a Crystal Mark for being written in plain English.

Lettings agents can now access a form of referencing whereby CCJs show up on the checking system, and no reputable agency will take such a tenant onto their books. The referencing system cuts down the risk of non-payment to almost nil, but there will always be determined fraudsters who slip through the net.

You may be in a difficult position, however, where your tenant is a visitor from abroad and simply vanishes into the ether without paying. To avoid such an eventuality you can, if you think it is worth it, take out insurance cover. As with any insurance cover, only you can decide whether it is money down the drain or money well spent, bearing in mind that all insurance covers you against things that are extremely unlikely to happen.

If you are in the process of taking a defaulter to court, a word of advice: never, ever discuss the matter with them either in person or on the telephone. If they have not paid and they have ignored your reminder, you have nothing further to say to them. In my experience, non-payers fall into two main categories: those who bully and blackmail, and those who have a sob story. Very often, a defaulter will try both tactics. Don't be browbeaten and don't be swayed by hard luck stories. There is nothing personal involved: you are simply doing your utmost to recover money promised and owed to you, but not paid.

All you have to do, if a non-paying tenant tries emotional or other blackmail, is to repeat, 'Let the court decide.' This is known as the 'broken record' technique and is extremely effective. But never enter into any justification, argument or discussion directly. You could be putting yourself in the wrong. Also, there is no need to justify your action. Non-payers have to be taken to court. If they cannot afford to pay the rent, they should not have taken the property in the first place.

Where there is genuine hardship

It may be that your tenant, while having perfectly good intentions, has lost her job, been made redundant, or become ill and simply cannot pay the rent that she was perfectly well able to do at the start of the tenancy. In this case, if she is otherwise a good tenant, she will let you know her position, and ask what you are prepared to do. Then you can decide either to let her go before the end of the tenancy, waive the rent until her Housing Benefit is payable, or demand the full rent as agreed.

A tenant under an Assured Tenancy cannot be made to leave until after the court has made an order saying that the plaintiff can have possession of the property. If the tenant disagrees with anything said in the affidavit, she may be able to get help with legal costs via legal aid. A parallel leaflet for tenants to the one produced for landlords, available free from County Courts, advises tenants to act quickly once a court order is received.

You as the plaintiff will have to produce written evidence that the tenancy was an Assured or Assured Shorthold made on or after 15 January 1989, when the Housing Act came into force.

If the judge decides that the tenant must leave, she will be sent a form saying when. If the tenant does not leave when told, the plaintiff can ask a court bailiff to evict her. Should the matter proceed to a court hearing, both parties should be present to put their side of the story. Tenants who are unsuccessful in asking the court to set aside the eviction order may have to pay the plaintiff's costs. If ordered to pay, the defendant must pay the plaintiff directly, and not through the court.

It has to be said, though, that only the most determined tenants will go this far. It goes without saying – or should do, at any rate – that landlords should not go to court unless they are absolutely sure of their ground. It is unlikely that a court will issue an eviction order for, say, a friend who you took in out of the kindness of your heart, who did not sign an agreement and who now insists on staying put.

The possibility of non-payment or other unsatisfactory behaviour on the part of tenants should encourage you as a landlord to protect your investment by making sure any arrangement to let out your property to others is executed according to current laws on the matter. It cannot be said too often: *never have an ad hoc or open-ended arrangement.*

Remember: a bad tenant is a bad tenant is a bad tenant, and a good tenant is a good tenant is a good tenant. In other words, a bad tenant is a bad tenant all the way through: not only will she not pay the rent, she will also not take care of the place and will return the flat to you in bad condition. When I finally regained possession of a flat inhabited by a tenant from hell, not only was the bathroom clogged up with hairs, there were cigarette burns and worse on the sofas and chairs, and the fridge and cooker were filthy.

Good tenants – ie those who pay rent on time and who are polite and courteous – always, in my experience, leave the place impeccably clean and tidy, and have a list of anything soiled or broken.

Mostly, I must say, tenants are a decent species, and it's only the occasional one who turns out to be terrible. Usually, I find, they are terrible in all other aspects of their life as well. My own hellish tenant was, I discovered later, undergoing psychiatric treatment, although she carefully concealed this when her references were being checked.

If your tenant dies

There are tenants who don't pay their rent. Tenants who outstay their welcome. Tenants who bring in their pets. But what about the ultimate horror – a tenant who actually dies in your property?

Surprising as it sounds, this is not as uncommon as it might seem. Most lettings agents have experienced a situation where a tenant has died whilst in the rental home.

Letting agent Mary Hennigan-Lawson said: 'Once I had let a flat where the tenant died just a month later. The landlord in the case pointed out that the deceased tenant had signed a contract for six months and he would hold him – or at least his estate – to that.

'In the event, we quickly found another tenant, but the landlord held the deceased's estate responsible for fees, inventories and cleaning, even so.'

Although most tenancy agreements do not make provision for a death, there are clear legal rules to follow when this happens. The landlord can demand full rent until the tenancy officially ends, although this might be contested by the deceased's solicitor. It may be possible for the tenant's representative to give two months' notice to the landlord, but normally this cannot be done within the first six months of an agreement.

Landlords who take out rent guarantee insurance should ensure that it covers this possibility. One friend of mine whose tenant died whilst in her property had taken out, on her agent's advice, a cheaper form of insurance that did not cover death. Also, as luck would have it, her tenant died on the very day that his tenancy agreement ended.

My friend takes up the story. 'I got a call from the police one night. The tenants in the flat above, which I also own, had rung the police to say the television in the flat below had been on all day and all night.

'The tenants upstairs had rung the bell but could get no reply. The police took a key from me and went in, finding my tenant unconscious on the floor. He was taken to hospital and recovered.

'But then a fortnight later I got a call at eight in the morning from my tenant's girlfriend, who also had a key, although she did not live with him. She said she had gone in to find him dead in a pool of blood. She was, not unnaturally, in a terrible state.

'By the time I arrived, the police were there, and confirmed that my tenant was dead. They said that nothing must be touched as we had to wait until they had ruled out any suspicious circumstances.

'It was the most horrific sight imaginable. There was blood everywhere, pools of blood at the side of the bed, and a trail of blood to the bathroom. It looked as though he had vomited at the side of the bed and then haemorrhaged to death. The social worker gave the cause of death as heart attack, and the coroner later ruled out any suspicious circumstances.'

The question was, what to do next? My friend contacted the deceased's ex-wife, who didn't want to know, and was unable to get in touch with any other relatives. The flat also had to remain as it was until the coroner released it, a month after the death.

The tenant's belongings then had to be dealt with. There was a large bed, lots of hi-fi equipment, CDs and so on that nobody would claim. In the end, the police had to clear it away.

The tenant, in his forties, had lived in the property for six years and there had never been any problem over the rent. He was known to suffer from ill health, although death was not expected.

Lettings agent Jane Salthouse, of Lane Fox, advises: 'In the case of somebody living alone, look for work numbers and next-of-kin details. Otherwise, contact the person who supplied the character reference and take it from there. As a last resort, search the flat for address books, credit details and so on.'

As it was, my friend had to replace all the carpets and redecorate completely, at her own expense, before the flat could be re-let. It is not advisable to tell an incoming tenant that the previous person died in the property, as this may put them off taking the place.

Although over 80 per cent of tenants are absolutely fine, and don't die or commit any other horrors in your property, it's as well to remember, as a landlord, that all human life is likely to be there eventually, and no weirdness can be completely ruled out.

7

Becoming a portfolio landlord

Be warned: investing in property can become so addictive that no sooner have you got one flat up and running than you are looking for another to buy, with a view to renovating and letting that one out as well.

I admit that I have become such an addict. Every week I scour through property magazines and newspapers, asking myself: would that one let? What would be my gross yield on that one? I then get my calculator out and do quick sums to determine whether, in theory, this or that particular property would be a good investment buy. In this respect, I am rather like a racing fanatic who is always studying form, whether or not he actually places a bet.

Mostly, I'm glad to say, I can control the addiction, especially where it comes to paying out £50,000 or more. I am prevented from indulging my habit to the full by the simple fact that I have very few chunks of fifty grand plus to play around with, and also because I have an emotional aversion to borrowing large sums on which I have to pay interest. But every now and again, the urge to buy, renovate and rent out an apartment becomes irresistible.

I believe most investment landlords are like this. What begins as a little hobby, an interesting way of making some money (with any luck) can soon turn into a way of life and, as with most enjoyable pursuits, the income received from rents is only part of the fun. There is the excitement of the chase, the possibility that you are hunting down a bargain, the adrenalin rush when you make an offer, and the thrill combined with the intense stab of fear when your offer is actually accepted and it finally sinks in that you now have to go through with it and buy the damned thing.

I went through such a scenario a few years ago. On seeing a property that I felt I absolutely had to have, whatever, I first of all took down the name of the estate agent, thinking to myself: oh well, no harm in asking the price. On discovering the price, I arranged to view, telling myself that there was no harm in viewing, and that viewing didn't commit me to buying the place. On viewing, I made an offer, telling myself now that there was no harm in making an offer, and that making an offer didn't constitute any form of commitment. The offer was rejected and I heaved an immense sigh of relief. My money was safe after all.

But then the estate agents came back with a lower price. I haggled and bargained a bit, and in the end the owners said yes. Damn! I had to have it now; there was no getting out of the deal. Thankfully, time has proved that this particular property was a good buy, but I have now recognized the danger signs, the times when I am in the grip of a house-buying addiction.

Once the many fears involved in actually buying a place and parting with the money have been allayed, there is the tremendous excitement involved in doing the property up. But even that is mixed with fear as you keep asking yourself whether you are overspending, whether you could have done better by going somewhere cheaper, or not taking quite so much trouble.

You may be torn between charity-shop curtains that are nearly, but not quite right, and going to the expense of having curtains made specially. These, you know, will add greatly to the look and appeal of the place, but at the same time there is a risk that you will go over budget. I know I always worry when I edge dangerously near the 5 to 6 per cent of the purchase price that I allow myself on renovation. I start to panic if I go over 6 per cent, especially when I have yet to buy a sofa, a washing-machine, a fridge-freezer...

There may be some investment landlords for whom these fears, these lurches of alternate terror and excitement, stress and peace of mind, do not exist, but I don't know of any. Perhaps ice-cool Hong Kong businessmen can buy investment properties without a trace of emotion, but most people aren't like that.

When I bought my first investment flat, a small studio in a 1930s block, and had overcome my initial terrors of being a landlord and spending huge sums of money to induce a paying tenant into my lair, I was soon looking for a similar flat to buy. Nothing to this property-buying lark, I thought. Within a few months, I was the proud owner of an identical flat just below my first one and, as with the first, I soon found an ideal tenant who appreciated the place very much. I was very fond of my two little flats, both done up simply but effectively, I thought. So, as soon as I had some spare funds again, I was looking for a third. I was well on the way, in my mind at least, to becoming a property magnate.

I discovered that buying properties to rent out was so much more fun than any other type of investment I might be able to make. OK, it wasn't entirely risk-free, and it was certainly not without effort, but here I was, creating lovely little homes for people, and making some money into the bargain. When, a couple of years later, I sold my two studio flats to buy other properties (the service charges on the studios had gone through the roof, and meant they were no longer a good investment), I made a useful profit on resale, even after the dreaded Capital Gains Tax had been levied.

Yes, there are heart-stopping, anxious moments, but there are also wonderful long periods of calm as well, where you do nothing but watch the money come in. Although the money I receive in rents is a useful bonus, buying investment properties is certainly not a way to get rich quick. Although now a 'portfolio' landlord on a small scale, I still regard myself as an amateur, doing it as a hobby-plus rather than as a means of becoming a 'Rachwoman'.

The multiple landlord

Most portfolio landlords, even those with many more properties than I possess, still regard the business as a more or less lucrative sideline rather than anything else. They do it because they enjoy it, get a buzz out of it, and although of course the books must balance, most people are not, contrary to the view of certain tenants, making vast amounts of money out of being a multiple landlord.

Multiple landlord Greg Shackleton, the owner of over 40 rental properties in Brighton, who has it all down to a fine art, became a 'reluctant landlord' when he acquired a property from a client. His day job is as a loss assessor, and this particular client offered him the property, a former shop that had been gutted by fire, instead of his fee. Greg took possession of the property and turned it into a smart one-bedroom flat. The flat let instantly and, within a few months, Greg decided he had enjoyed the process so much that he started looking round for another property to buy.

As he does not have the funds to buy his properties for cash, he calls in a bank official to value a potential new property. If the loan is approved, Greg buys the property, usually in dilapidated condition, and sets about renovation. Then the bank official returns and revalues the property.

Greg made the point that if you own 31 properties, you can receive a cheque for every day of the year – 365 cheques a year, provided every tenant pays up on time, of course.

On average, Greg reckons to have bought one property a month in this way since becoming a super-landlord, and he lets out all his flats unfurnished. Otherwise, as he said, he would own 40 washing-machines, 40 sofas, 40 dining tables and so on – rather an encumbrance for anybody. When you operate on that sort of scale, it becomes impossible to furnish the properties. Greg just puts in a new kitchen (often without washing-machine, as the tenants can hire these) and a new bathroom, carpets the place and rewires if necessary. Because of the need for a yearly gas certificate, Greg makes sure the heating and all appliances run on electricity.

All his flats are let through Leaders letting agents in Brighton, and Greg is constantly adding to his portfolio. He is on the books of all local estate agents, who now know just what he is looking for, and contact him when a flat which may be suitable comes onto the market.

Greg is very clear on what he's looking for: a dilapidated flat in a conversion, rather than a purpose-built block, near to public transport and shops, and going at a cheap price. He does not buy into purpose-built blocks because of the high service charges and the propensity of freeholders to add extra levies all the time, which just take away from profits if you're a landlord.

As Greg goes for high rents rather than capital appreciation, he does not expect his properties to increase greatly in value. Therefore, the bulk of the return on his investment will come from rents rather than resale. Also, as Greg keeps buying more properties, he is constantly ploughing money back rather than sitting on his laurels and watching the rents come in.

A point to bear in mind if you are collecting up properties: you must keep a beady eye on the length of the lease. Although the general trend of properties is to rise in value, this is not the case when leases get progressively shorter. This is why, unless the lease is extremely long, it is important to have a definite time-scale in mind for the properties to pay for themselves in rent. If you bought a couple of flats with 80-year leases and kept them for 20 years, you might find it hard to sell properties with only a 60-year lease on them. This, of course, is not the case in central London, where leases of 60 years can be considered long. But it does not apply in the rest of the country.

Money

If you are interested in becoming a multiple landlord, the first thing to do is to work out the figures. Otherwise, you could easily find yourself paying out far more in costs than you have coming in in rents. As I only ever buy rental properties for cash, obviously I proceed very slowly compared to some. I have passed the age and stage where I can calmly contemplate having long-term mortgages and loans. By nature I am not a great risk-taker with money, maybe because I don't really understand money, or at least, high finance. And although I will take a calculated risk, I would not like to be burdened down with huge loans.

Loans

Like most people these days, I constantly receive 'offers' of loans from banks and other financial institutions through the post. They all go straight into the bin without even being opened. I know that loans are not gifts, but sums of money which have to be paid back at usurious rates of interest.

Other people may not have such a strong aversion to loans, believing that the modern way to riches is through credit. They may well be right. So, if you have a steady enough temperament, and can sleep at night knowing you owe people sums into six figures, it is possible to build up a large property investment portfolio quickly, as Greg Shackleton has done.

When interest rates are low, you can start to acquire many properties extremely quickly, maybe on the Buy-to-Let scheme explained earlier. As you are, with any luck, receiving regular rents, it should only take fairly elementary arithmetic to work out your outgoings and incomings to see how much there is left over when everything else is taken into account.

Other ways of becoming an instant multiple landlord include buying a dilapidated building and turning it into flats, or buying a block of flats in its entirety. Many modern landlords have done this with spectacular results, but as with the Greg Shackleton method, it takes a lot of nerve.

Going into partnership

As I don't have the nerve to buy a large dilapidated building or to borrow to buy a block of flats, I used another method of acquiring more properties than I could readily afford in cash, and that was to go into partnership with a friend who was of a similar turn of mind.

My friend had already employed this method, some years previously, of buying a place he could not afford on his own. He had his eye on a house which cost more than he could raise, and approached a friend of his to put in a proportion of the price with some spare funds he, the friend, had at the time. (This was, of course, how The Body Shop International started out. Anita and Gordon Roddick were quite unable to raise a bank loan to start their business, and in the end managed to borrow £4,000 from a friend. The rest is history.)

The whole thing with my friend and his co-purchaser was drawn up legally and some years later, the property was sold for a handsome profit. Both my friend and his co-purchaser made a useful sum of money from the sale, and were well pleased with the result.

It was this method of property buying that Labour MP Peter Mandelson used with such disastrous and public results, when he borrowed over £350,000 from fellow socialist Geoffrey Robinson. Although, as Mandelson continually pointed out, he had 'done nothing wrong', in his case the whole thing smacked of naked capitalism and a desire to beat the system, rather than the socialism the two men supposedly espoused. Where my friend and I were concerned, however, nobody was likely to report us to the papers if we put our financial assets together in this way.

We sat down one night and worked out the figures. We discovered that, if we joined forces, we could just afford two more cheap properties without having to resort to borrowing. We drew up a Deed of Covenant with a solicitor, and bought them. We set up a separate bank account to deal with money relating to these properties, and the enterprise, embarked on so tentatively and nervously a few years ago, has worked out so well that we are now looking for more properties to buy jointly.

The advantages of joining with a friend in this way are that you don't have to borrow money from a bank at punitive interest rates which has to be paid back, whatever, and you are both able to share the worry and the rewards. When things go wrong, it is not anything like so bad if you don't have to shoulder the whole burden yourself. There is also the distinct advantage that you can have another perspective on the property when buying, and so can make a more informed and objective decision. Where somebody else's money is at stake, you are less likely to make a purchase you later regret.

The friend with whom I have been buying properties has a good eye for building defects, which I do not possess. I, on the other hand, can look at a flat and visualize how it could look. He does not have this kind of imagination or colour sense. So, by buying together, we are doubling our expertise quotient. In fact, we are more than doubling it as the whole is often greater than the sum of the parts.

My friend and I have also discovered that we can save a lot of money on refurbishment by doing it together. My heart tends to sink when I contemplate redecorating a room by myself, and the prospect of getting out brushes, paints, newspapers, white spirit, ladders and so on fills me with despair. But if I am doing this same task with a friend, it can even be enjoyable. The other advantage is that with two of you working away, the time spent on redecoration is halved. Also, I find that I take more care when somebody else is involved. I paint more painstakingly, and try to do a much more professional job than I could probably be bothered to do entirely on my own.

Is it a good idea to join forces with your spouse or intimate partner? That depends on the kind of relationship you have. It can work, but in so many ways spouses are hardly considered separate people. To my mind, the situation works best in a relationship where not everything is joint, but where a certain amount of your life is kept separate from each other. If you're too close all the time, investment properties can easily become just another area of friction, and cause immense trouble to apportion fairly when and if you split up.

Of course, you must choose your co-investor wisely. It must be somebody who you can trust absolutely and about whom you have no misgivings. The friend should also be somebody who can put in an equal amount of time and effort. Otherwise, if one partner feels they are doing more than the other, resentment can set in.

Buying a property jointly with a friend can be the quickest way to ruin a beautiful friendship. But if it works, it can work wonderfully well. One reason that many immigrant Indians, for instance, have done so well in host countries is that they work together and stick together. Instead of borrowing money from a bank, they will try to borrow from family members or those within their own community. By keeping business transactions private, and by not using banks, they have been able to expand without paying crippling interest rates, or being ripped off by outsiders.

When everybody concerned has a stake in the enterprise, it is more likely to be successful than when you are using outsiders who don't care and who are only interested in their wages or repayment of the loan.

Being a multiple landlord can be a lonely business, especially when a tenant rings with a serious problem in the middle of the night (as they tend to do). But if you join up with somebody else equally enthusiastic, it can become exciting and challenging.

According to the Law of Property Act 1925, the maximum number of people who can buy a property together is four. The best way to secure the position legally is to draw up a Deed of Covenant with a solicitor whereby all the parties become Tenants in Common. The percentage of the purchase price provided by each partner is entered, and they own an equivalent share in the property. For instance, if one partner provided 75 per cent of the purchase price, he would have a 75 per cent share.

With a Tenancy in Common, there is provision for one partner to get out of the deal, should they wish to. If one partner wishes to sell his share, he must offer it to the other partner at the current market price, or find another partner. If another partner cannot be found, the property can be sold within three months. If one partner dies, the other share passes to the survivor, unless arrangements are made for somebody else to inherit that share.

If you do not have the full purchase price, you may be able to get a mortgage between you. NatWest, for instance, will lend on a maximum of three gross annual incomes. The amount borrowed can be up to three times the main income, and one times the second and third incomes. In some cases, two and a half times the joint incomes of two people and one times the third may also be allowed.

Whenever buying property with somebody else, whether a close friend or business partner, the legal agreement must be drawn up very carefully. Even then, the arrangement can come to grief. Problems tend to arise when the property drops in value and partners risk losing their stake.

Working with agencies

Yet another way of becoming a multiple landlord is to contact a company that specializes in this type of investment property. A number of estate agents are now turning their attention towards this, and some have put together a very professional-looking package aimed at the investment landlord.

Hamptons International, for instance, have a dedicated Investment Lettings Consultancy, which will advise clients on every aspect of rental investment. They will, among other things, advise on suitable rental investment properties and prospective rental levels, report on tenant profiles and prepare rental investment appraisal reports. All at a cost, of course. They can also provide an independent rental investment service, advise on newly built and newly refurbished properties and all aspects of design and specification of the development.

This type of service is aimed mostly at the big-time invest-ment landlord with a lot of money to spare, rather than the person interested in just one or two properties. It is a sophisti-cated service for very professional landlords, but you never know – even the biggest landlords started off small.

Andrew Reeves Property Investments is a company special-izing in acquiring and managing residential property portfo-lios for clients. Founder Andrew Reeves, a former accountant, believes it is better to borrow to buy three investment proper-ties rather than buying one outright, as within five years you stand to make far more money by borrowing.

As against this, for the crucial five years you will have neither usable capital nor income, as all rents will go on servicing the buy-to-let mortgage. Andrew Reeves points out: 'Assuming property prices go up 10 per cent per annum, if you buy one property outright with £80,000 capital, in five years you will have achieved capital growth of £39,178, or 49 per cent. Plus you will be getting a useful income over that time as well.

'But if you use that same capital to buy three properties, your net capital growth will be £117,543, or 147 per cent, in the same timescale.'

Of course, by the time you've paid the mortgage, letting and running costs, you can say goodbye to any income, as this will amount to no more than four pounds for each property.

Taking everything into account, Andrew Reeves, who was responsible for launching Buy-to-Let for ARLA, advises: 'If you absolutely need to get an immediate income from your property, then you should not consider borrowing. It is not easy to get a usable income from buy-to-let properties when you borrow.

'On the other hand, if you don't need the income and can tie the money up for five years, you will see a substantial return on your investment that nothing else can match.'

It is true that those who have long since paid off the mortgages on their own homes are often extremely reluctant to take on another one voluntarily, but you have to view it, says Reeves, as a mortgage on the investment property, not on your own home. Then, if disaster strikes, you can sell the rental properties without losing or risking your own home.

You should, adds Reeves, always try to hang onto an investment property for five years, to minimize Capital Gains Tax.

Becoming a portfolio landlord is a matter of jam today if you don't borrow, or jam, cream and butter in five years' time (with any luck) if you do.

Other things to bear in mind

If you are interested in becoming a multiple landlord, there are some other factors you should bear in mind.

Flats or houses?

One is to have a very clear idea indeed of the kind of property you are looking for, and how much you are prepared to spend on the purchase and renovation. Never let your heart rule your head.

Generally speaking, if one property in a block of flats lets well, then another property in that same block will also let well. For this reason, it is very common for portfolio landlords to buy up more than one property in the same block. Once you get to know a block and its ways, it can be a case of the devil you know. Against this, there is something to be said for not having all your eggs in one basket.

If you have all your properties in one block, any problems arising with the block can adversely affect your entire investment. One friend, who has three flats in the same building, found himself with a bill totalling £8,000 as his contribution to the exterior decoration. As he was unable to put the rents up any more, this amount made a severe dent in his profits. In fact, the £8,000 knocked them out altogether.

Another idea is to buy investment properties in a building where you are already resident. Then you have a greater interest in the place and benefit from any general improvements – unlike my friend above who paid out £8,000 on a property he did not occupy and in which he had no personal interest. A 'living flat' and a 'letting flat' in the same building can make good sense.

It's important to bear in mind, if buying leasehold properties in blocks, that few blocks seem to run well for any length of time. Also, the older the block, the more acute the problems are likely to be, as elderly blocks suffer a similar to fate to all elderly institutions and people, in that they tend to get set in their ways and become resistant to change. Also, they start to become extremely decrepit and need expensive medication. The older the block, the more you are likely to have to fork out in repairs and renovation. And if it is a listed building, your problems are compounded, as you have to get listed building consent before embarking on any repair work. That can take ages.

It took over two years to get planning permission for essential repair work on a listed building I once owned. The council was quite happy to let the place go to wrack and ruin, which it had been in the process of doing for very many years, but when it came to try and improve it, this was a different matter altogether. If you do try to improve listed buildings without consent, you can find yourself ordered to undo the good work and start again in the proper fashion. So, although listed buildings are attractive, they may not be the best places to build up a property portfolio.

Anything in a block of flats can change at any time. The freeholder may decide to sell, the managing agents may change, or there may be problems with longstanding debtors or planning permission.

In some ways, it may be better to concentrate on freehold houses. These do not attract the problems of blocks of flats, and of course there are no service charges, no overwhelming problems of maintenance and no risk of high extra charges from the freeholder or head lessee. Charges for lift maintenance alone can add up to several hundred pounds a year – for each resident.

Against this, it has to be remembered that houses on the whole let less well than small flats and tend to have longer void periods. On the plus side, houses are more likely than flats to increase in value, especially as with a flat you can run into problems when the lease starts to run down.

The rental return, percentage-wise, is usually greater on a flat than a house, and flats tend to be more secure than houses, especially in blocks where there is a resident porter. So, there are many pros and cons with, perhaps, no outstandingly 'best buys'.

If you are considering letting to students, it might make more sense to buy houses than flats, as students almost always want to share, and in a three-bedroom house a downstairs room can double up as an extra bedroom. Investors in student accommodation tend to buy new, rather than old, houses, as the new ones tend to need less maintenance. If you are interested in the student market, it is worth looking at new developments being built right near colleges and universities.

Anybody seriously wishing to build up a property investment portfolio should probably go for a mixture of types of properties in much the same way that investors in stocks and shares are advised to build up a mixed portfolio.

Watch the market

A very important aspect, as with all investments, is to keep an eagle eye on the market. If you find you are getting long voids, or cannot seem to command the same rents as a few years ago, it may be time to consider cutting your losses and selling up. Don't think that, because it's property, it has to be on your books for all time. It may be that in order to acquire three or four properties that are a genuine bargain, you have to sell existing ones that, for you, have passed their 'let by' date. Always be prepared to do this, and never become sentimental over your existing properties, however attractive they may be. Properties, like anything else in life, can outlive their usefulness.

It is vital to become a friend of all the local estate agents. Get onto their mailing lists, tell them what you are looking for and keep reminding them that you are still looking. Otherwise, with many other people on their books, they will tend to forget about you. Professional property developers are always badgering estate agents, and you must start doing the same. Make sure they remember you, and know precisely what market you are in.

Many estate agents now advertise properties on the Internet, so do get into the habit of checking the net daily, as very often properties are put on the net which are not advertised in brochures or windows.

House auctions are good places to look for bargains and if you are a novice, get your hand in by attending a number of auctions before you intend to make an offer.

It goes without saying, or should do, that you should never buy any property or properties, however cheap and however much a bargain they seem, without first checking that they will let well. The nearer to shops and transport links, the better they will let – always. Properties right in the centre of town, where shops and facilities are, make the best rental propositions.

Two voices of experience

Here are views from two multiple landlords of very long standing. Jean, a friend who has let out several properties for many years, said: 'I've discovered that being a landlord doesn't really make you a lot of money. If you sold the flat and put the money in a building society, you would probably be making as much as you take in rent, by the time all expenses have been taken into account.'

But, she added: 'The huge plus is that the money you invest in property is going up in value all the time. To my mind, the gross yields quoted by agents and others trying to sell you investment schemes mean nothing whatever because if the roof collapses, that could be your year's yield completely wiped out. Having said that, property is a good investment as it goes up in value faster than anything else and is relatively low risk. If you just put the money into the building society your capital sum never increases, but the value of my flats is enormous compared to what it was when I bought them.

'I think that if you are to be a landlord, you must have a fairly tolerant outlook, and you have to be able to smile at the vagaries of tenants. I would also say that although I always use agents, you can never expect them to do everything or to be there all the time. Full management is hugely expensive and wipes out just about all your profit, so I never go for this option. In the end, something always comes down to you, especially when tenants ring you to ask you to come and change a lightbulb. Tenants tend to contact you with the most trivial enquiries, and you have to be able to cope with them.'

Geoff, who owns a number of letting properties on the south coast, said: 'The more properties you have, the more lucrative the business becomes. If you have 400 properties, you are bound to make money. I think that in order for the business to be genuinely profitable, you need a great deal of properties. Otherwise, it's vital to take the possible capital increase into consideration. Properties bought on a short lease will almost certainly not increase in value, and it is difficult to make a killing on rents alone as so many things can go wrong.'

If you talk to estate agents, you will discover that very many of them are investment landlords themselves. One estate agent I know owns properties all over London. All of them are small one-bed flats or studios. Some agents have 20 or more properties they let out, and while they are showing you round a property, they may well be wondering whether they might be better off buying it themselves instead.

My hunch is that if estate agents, as true professionals in all aspects of the house business, are becoming investment landlords, there must be some advantage in it.

Buying and letting property abroad

It has long been a dream of many Britons to buy a place in the sun in which to rest and relax, and maybe retire. And a potent part of that dream can be the prospect of making the place pay for itself by letting it to others when you are not there yourself.

For most people, the starting point of buying a holiday villa in a favoured foreign spot is the experience of a blissful holiday there, or maybe several blissful holidays there. When you never want the holiday to end, you can fantasize about how wonderful it might be to return there at any time you liked, to your very own villa or apartment, your very own place in the sun.

Beware!

Those who have actually turned their dream into reality warn that although the perfect holiday may be the trigger to buying a home in the locality, your judgement, lulled by warm sunshine and local wine, may be temporarily clouded.

Buying a place in the sun can be rather like trying to make a holiday romance permanent. What works wonderfully well for two weeks, when you are relaxed, happy, stress-free and optimistic, may not look so good when you try to turn it into a lasting relationship. As with romantic holiday lovers, the defects of romantic holiday villas can soon start to show up once you realize that you are saddled with them year in, year out, and cannot just go home and forget about them once the heady excitement has worn off.

George East, author of *Home and Dry in France: A year in purgatory*, believes that many people start to suffer from what he calls 'French Property Brain Loss Syndrome'. His advice, based on his own bitter experience is: don't buy in the dark, or after you've been drinking.

But the brain loss syndrome doesn't just happen in France. It can happen in any country where you have just had a wonderful holiday. You naturally want to hold on to the dream by making the temporary situation permanent. Some people even buy properties while they are on holiday, before it all fades away.

One friend went to Canada for a holiday and loved it so much that while she was there, she bought a log cabin by a lake. That must be the impulse buy to beat all impulse buys, especially as whatever the reality eventually turns out to be, she will not be able to pop over at a minute's notice and keep an eye on it. And though it may be wonderful in summer, what will it be like in the middle of a typical Canadian winter, with snow up to the roof?

Although such gestures are romantic and make life exciting, it is most probably a good idea to wait until you're home and back to your normal routine before taking the plunge. Then ask yourself whether that wonderful holiday home is, in fact, such a good idea:

- Do you have the finances, not just to buy the place, but to run it?
- How often would you actually use it? For two weeks, four weeks in a year, or more?
- For how many weeks in the year, realistically speaking, would it let to paying customers?

- What about getting there? How cheap or expensive are the air fares or train fares? How much is petrol?
- What considerations have to be taken into account if you are interested in letting it out for part of the year?
- What, if any, is its letting potential?

Of course, the opening of the Channel Tunnel has made 'abroad' seem far less distant and intimidating than it used to be. When you can board a train at Waterloo and be painlessly deposited in the middle of Paris not long afterwards, with no fuss and no discomfort, the prospect of owning a holiday home in a country which can actually guarantee some sun becomes ever more appealing.

The main thing that tends to go wrong when buying property abroad is that you purchase a picturesque tumbledown farmhouse or chateau, say, only to discover that renovation is way beyond your means. Either that, or you get hopelessly bogged down in the bureaucracy of the country as you try to get planning permission and satisfy all the requirements of the building regulations in that area. It is all too easy to become entangled in the red tape of another country, and if you are not conversant with the laws, or do not speak the language fluently, you can end up in a hopeless impasse.

There can also be endless bills not anticipated when the property was bought in that first fine careless rapture. One former owner of a French holiday home said: 'We found we were sitting outside in the sun with a bottle of wine – paying bills.' In fact, some sound advice when contemplating buying *any* holiday home, wherever situated, is to add up all the costs you expect, and then double them. When I bought a holiday home, I estimated the yearly running costs (without letting the place) at £1,500, which I thought a generous estimate. In fact, the place costs over £3,000 a year to run, whether occupied or not. .I had forgotten about council tax, the TV licence, the enormity of the water rates, cost of transport, repair bills. Even something as apparently minor as replacing lightbulbs in a second home can add up.

There is also the question of who looks after the place while you are not there. Some owners of holiday apartments outside

Moving into the
global village?

Linguaphone's self-study language courses are the best way to learn a new language. Our method "Listen, Understand, Speak" has already taught over 7 million people how to start speaking another language.

There are over 30 major languages and a wide range of formats to choose from. Using books, tapes, videos, CDs, CD-ROMs or even our new Online resources. So, we're bound to have the right course for you. Study where and when you choose: at home, in the office, even on the move.

Receive **free Language Support**, anytime, to answer any problems you may have by phone, post or e-mail. Put us to the test with a 21-day home trial. Or ask for a free information pack. **Call free on 0800 282 417** or fill in the coupon and post today.

Post to: Linguaphone, FREEPOST LON17579, London SW13 9BR

Language of interest:_____

Mr/Mrs/Miss/Ms:_____

Address:_____

_____

_____ Postcode:_____

Tel:_____

E-mail:_____

Please tick here if you do not wish Linguaphone Institute Ltd to make your details available to other companies ☐   PG2001

 **Linguaphone**

www.linguaphone.co.uk
0800 282 417

Advertisement feature

the UK retain friendly locals to keep an eye on the place and make sure, for instance, that pipes do not freeze up in the winter. Some properties may need annual refurbishment to make them suitable for letting, so this has to be taken into account as well.

Buying to let

Estate agents are reporting that second-home buyers are now representing a considerable chunk of the Buy-to-Let market, and that this is increasing all the time. But what about the property you buy? Many people who have enthusiastically bought abroad have sobering tales of buying a wonderful-seeming flat or villa only to discover later that the block or estate had been built without the permission of the landowner, or was in a protected area. When this happens, for instance in Spain, the deed, the *escrita de compraventa*, is either non-existent or meaningless, and the entire investment is wiped out.

Because of the capital cost of buying a second home abroad, the possibility that you may not use it as much as anticipated, and the fact that bills don't go away simply because you are not there, you may wonder whether you can make the place pay for itself by letting it out to paying tenants, at least for part of the year.

In fact, such is the propensity for second-home owners to let their properties, that in some countries it is actually assumed, if you are a British buyer of a holiday villa, that you will be letting it. One British owner of a Spanish villa said: 'The Spanish authorities assume that I will be letting my villa, even though in actual fact I don't.' This particular owner, who is retired, finds he spends at least six months of the year in Spain, and at the times when it would be a good letting proposition, he wants to be there himself. So, for the moment, he does not feel he can bear to let it, even though he might make some useful extra cash by doing so.

This certainly is yet another of the many problems besetting those who would buy a place in the sun. They buy with a view to letting the place out, and then discover that they can't bear to have strangers in when they are not there themselves.

In the main, though, owners of holiday homes abroad *do* want to let their property out to others. Or, even if they don't exactly *want* to let it, they often find they have to, simply so that they can afford to keep it on. So, if you buy with a view to letting, either temporarily or permanently, it is essential to make sure that you are buying in an area where you are actually allowed to let for profit.

Making your choice

Do your homework first. For instance, in some areas of France you may not be allowed to rent your home out as a holiday let. You may be classified as a 'professional' landlord if you are letting out property in certain areas, and under the French Planning Code, you are not allowed to let out property in some places if you are deemed to be such a 'professional'.

It's a good idea, before signing on any dotted lines, to contact the tourist board of the relevant country, so that you can avoid falling foul of any restrictions well in advance. Estate agents in your chosen locality or country can also help you to decide on a property that has letting potential, as well as being a place that you want to inhabit yourself.

If you are interested in buying a property in another country with letting in mind, what factors should you consider? One very important aspect, according to Stephen Smith and Charles Parkinson, authors of *Letting French Property Successfully*, is that a place which appeals to you because it is beautiful, tumbledown and remote, may not seem so attractive to paying tenants.

You must make sure that the place you buy has good rail and air links, and that potential tenants do not have horrific journeys to make before reaching their destination. There should be nearby shops and other facilities. Climate should also be taken into account, as places will not let easily when it's freezing cold, when there are biting winds, or other extremes of weather. It can be very cold in the winter in many European countries and this could mean either a lengthy void period or a lengthy period when you as the owner don't want to be there either.

BUYING A VACATION HOME IN FLORIDA

By Kevin W. Lumb, Licensed Realtor®. AHN Realty Inc.

Compared to the UK buying a home in Florida is relatively simple, there are more than 12000* Vacation Homes in the areas close to Disney and most of those are owned by UK residents. Florida attracts more than 44 Million tourists each year and is the most visited City in the world.

It is possible to buy a Vacation Home and once you have paid your deposit and closed (completed) the transaction, to rent the home out on a short term basis to tourists (from the UK Europe and USA) or UK tour operators and the home can pay for itself with little or no money out of your own pocket. With the advent of the internet and the many sites offering these homes for rent some people have purchased two or three homes or more and actually run them as a business from the UK.

It is very important that you select a Licensed Realtor® to represent you in your purchase, a Realtor® is there to represent you and will deal with all aspects of your purchase ensuring that you are buying a home for the purpose it is intended on a development which is properly Zoned, the services of a Realtor® cost you nothing but could save you thousands in the long term. Your Realtor® will spend as much time with you as necessary and before showing you any properties will talk with you for some time finding out just what your requirements are, after all there is no point looking at homes that are outside your budget or that may not be in the area you want to be in. Your Realtor® should be knowledgeable in all aspects of the market in which you are considering purchasing in and should be confident, courteous and helpful, he or she is bound by law to deal with you Honestly, Fairly and Truthfully, if you are not confident with your Realtor® ask the office to assign someone else or find another firm.

Once you have purchased your home you will need to think about Property Management and whilst your Realtor® will not be able to recommend a Management Company to you he can point you in the right direction and supply you with contact details. The selection of a Management Company is just as important as the selection of your Realtor®, you need to be confident that whilst you are thousands of miles away your home is being looked after properly and that the rental opportunities are maximised.

There are many developments to choose from and you will find both new and pre-owned homes for sale, most UK buyers choose to buy a new home because of the peace of mind offered by the guarantees which come as standard. You will get a full year of warranty on ALL items supplied with your new home including, Swimming Pool, Air Conditioning/ Heating, all your appliances (Washer, Dryer, Fridge/Freezer, Dishwasher and Microwave) for the first two years all plumbing and electrical work is warranted and the home itself carries a 10 year structural warrantee, these are items which may not be covered if you buy a resale home and could prove to be costly if you have problems, the advantage of buying a resale home is that you will save money on the purchase, you will have to weigh up the options and decide which is right for you.

Typical costs to run a 4 bed rental home in Florida are around $500-$600 per month and the current interest rate at this time are around 6.75%.

We hope you find your Dream Home in Florida and wish you many happy vacations in the Sunshine State.

The competition

It seems that when it comes to letting holiday properties abroad, there are often two stark choices to face:

1. If you buy a remote, hard-to-reach property you may find it difficult to let.
2. If you buy a property in an already popular tourist area you stand to face intense competition from other holiday apartments.

In the latter case, your property will be hard to let if it is vastly more expensive or less well equipped than similar holiday properties in the area. In extremely popular tourist areas, you will also face competition from international holiday companies who may be in a position to offer huge discounts on holiday packages.

An Englishman I met while on holiday in the South of France had bought an apartment in a holiday village some years previously. The idea was that he would live there for some months of the year, then let to holiday-makers at other times. In this way, he would have an ideal retirement, as he would be getting income from his apartment as well as having it for his own use, as he thought.

Theoretically this was fine. The only problem was that there were four or five big holiday companies also operating there, in intense competition with each other. While this was good news for the holiday-maker, as huge discounts were being offered on apartments, it meant that my new friend could make nothing whatever from letting his own property. In fact, he soon decided it was not worth the bother of even trying to let it, and so just kept it for his own use.

It was one reason, he realized with hindsight, why the apartment had been suspiciously cheap. There was just no money to be made from letting it out in the season, even though it was in a prime holiday spot. And out of season, nobody would want to be there anyway, as this place was suitable only for seaside holidays.

You must make sure that your apartment or villa is not inferior in any way to others in the same area. For instance, if all the villas in your area have private swimming pools, yours may not attract many paying customers without one. But if you want to put in a swimming pool or make other structural alterations, you may have to get planning permission and satisfy the authorities that the construction conforms to local building regulations.

When thinking about letting property in another country, more or less the same considerations must be taken into account as when buying investment property in your own country. The numbers must add up, and at the end of the day you should not be out of pocket from your investment. The additional factor is that the market for holiday lets in popular tourist destinations is extremely competitive, and you may well be up against many properties that are very similar or even identical to your own, but much cheaper.

Local customs and practice

Don't forget also that you will be dealing with customs, laws and traditions that may be very different from those you are used to. If your property needs alterations or renovations (and these may be essential if you are to appeal to the lettings market) you will have to deal with French, Spanish or Italian workmen, for instance, who have their own methods of doing things, as we learned when reading Peter Mayle's *A Year in Provence*. Then you have to ask yourself whether you will be on hand to supervise all refurbishment work. Most owners of property in other countries maintain that it is not a good idea to engage local workmen and then disappear for months on end while the builders work on their own initiative. So, large amounts of time have to be made available for supervision of the workforce if your property needs adaptation for letting purposes.

In most countries, public liability insurance is compulsory, and you may have to have fire insurance as well. If you are letting, your insurance may have to be extended to include third parties such as tenants temporarily staying in the place. Your insurance company must also be notified if you are using the property for holiday lettings.

With holiday lets in other countries, there is usually not the choice of letting furnished or unfurnished. A holiday apartment must be fully furnished and include linen, kitchen equipment, tea towels, crockery and cutlery.

Fitting out the property

As with letting properties in the UK, you can get away with any standard of furnishings, provided somebody is willing to pay you rent, if you let privately. But if you let through an agency, certain standards regarding equipment, fire and safety regulations and so on must be honoured, again in the same way as letting through agencies in the UK. In France, for instance, you may not be allowed to let on a commercial basis if the property or equipment fall below a certain standard. Having said that, in my experience the standards must be pretty low, as I have stayed in some truly terrible 'commercial' apartments in France which, presumably, met legal requirements.

If you want your property to be attractive to paying tenants, then the furniture and fittings should be of good quality and above all, *comfortable*. In very cheap apartments, the beds tend to be uncomfortable and flimsy, and the utensils may be all but useless. In fact, the two commonest complaints of holiday apartments are the discomfort of the beds and the poor quality of the kitchen equipment. Another common complaint is the lack of easy chairs. Of course, beds, easy chairs and good-quality utensils are all expensive to provide, which is why they are frequently not found in cut-price apartments.

If the apartment is equipped too cheaply and nastily it may not encourage repeat bookings. Some experts advise not providing linen, as it is 'not unreasonable' to expect tenants to provide their own. Well, I don't know about you, but I don't want to travel to another country with my suitcase full of bed linen. I believe that it is absolutely essential for landlords to provide plenty of linen for tenants. The bed(s) should be already made up when visitors arrive, as they are often exhausted after their journey, and there should be at least one change of linen for each bed in the apartment.

In recent years, I have stayed in two holiday apartments in Spain and one in the South of France. Although all were in idyllic settings, in each apartment the beds were absolutely terrible, the cheapest possible sleeping arrangements, and the kitchen utensils so bad that I had to go to the local supermarket and buy knives, can openers and so on. Although the climate, the scenery and the ambience at each of these places was wonderful, the furniture in the apartments was so gimcrack that I would not want to book those particular places again. A fortnight of sleeping on a bed that kept coming apart and collapsing is an experience I do not wish to repeat. Also, the sheets were so skimpy that they would not tuck in the bed, with the result that each morning I woke up mummified, tightly wound up in a sheet that refused to stay in its proper place during the night.

If you are letting out a place which is essentially a holiday home for yourself as well, you also have to make sure that there are not too many personal items lying around. This is not so much for fear of burglaries, but simply because personal possessions tend to clutter up apartments so that the tenants have nowhere to put their own stuff.

The problem of how to have a holiday home that you can happily live in yourself at the same time as being lettable to others is not one that is easily solved, as in a home you naturally tend to collect favourite objects around you, and few people want to live in a completely sterile minimalist environment.

I have a holiday home that I originally bought with letting in mind, but almost imperceptibly it has filled up with personal objects, so much so that it is now unlettable unless a massive cull is made of the contents. Objects, paintings, ornaments, have somehow appeared which now have no other home, and the bookcases are full of my books. The wardrobes have also filled up with my clothes and shoes, the bathroom has my toiletries in it and the kitchen is full of my spices, herbs, pasta, rice and so on. I soon realized that I could not keep the place in a permanently lettable condition as well as living in it myself, as to do so would severely truncate the quality of my life while I inhabited my own place.

SUNBELT®
BUSINESS
BROKERS

Sunbelt Business Brokers is the largest Business Brokerage in the world, from our offices in Florida and the UK we specialise in representing buyers who would like to live and work in Florida. Below is a small sample of the business we are able to offer. All our businesses are compatable with either an E2 or L1 Visa.

	Net	Price
Safe Rentals near Orlando	$40,000 p.a.	$140,000
Jet Ski Rentals in Kissimmee	$38,000 p.a.	$140,000
Vacation Home Booking Company	$38,000 p.a.	$120,000
Used Car Sales on US 27	$50,000 p.a.	$150,000
Motel on US 27 (inc. property)	$85,000 p.a	$565,000
Home Improvements Palm Beach	$92,000 p.a.	$149,000
Pool Service Kissimmee	$65,000 p.a.	$150,000

We have hundreds of businesses available and would be happy to speak with you about Purchase, Financing, Visa requirements etc. We can guide you through the whole process and ensure you get the business you want at a price that is right.

We are licensed by the State of Florida as Real Estate Brokers, make sure you make the right decision when selecting representation by using a Licensed Company.

Please call either our UK Office on
01244 579 076 or our Florida Office on
001 863 557 0775 we will return your call
immediately to minimise your costs.
E-mail: ahnrealty@aol.com
general@floridahomes.uk.com

**SUNBELT®
BUSINESS
BROKERS**

RELOCATING TO FLORIDA

By Kevin W. Lumb, Realtor®. Sunbelt Business Brokers

Many UK residents would love to sell up and move to Florida but do not realise how realistic and achievable this is.
Florida is the State most visited by Brits and is the most popular place to move to in the US.
There are several important factors you must be aware of when considering your move and we will endeavor to give you the guidelines you should follow, remember we cannot tell you all need to know in this short article so consult a licensed Business Broker who will be able to help you through the whole process.
Business Broker: Your selection of your Broker is most important he/she should be someone who is reputable and who you feel comfortable with, his/her role is to find you a suitable business which meets your requirements and will satisfy the INS (Immigration and Naturalization Service) guidelines for your future residency, find a Broker who is knowledgeable in ALL these aspects, any Broker can sell you a business but if it does not qualify for residency status you could end up wasting time and more importantly money!, your Broker will be able to find hundreds of businesses and will represent you in any negotiations, make sure your Broker is a member of the FBBA (Florida Business Brokers Association) and

is properly licensed to represent you.

INS: This is the Government agency that will determine whether or not your investment/business meets the requirements for residency, we cannot stress how important it is that your application is submitted correctly, any errors and you go back to the beginning, your move could be delayed by months or even years.

The First Step: Select your Broker and work with him/her to find a suitable business, once you have found what you want you will enter into negotiations, you will discuss price, terms, Real Estate (if any is involved) lease conditions or even relocation of the business. Many owners will help you finance the business with a fair down payment and we suggest you look for these owners, after all if the owner is willing to give you a loan on his existing business it is a good sign of his confidence that the business is good and that you are the person to operate it. Commercial finance is not available to you if you are not a US citizen or Green Card Holder or if you have not resided here long enough to build up credit, again your Broker can help with this process.

Type of Business: There are hundreds of businesses for you to choose from with prices ranging from $40,000 to $Millions, not all of these business will be suitable for you and not all of them will enable you to qualify for a visa, you may want to continue in the line of work you have been in while living in the UK or you may want a complete change, whatever you want there is a business waiting for you in Florida AND a licensed Business Broker can help and protect you.

Many Brits have successfully moved to Florida and enjoy a fantastic lifestyle which they can only find in this beautiful State, follow our guidelines and make sure your Dream does not become a Nightmare.

Sample Business Available:

Motels in Orlando Area from $565,00 to over $5,000,000
Jet Ski Rentals in Kissimmee $140,000
Vacation Homes Booking Service Orlando Area $120,000
Manufacturing South Florida $1,500,000
Safe Rentals Orlando Area $140,000

But tenants will not be impressed by a lot of your personal objects being around, not just because these take up space, but because it makes the tenants feel like intruders, and uncomfortable. A place which is suitable for letting should look exactly like a hotel room, spotlessly clean, with a few bland pictures on the walls, maybe one or two books in the bookcases but with absolutely no personal items of any kind lying around. The kitchen should be completely clear of old herbs, spices and jars of salad dressing, tomato ketchup and so on, and there should be no personal papers in the place.

It is an effort to keep a holiday home in this condition, so if you want to let it as well as live in it yourself, you yourself may have to live in it like a tenant – in which case, much of the fun of having your own holiday apartment is lost.

Marketing your property

After you have satisfied all the building, insurance and maintenance regulations, and fitted out the property ready to let, the next matter to address is the marketing of your holiday property. You may, as in the UK, decide to use a specialist agency for this, and this will in a sense take care of your problems, provided that a reputable agency is prepared to take on your property. As with UK rented property, lettings agencies that handle foreign properties will not take you onto their books unless the property satisfies local regulations and conditions. Also, of course, they will take their percentage, although in high season they may be able to achieve a higher rent than you could do on your own.

Most lettings agencies in Europe require your written authority to let the property (as in the UK), and have their own standard form for you to sign. This is very similar to a short-let or holiday-let contract in the UK, although there may be some local differences, as there may be slightly different laws and regulations in the particular country.

There are of course many UK letting agencies that handle foreign properties and usually there is a sliding scale of services and charges. Some offer a complete marketing and fully insured management service while others simply find tenants for you but do not provide any local service in the country concerned. In this case, you will retain responsibility for cleaning, maintenance and repairs. A usual fee for a complete management service is 20 per cent, plus the local equivalent of VAT, as in the UK.

In most European countries, similar laws to those in the UK govern holiday lets. Those to whom you let on this basis must have a permanent home elsewhere, and the letting period must not extend beyond the 'official' holiday season. In most countries the property must be let purely for holiday purposes. Tenants are not allowed to carry on any kind of business in a property designated a holiday apartment. Otherwise, the standard terms are very similar to those found in the UK Assured Shorthold Tenancy agreement.

Should you wish to let your property to somebody for six months or so, then you have to enter into a different kind of agreement. An extended agreement of this kind must be drawn up by lawyers and usually has to be in the language of the country concerned. Otherwise, you may not be able to get your tenant out when you want to reclaim the property. There may also be difficulties over obtaining rent without a legally binding agreement.

If going it alone, proper marketing is extremely important. You can get your hand in by reading a publication such as *The Lady*, which advertises dozens of holiday properties to let every week. Advertising in newspapers and magazines can be expensive though, and it may actually work out cheaper for you to use an agency.

The authors of *Letting French Property Successfully* advise that foreign advertising is risky for the inexperienced, and suggest instead contacting the English Tourist Board's offices in Europe. In any case, if you are very new to letting property in another country, it is probably safest and best to go through an agency, at least at first. If you find you are getting repeat bookings from the same people, you may decide you can go it alone without any problems. What you must never do is let your precious property to friends and hope for the best. As with letting property in the UK, proper, legally binding agreements detailing when and how the rent is to be paid, what is to

SO YOU ARE THINKING
OF BUYING A PROPERTY ABROAD!

Buying and letting a property abroad can be a worthwhile investment but, if care is not taken, this could result in a potential nightmare.

As a starting point consider the country you have in mind and the type of property. You must be satisfied that the country is both politically and economically stable and that the location is where you genuinely wish to spend your time and money in the medium to long term. After this, consider whether the property is served by an adequate infrastructure, such as airport, roads, utility supplies, shops, doctor/hospital and so on. So far as the type of property is concerned, should it be a villa, chalet or apartment? Should it be coastal or inland, in a busy location or secluded?

It is very important that you should have visited the general location, say for a holiday, on a few occasions since there is no substitute for first hand knowledge. There will doubtless be agents and property companies who will provide much in the way of glossy brochures and hand-sheets but they might omit what for you is important information.

You should also decide whether your intention is to buy a property outright or alternatively, a timeshare or co-ownership scheme.

If you buy the property outright, you would need to consider realistically the amount of time you would spend occupying the property and what should happen to it when you are not there.

Assuming you have set your sights on a suitable property and its price is affordable, what funding is required? If you have the resources to buy the property for cash, all well and good. However, it may be appropriate for you to take out a loan. Most people feel comfortable with a lender whose terms would be set out in a language they can understand. Many U.K. lenders now have interests abroad and you also have access to financial centres such as Gibraltar.

An investigation must also be carried out into the legal title. If comparisons are made with buying a house in England, your solicitor would need to look at the title deeds and documents to ensure firstly that the person from whom you are buying the property is the person who actually owns it and secondly, that he has the right to sell it to you. He would also need to see what rights attach to the property, for example, the use of roads and accessways, water and other communal facilities. In addition, he would need to concern himself with mortgages that might have already been created on the property and to ensure that these are properly cleared off the title before ownership passes to you. Your solicitor would also need to check with the local civil authority, the equivalent of your Town Hall, to ensure that problems do not arise with local planning or development laws. Failure to investigate these matters might mean that you are saddled with your vendor's mortgage or find that an unsightly development takes place close by or that you do not have the right to use the water supply or a particular swimming pool. All of these things could turn out to be an inconvenience or worse and may well have a detrimental effect on the value of your investment.

If your intention is to rent it out, consider if there is someone locally upon whom you can rely to manage the property. If not, you may wish to engage the services of a local managing agent. Consider what are the costs in each case and what insurance arrangements you should put in hand. If a time share is your choice, many of these questions might be answered for you.

In letting or renting your property it is important to take into account local laws which are designed to provide secure tenancies for tenants in the letting market. In general terms it is essential to have a written agreement which conforms with the local laws and which does not unwittingly confer security of tenure on the tenants. Expert advice should be sought prior to entering into an agreement or allowing a third party to occupy your property, however short the period of occupation may be.

Michael Cornish, the author of this article, is senior partner in Cornish & Co.
Solicitors, which he founded after qualifying in 1975.
Michael is often quoted in the national press, and is widely regarded as a leading authority on legal matters concerning overseas property transactions.

EXETER FRIENDLY SOCIETY

TOP TIPS FOR A HEALTHY LIFESTYLE WHEN MOVING OVERSEAS

With increasing numbers of people choosing to live abroad, one of the many things on a pre-departure check-list should be private medical insurance. This is essential for expats whether they're planning to live temporarily or permanently overseas. Private medical insurance is designed to cover the costs, or majority of costs, of medical treatment. The advantages of taking out such cover are speed, quality of service and convenient location of treatment.

A recent review of developments in the European market highlights the rapid re-positioning occurring within the PMI marketplace in Europe and, because of different legal requirements, Exeter provides "localised" policies throughout Europe. Indeed, Exeter has plans to go further down this route in ensuring that policies are totally relevant to the medical needs of members in their particular country of residence.

Spain is a good example of this where some policyholders with generalist PMI plans have been very restricted as to where they can undergo treatment due to the regional nature of the Spanish health service.

What sets Exeter apart from the majority of other international PMI providers is that premiums don't automatically increase with age. Premiums are based on the age members are when they join. Therefore, the younger people are when they take out an Exeter plan, the Society the lower their subscription will be in later years, making quality medical cover more affordable.

So, what should you do before you move abroad:

Have a pre-departure health check – particularly important if you are elderly or have a poor health record

If taking regular medication make a note of generic names of drugs and medicines

Keep copies of all health records and policy documents from your medical insurer such as level of cover, acceptance terms, claims procedure etc.

It is in your best interest to take action, ideally before you leave the UK, to safeguard your entitlements. Write to, or telephone the DSS Pension and Overseas Directorate, Newcastle Upon Tyne, NE98 1BA (0191 218 7547 – if retired or non-working; 0191 225 4811 – if working) and advise them of your intended emigration. Ask them to register you and your dependents with the necessary authorities for Medical Benefit purposes under EU regulation.

And when buying medical insurance:

Decide what you can afford and which benefits you most want

Ensure you fully understand **what isn't covered** by the policy you are choosing

Check on the claims process and efficiency of the company you are considering and ensure that the company you choose has sensible complaints procedures. This is particularly important when living overseas

Understand the terms and the cover provided before finally accepting the offer by the insurer

Does the policy provide benefit for pre-existing conditions? If not, is the insurer prepared to review any exclusions that may be applied after a suitable period of time

Make sure that your policy covers all your health requirements. This should include cover for accidents and injuries.

Making adequate provision for private medical insurance before you move abroad will ensure peace of mind and, with increasing flexibility and choice of PMI products, the need for the right advice is paramount. A specialist adviser will be able to highlight the appropriate cover for the country where a client will be living or working.

Neil Armitage
Marketing Director
Exeter Friendly Society
01392 353500

happen to the deposit and what happens if a tenant refuses to pay rent or to leave the property when the agreed time is up, must all be sorted out before you hand over the keys.

Never, ever allow yourself to take in friends who 'need a holiday' or who are in poor circumstances, just because you are lucky enough to own a property in another country.

Finance

If you want to buy a holiday property in another country and do not have the ready cash, there are a number of ways of financing the purchase. In many European countries prices have not shot up as much as in the UK, and standard mortgage providers might well be prepared to lend you money to buy property in another country. You can take out a mortgage in the currency of the country concerned, where there may be lower interest rates. But as with buying a property in the UK, interest rates and exchange rates can change, and monthly repayment costs can go up after you have bought.

Abbey National, for instance, offers foreign currency mortgages to people buying properties in France and Italy, and loans in Sterling for those interested in buying in Spain and Portugal. In order to secure one of these mortgages, you will have to provide at least 20 per cent of the purchase price.

You will also have to inform the mortgage provider if the property is going to be available for letting for at least some of the year. Some people may decide to buy a holiday home in another country for their future retirement, and in the meantime make it pay for itself through lettings. If the property is going to be available for letting for at least 140 days a year, and perhaps actually let for 70 days in the year, tax relief can be obtained on mortgage interest payments and other expenses related to the upkeep of the property. If you are looking to buy a holiday home for your future retirement, you can also avoid Capital Gains Tax through 'retirement relief'. If this is your plan, ask about this when you talk to your mortgage provider.

If you let out property in another country for profit, however small, you will of course be liable for tax, both in the UK and in

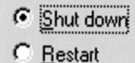

Advertisement feature

Managing finances when buying to let abroad

by Mark Johnson

Head of Sales and Business Development at Bank of Ireland Fsharp

Buying a house to live in or let is a stressful experience at the best of times. Buying a property overseas, with unfamiliar regulations, complex bureaucracy and often coupled with a language barrier, can be enough to put people off even considering buying abroad.

However, there are ways people can manage this process effectively, making it quite straightforward and even providing a good investment for the future.

Generally, there are two scenarios for those who are buying property to let abroad. In one scenario, there are those who wish to buy solely to let, 12 months of the year. Alternatively, there are those who buy to live abroad but who lease their property in the peak season, when they can make substantial rent from holidaymakers on short leases. In either scenario, how the owners of property abroad manage their banking and finances can be very different from what they are used to.

Buying to let all year round

For landlords living in the UK but renting their overseas property, managing finances can be burdensome.

Firstly, rent is usually paid in the local currency which means that if you are a resident of the UK with a property in Spain, for example, your tenant is likely to pay rent in euros. Although this does not cause enormous problems, the costs incurred through foreign exchange can be considerable, especially when one currency is substantially stronger than the other, as sterling has been for some time.

One solution to this foreign exchange issue is to open a euro account into which your tenant can pay rent and from which you can pay bills for your overseas property including, for example, local taxes or rates or annual charges such as ground rent.

A second difficulty encountered in buying to let abroad is dealing with time differences and/or local bank and office opening times. If you open an account online, this becomes easy to manage. As the internet is accessible 24 hours a day, it means you can make transactions at any time of the day, regardless of time differences and/or local bank opening times, which are often very different from those in the UK. It is also easy to pay bills, either through a standing order or by money transfer from your online bank account.

Third, if you are able to open your account in more than one currency, for example in euros as well as sterling, then managing your affairs becomes easier and costs of foreign exchange can be cheaper. With multi-currency accounts, money can be transferred from one account to the other with no charges incurred and it also means that money can be transferred more efficiently to take advantage of fluctuating exchange rates. Bank of Ireland Fsharp offers Currency Manager, a unique commission-free, multi-currency account facility available online at www.boifsharp.com.

Multi-currency accounts are also great if you wish to use the same account to pay bills in both the UK as well as abroad. For example, if the mortgage for your property is paid to a bank in the UK, while all other bills are paid abroad, money can be transferred between accounts at the touch of a button.

In some countries, such as Spain, it is a legal requirement to have a local bank account. This can be used to pay local bills or can simply be used as a back-up for any unforeseen circumstances. It is easy to transfer funds from your online bank account to a local bank, particularly if that account is in the same local currency.

It is important to get legal and financial advice when buying to let abroad as regulations are often very different than in the UK. Some property developers and estate agents are aimed specifically at UK residents buying abroad, and can help steer you through the minefield of legal issues. Fees involved with buying a house abroad are often higher than in the UK and should be taken into consideration when buying overseas.

Buying to let for 6 months of the year or less

Moving abroad is many peoples' dream, but some miss home and prefer to spend at least a couple of months a year back on their home soil. While they are away, many chose to take advantage of the situation and rent out their property to holidaymakers who rent properties for two to three weeks at a time. Rather than arrange for payment through an agent, who can often charge exorbitant prices for the privilege, it makes more financial sense to set up an account into which your tenant can transfer money in any currency.

Again this account can be used to pay bills that become due during your absence and, if your account is online, you can keep an eye on all of these payments.

If you live abroad, an offshore bank account should be of serious consideration. Interest would be paid gross on monies held and you would have access to bespoke products for expatriates.

The idea of buying a home abroad, particularly in retirement, is a great one, but the reality of actually doing it can often be very complicated. It is important that people seriously consider the financial implications and make sure they seek proper advice on the best methods and what can be done to make the process easier.

About Bank of Ireland Fsharp

Bank of Ireland Fsharp is a registered trading name of Bank of Ireland (I.O.M.) Limited, which is incorporated in the Isle of Man under registration company no 17696C with its registered office at 4 Christian Road, Douglas, Isle of Man. Bank of Ireland (I.O.M) Limited is registered with the Isle of Man Financial Supervision Commission for Banking and Investment Business. Paid up Capital and Reserves exceeds GBP 48 million.

Bank of Ireland Fsharp is a member of the Isle of Man Depositors' Compensation Scheme, which guarantees 75% of most depositors' funds, subject to a maximum compensation payment to any one depositor of £15,000.

Bank of Ireland Fsharp online services are not available to residents of certain jurisdictions.

the country where the property is situated. In France, for instance, a UK resident who lets out a property in France will have a UK liability to income tax under Schedule D, and will be entitled to credit against his UK tax bill for the French tax which he has paid on his French rental income.

Income from letting property must be declared to the authorities of the country concerned each year, even if neither the owner nor the tenant(s) of the property resides in the country. Under self-assessment or self-declaration rules, the onus is on the taxpayer, and not his letting or other agent, to make a complete and accurate return of profits and expenses from furnished lettings.

Many UK non-resident landlords do not declare their rental income to the local tax authorities, and although the country may take some time to catch up with you (or may never do so) there are penalties for non-declaration. In France, the tax office can assess up to three years in arrears, so you could be landed with a heavy tax bill plus interest, for trying to get away with it.

Of course, as with UK properties, there are very many deductions that can be taken into account with rental properties. Because the laws on taxation vary from country to country, it is worth discussing the situation with your accountant, or with somebody well versed in the tax situation of rental properties in other countries, before you make a decision on buying. If you have already retired, for instance, your tax position in any case will be very different from that of a working, or earning, person.

If the property being let out from time to time is your main residence, then you may be exempt from paying any tax on rental income. If the annual income is extremely small, you may also qualify for exemption. There will also be differences in the tax position according to whether you are treating the property as a business proposition or as a personal asset. This will normally be assessed on the amount of rental income achieved over a year.

Once you have declared your rental income in the country concerned and paid any taxes due, you must then declare your rental income to the UK Inland Revenue. You can claim a credit for tax paid to another country, and your total liability will be determined by your liability to UK income tax.

Advertisement feature

Before the 1995 Finance Act came into force, the UK Inland Revenue was reluctant to accept that the letting of a holiday home in another country qualified as a business for UK tax purposes. Therefore, there was no relief available for any interest on money borrowed to purchase the property. Section 41 of the Finance Act changed the whole basis of taxation of rental income from overseas properties. This income is still assessed under Schedule D, but now, income on one property may be relieved against losses on another, and interest relief is available as on any other genuine expense. For instance, relief may be available for interest on loans taken out to repair a non-UK property.

As this subject can be hugely complicated, and depend on your tax liability in the UK, it is best to discuss the matter with a financial expert so that the extent of any liability and the relief available are known in advance.

A few tips for buying overseas: always buy through a qualified and licensed agent. By law, agents in most European countries must be licensed, but if you buy through an unlicensed agent there may be no comeback if things go wrong.

Don't sign any document until you are sure you understand it; property buying can happen much more quickly in some countries than in the United Kingdom. Make sure you hire an English-speaking solicitor if you are not fluent in the language, as it's important to ensure that there are no debts attaching to the property and that planning regulations are in place.

9

Mostly for tenants

Although this guide is aimed mainly at prospective and actual landlords, we must not forget the tenant, the person who makes rental investments possible. Without paying tenants, the letting market would not exist, so landlords must do all they can to keep their tenants happy. So, this book ends with some advice and information aimed at tenants. Landlords will also find it useful as a checklist when contemplating renting out properties.

Very often, tenants and landlords are one and the same people, at different stages of their lives. Or even, sometimes, they are both landlord and tenant at the same time. It is not at all uncommon for owners to let out their own property at the same time as renting somewhere else. This can happen if you move to another part of the country, for instance, and for one reason or another do not wish to sell your home. One friend decided to rent out her flat in Brighton when she landed a job in London, and to rent, rather than buy, a property in London.

Another common situation is where an owner moves in with a partner, then rents out his or her own property while sharing costs with the partner. Most people will have had at least some experience of being both landlord and tenant, in much the same way that most adults will have had experience of being both child and parent. So, theoretically at least, people wishing to become landlords should be able to see the picture from the tenant's point of view as well as their own.

The inventory

If you are a tenant viewing prospective apartments, it is important to understand that the property, unless otherwise stated, is being let 'as seen'. You cannot demand a microwave, for instance, if one is not present or not listed on the inventory. Generally speaking, items that are not included and not listed are not available to the tenant. If the place does not include an iron and ironing board, for instance, you cannot demand one, although there is nothing wrong with making a request, as the landlord might have spare equipment and utensils lying around for all you know.

If you wish to rent a fully furnished and fully equipped property, it is up to you as the tenant to make sure that linen, crockery and so on are included in the inventory. You cannot sign the inventory and then complain later that there was no duvet, for example. (As a landlord, I always keep a spare duvet and set of bed linen in my home for tenants' emergencies, but not all landlords do this and it cannot be expected.)

References

Once you have chosen the property that you are interested in renting, the next step is to provide the landlord or agent with satisfactory references. Most agencies require separate references from your bank, a previous landlord or agent and a personal reference, usually from an employer. Your agent will apply for these directly; you cannot supply them yourself, as they could be faked.

Some agencies use a credit reference agency for this purpose, and you as the tenant may be charged for this. Once the references are checked and found to be satisfactory, they will be presented to the landlord. Don't forget that the landlord has the final say on whether or not he decides to accept you as a tenant, and there is not much you can do about it. If your prospective landlord has an aversion, based on previous negative experiences, of letting to somebody of your profession or appearance, you may be refused, even though you are otherwise a perfect tenant. There is little you can do about this. The property remains that of the landlord and he has a perfect right to refuse admission, with no reasons being given.

The tenancy agreement

Provided both you and the references are acceptable, the next step will be to draw up a tenancy agreement. You should read this through very thoroughly, including the small print.

Embedded in the document will be break clauses and renewal options. Do not sign unless you are happy – your signature means that you agree to the terms. Once it has been signed and witnessed it should be returned to the landlord or letting agent. If an agent is being used, it is standard to ask for a holding deposit of £200 or so to secure the tenancy. This amount is deducted from the final amount you hand over.

Before the tenancy can commence, you will receive an invoice detailing all monies to be paid over before you can take possession. These will include:

- The initial rent, usually one month or one-quarter, depending on the terms of the agreement.
- The deposit, which will be not less than one month's rent, and could be the equivalent of six weeks' rent. This deposit covers dilapidations, breaches of contract which may arise, and repairs. It cannot be used as rent payment during the tenancy, and is refundable in full at the end of the tenancy if there are no deductions.
- The inventory contribution fee. Usually, unless the tenant is a company, the landlord will pay for the inventory.
- The credit reference fee, if applicable.
- The tenancy agreement fee. This is non-refundable should you, for any reason, decide not to proceed with the tenancy.

Most agencies will only charge the tenants for the agreement if it deviates in important ways from the Assured Shorthold agreement, ie if the tenancy is for a short let, if it is a company let, or if the rent exceeds the current £25,000 per annum ceiling which puts it outside the terms of the Assured Shorthold. This fee is usually around £100.

Before you move in, the deposit, initial rent and any other fees payable must have cleared into the landlord's or agent's bank. A standing order for subsequent payment of rent, directly payable to the landlord or agent, must also have been set up.

Moving in

On the day the tenancy commences, but not before, your landlord or his agent will check you into the property. Sometimes this check-in will be carried out by an independent inventory clerk. You will be asked to sign a document detailing the furniture and equipment and also the condition of the property. Factors such as missing tiles, stains on carpets and so on should be noted, in case of disputes later.

Once the check-in has been completed and you are satisfied as to the inventory contents, the keys will be handed over to you. Now the place is yours, until the tenancy agreement ends.

Meter readings will be taken at the check-in, and the landlord or agent will notify the companies concerned of the new account holder and make arrangements for the utilities to be changed into your name. From the day you move into your property you will be liable for all gas, electricity and water used and also any standing charges levied.

You will be responsible for organizing the telephone reconnection. Sometimes this is done by the inventory clerk or agent, but you remain responsible for all telephone use. All the landlord has to provide is a telephone point. There is no law which says a telephone itself has to be provided, although usually there is one. Even if the landlord or agent has contacted the telephone company, it is still up to you to contact them to confirm the start of your tenancy.

Now you're a tenant

You will, in most cases, be responsible for council tax. There may be exemptions where you are renting a bedsit in the owner's house, or where you rent a flatlet which includes payment of council tax. This tax is payable, though, on all self-contained properties. The local council will advise you of the tax band relevant to that particular property, and you will be liable to pay from the moment your tenancy commences. If you are a single occupier, there is a 25 per cent discount on the full charge.

It is the law that you must obtain a television licence to watch TV. Whatever you may personally think of the pros and cons of the licence fee, you cannot wriggle out of it unless you decide not to have a television. The TV licensing company comes down very hard on non-payers, and it has been estimated that a high proportion of women currently serving prison sentences are there for not having a TV licence.

Once you have moved in you are responsible for paying the rent in full and on time. Most tenancy agreements state that rent is due, whether demanded or not, and it must be paid these days by standing order. Few landlords or agents will accept anything else. You should arrange for the funds to leave your account five days before the due date to ensure that it reaches the landlord's or agent's account on time. Interest may be legally charged on late payment of rent.

The rent you pay is calculated as follows: monthly rent equals weekly rent times 52, divided by 12. A rent of £200 per week works out thus: £200 times 52 divided by 12 = £866.67. Rents are usually calculated 'pcm' – per calendar month.

While you are in occupation you are responsible for the upkeep and maintenance of the property. This may include replacing broken glass, changing fuses and lightbulbs, and repairing any damage to appliances caused by misuse. You will also be responsible for keeping drains and guttering free from obstruction, airing and ventilating the property and taking steps to prevent pipes from freezing should you be absent during winter months. If there is a burglar alarm it is your responsibility to ensure that it is set when you go out of the place. Should any problems arise, you must report these at once to your landlord or agent, so that they can be dealt with instantly.

If you are sharing, you and the others have 'joint and several' responsibility. This means that should one tenant default, the others become responsible for any unpaid rent or bills. If one tenant causes damage, the other tenants are held jointly responsible. Because of this, any disputes involving sharing tenants must be sorted out by the tenants. It is not the landlord's or agent's responsibility to intervene in these matters.

If your property is managed and you do not have direct contact with the landlord, you should be provided with the name and details of the property manager at the check-in. The managing agent will normally also hold a set of keys. If the landlord is managing the property himself, the agents cannot enter into any communication with the tenant on maintenance issues.

All landlords complain of tenants who ring them up to say a lightbulb needs changing. Before contacting the landlord or agent, it may be worth your while to see whether there is a simple solution to the apparent problem. Vacuum cleaners, for instance, should be checked for full bags and blockages. Boilers and heating arrangements should be checked to see whether the timers and thermostats are correctly set. Radiators may need bleeding occasionally. Washing machine filters need to be cleaned, and dishwashers must have rinse aid and salt kept topped up.

If you do need to contact the landlord or managing agent for more serious problems or repairs, necessary works should be carried out within 24 hours. At weekends and holiday times – when most problems seem to occur – there may be some delay. If new parts have to be ordered, machines or appliances may not be working for a few days or a week. You are not allowed to withhold rent because an appliance is temporarily out of action and repairs have been held up because of a hard-to-obtain part or the inability of an engineer to come out immediately.

Landlords or their agents have legal permission to visit and inspect the property from time to time, so long as written notice is given. You do not have to be present at these inspections, which are carried out for the purpose of keeping the landlord up to date with the condition of the property, and noting whether any expenditure seems likely in the near future. Any damage for which you may be responsible will be drawn to your attention and could, in some cases, lead to termination of the tenancy agreement before the due date.

The landlord may or may not be covered by contents insurance but it is possible for you as the tenant to take out insurance to cover your own possessions. Most letting agents can arrange this for you and it may be a good idea, especially if you have expensive computer equipment, for instance. Nothing of yours that goes missing from the property while you are in occupation is the responsibility of the landlord, nor does the landlord's insurance cover any accidental damage caused by the tenant.

In the case of unfurnished properties, it is up to the tenant to insure furniture and fixtures. Permission *must* be obtained from the landlord or agent before making minor alterations to the property such as putting up picture hooks or installing cable and satellite or shelves. This cannot be stressed too often, as these items are often the main cause of disputes over paying back the deposit.

Moving on

When you wish to terminate the tenancy, everything goes into reverse. You will be advised of a time when the check-out will take place and the meters read. Once the inventory check-out has been completed, you as the tenant are no longer allowed access to the premises, even if the tenancy has not been formally terminated.

As the tenant, it is your job to ensure that everything listed on the inventory is present and in the same condition as when you took the place. Allowances are usually made for reasonable wear and tear, although there may be disputes as to what constitutes 'reasonable'.

Tenants are responsible for cleaning the place and for making sure everything is as impeccable as can be. Some tenants arrange for cleaning companies to come in and clean the place professionally, as if it is not cleaned to the landlord's or agent's satisfaction, the cost of cleaning may be deducted from the deposit.

The cleaner and smarter the place at the end of the tenancy, the quicker your deposit will be returned to you. If the whole thing has been handled by agents, you will probably not see your deposit for at least a week after you have vacated the property. If dealing directly with the landlord, you may get your deposit back on handing over the keys, although some landlords still make you wait a week.

Make sure you leave a forwarding address with the agent or incoming tenant, so that post can be sent on to you.

Provided you stick to your side of the bargain and the landlord sticks to his, there should be no problems for either of you with the tenancy arrangement.

10

Useful contacts and publications

Contacts

ARLA (The Association of Residential Letting Agents)
Maple House
53–55 Woodside Road
Amersham HP6 6AA
Tel: 01923 896555
Web site: www.arla.co.uk

Provides details of Buy-to-Let schemes, nearest ARLA member, and the booklet, *Trouble Free Letting*, on receipt of stamped addressed DL size envelope marked TFL in the corner.

Information on short lets from:

Foxtons
1 Camden Walk
London N1 8DY
Tel: 020 7704 5005
Fax: 020 7704 5001
E-mail: isln@foxtons.co.uk

Information on rental investment packages from:

Hamptons International
168 Brompton Road
London SW3 1HW
Tel: 020 7589 8844
Fax: 020 7584 4365
E-mail: invlet@hamptons-int.com

Andrew Reeves Property Investments plc
3 Catherine Place
London SW1E 6DX
Tel: 020 7808 5566
Fax: 020 7808 5567
E-mail: ar@invest-in-property.co.uk
Web site: www.invest-in-property.co.uk

www.lettingbrokers.com
Tel: 020 8492 7472
Fax: 020 8343 8293
E-mail: info@lettingbrokers.com

www.froglet.com
Tel: 01903 837740
Fax: 01903 837741
E-mail: advice@froglet.com

General information on letting from:

Leaders
4th floor
Columbia House
Columbia Drive
Worthing BN13 3HD
Tel: 01903 837742
Fax: 01903 837741
Web site: www.leaders.co.uk

Information on French property from:
Prettys Solicitors
Elm House
25 Elm Street
Ipswich IP1 2AD
Tel: 01473 232121
Fax: 01473 230002

It is now possible to buy property abroad through the Internet. These sites can help:

www. french-property-news.com
www.spanishproperty.com
www.french-property.com
www.europroperty.com

Informed Property Services has produced *The Go-it-alone Landlord Kit*, which provides detailed information for landlords who prefer not to use a conventional agency. Information from:

Informed Property Services
1–11 Britannia House
Glenthorne Road
London W6 0LH
Tel: 020 8471 499
Fax: 020 8748 4250
E-mail: young@informed-property.com
Web site: www.informed-property.com

Useful information on letting matters, and other e-letting sites can be accessed via:

www.fish4homes.co.uk

Students can now find suitable accommodation through the following Web site:

www.thelsv.com

Publications

East, G (1994) *Home and Dry in France: A year in purgatory,* La Puce Publications, Portsmouth

Henderson, L (1999) *Tenant's Survival Guide,* Robert Hale

Mayle, P (1989) *A Year in Provence,* 89 Hamish Hamilton, London

Randall, G (1999) *Housing Rights Guide,* Shelter, London

Smith, S and Parkinson, C (1997) *Letting French Property Successfully,* Pannell Kerr Forster, Guernsey

Zebedee, J and Ward, M (1999–2000) *Guide to Housing Benefit and Council Tax Benefit,* Shelter, London

Other leaflets and booklets on housing matters are available from Shelter, 88 Old Street, London EC1V 9HU. *Note:* Shelter publications are aimed mainly at the tenant rather than the landlord.

A series of booklets collectively entitled *Housing: Key facts,* written in plain English and produced by the Department of the Environment, Transport and Regions (DETR) is available free from public libraries. Relevant titles include: *Letting Rooms in Your Home: A guide for landlords and their tenants* and *Long Residential Tenancies: Your rights to security of tenure.*

Leaflets on assured tenancies and gaining possession, aimed at both landlords and tenants, produced by the Court Service, are available free from County Courts.